EMOTIONAL WELLNESS FOR WOMEN
VOLUME III

Edited by Linda Ellis Eastman

Professional Woman Publishing
Prospect, Kentucky

EMOTIONAL WELLNESS FOR WOMEN VOLUME III

Published by:
Professional Woman Publishing
Post Office Box 333
Prospect, KY 40059
(502) 228-0906
http://www.pwnbooks.com

Please contact the publisher for quantity discounts.

ISBN 13: 978-0-9799711-5-0
ISBN 10: 0-9799711-5-2

Library of Congress Cataloging-In-Publication Data

Cover Design and Typography by:
Sential Design, LLC — www.sentialdesign.com

Printed in the United States of America

For Stacie Ellis Brandt, an angel who has walked the Earth.

TABLE OF CONTENTS

TABLE OF CONTENTS
-CONTINUED-

TABLE OF CONTENTS
-CONTINUED-

ABOUT THE AUTHOR

Linda Eastman

Linda Ellis Eastman is President and CEO of The Professional Woman Network (PWN), an International Training and Consulting Organization on Women's Issues. She has designed seminars which have been presented in China, the former Soviet Union, South Africa, the Phillipines, and attended by individuals in the United States from such firms as McDonalds, USA Today, Siemens-Westinghouse, the Pentagon, the Department of Defense, and the United States Department of Education.

An expert on women's issues, Ms. Eastman has certified and trained over two thousand women to start consulting/seminar businesses originating from such countries as Pakistan, the Ukraine, Antigua, Canada, Mexico, Zimbabwe, Nigeria, Bermuda, Jamaica, Costa Rica, England, South Africa, Malaysia, and Kenya. Founded in 1982 by Linda Ellis Eastman, The Professional Woman Network is committed to educating women on a global basis regarding, self-esteem, confidence building, stress management, and emotional, mental, spiritual and physical wellness.

Ms. Eastman has been featured in USA Today and listed in Who's Who of American Women, as well as Who's Who of International Leaders. In addition to women's issues, Ms. Eastman speaks internationally regarding the importance of human respect as it relates to race, color, culture, age, and gender. She will be facilitating an international conference where speakers and participants from many nations will be able to discuss issues that are unique to women on a global basis.

Linda Ellis Eastman is also founder of The Professional Woman Speakers Bureau and The Professional Woman Coaching Institute. Ms. Eastman has dedicated her businesses to increasing the self-esteem and personal dignity of women and youth around the world.

Contact:
The Professional Woman Network
P.O. Box 333
Prospect, KY 40059
(502) 566-9900
lindaeastman@prodigy.net
www.pwnbooks.com
www.protrain.net

INTRODUCTION

Linda Ellis Eastman

This final book in the 3-volume series on emotional wellness for women is filled with strategies for life survival. It reaches into the ways you can learn not only to love yourself, but to pamper yourself because you deserve it.

Women face constant pressure and stress from family members, the work environment, and self-imposed expectations. The purpose of this book is to allow you to take control of your life while creating peace, calm, and healthy relationships which are of such importance to your emotional health.

May this book be a life compass for you, gently steering you into the direction of self-love, self-acceptance, and forgiveness.

EMOTIONAL WELLNESS FOR WOMEN

VOLUME III

ABOUT THE AUTHOR

Lisa E. Van Essen-Vinton

Lisa Vinton is President/CEO and founder of Services for Success, Inc. (www.Services4Success.com), a business management consulting firm which specializes in taking the guess work out of business development and management, as well as providing unique solutions to ordinary problems. She has mastered the art of diversity and growth in new, small and medium-sized businesses and is well versed in all areas of business operations. Prior to starting her own company, Lisa served as Chief Operating Officer for a civil engineering firm and developed the structure alongside the owners to grow the business to over $35M per annum within 5 years.

She has identified a large need to reach out to the entrepreneurs and women in the business community to strengthen their operations with practical tips and applications required to succeed. She has always had a heart for serving the community and participates in several leadership roles, including founding and directing the Southwest Pregnancy Counseling Center, Inc. (www.sw-pcc.org), a non-profit organization to educate and support teens during a crisis pregnancy. She has also served as a surrogate mother for two couples.

While a single mother and working full time, Lisa earned a degree with honors in Business Management and Administration. She is a keynote speaker and certified trainer for business and women's issues. Lisa is also a television Business News Reporter/Analyst, published author and a co-host on her own online talk radio show at only2degrees.com.

She is passionate about family, business and community. She and her husband, Scott, are the parents of five children.

Lisa would like to extend a special thank you to Heather Vinton for providing the illustrations.

Memberships

- Professional Women's Roundtable
- The Professional Woman Network (Certified trainer)
- Court-Community Planning Committee
- DiversityBusiness.com
- Women's Business Enterprise National Council (Certified)
- Rotary International, Temecula, CA
- Chambers of Commerce (California, Temecula, Murrieta and Oceanside)
- Engineers Joint Contract Documents Committee
- Notary Public (California)

Contact:
Lisa Vinton
Services for Success, Inc.
38770 Sky Canyon Drive Suite A
Murietta, CA. 92563
951.698.2500
lisa@services4success.com
www.services4success.com
www.only2degrees.com
951-698-2500

ONE

SINK, SWIM, OR FLOAT: THE ART OF BEING A SURVIVOR

By Lisa Vinton

"I'm a survivor of life. I try to give the glory to God and appreciate what's happening to me." —Mike Epps

For as long as I can remember, my family and friends have told me that I'm a survivor. Most times, I'm flattered and accept it as a compliment. But there are still other times when I am offended, annoyed, or hurt by it. It's not their fault that I don't always see it as a compliment. There are just moments or days when I am tired of being a survivor. It can be a lot of work. It's an art, you know, and there is no manual. To be a survivor, with no previous instruction, you must learn how to face life's challenges head on and win. You must earn your badges and gain your survivor skills, one experience at a time. You must know what to do when times are rough and tough. It's the way we handle those times that make us a survivor. It's those so-called opportunities in life that force us into survivorship.

I'm a professional survivor. Many women are. We survive because we have no other choice, and because sometimes it actually feels good. It's an accomplishment to survive a difficult time. It makes us winners! God deals us a hand and tells us to survive it. But why does it always have to be so darn tough? We certainly don't have to survive the easy times…or do we? Believe it or not, even the easy times need some survival skills. We need to know how to prepare for the storm after the calm. We need to learn how to have eyes in the back of our head and super-human hearing. We need to figure out how to dig deep into the depths of our heart and soul when we need to the most. We need to learn how to trust our instincts and understand the people around us.

Welcome aboard the ship of survivors! Put on your life preserver and hold on. There are going to be times when it's a rough ride. Be prepared, say a few prayers, and you'll be just fine…you will survive…

Being the oldest of three girls, I suppose it was inevitable that I would be the one expected to be strong at all times. I was a "big girl" from the moment I was born. I was a daddy's girl who learned how to garden, lay hardwood, and fix cars. I was a mommy's girl who learned how to cook, sew, and serve the community. I was a big sister who protected and raised two young girls in the home of an alcoholic mother and abusive father. I was a teacher's pet who stayed after class to help grade papers and decorate the classroom. I was a friend who helped with homework and listened when other friends had a bad day. I was the favorite niece, granddaughter, and cousin.

Now, I am a mom (and dad) to two adult children who continue to count on me for stability and security. I am a wife who manages the home, pays the bills, and tries to find time to enjoy my husband. I am a business owner who works hard to make sure my employees receive their paychecks and my clients receive excellent service. I am a volunteer who gives up "me" time to serve others in need, even in times when I need my "me" time. And when I think I've had enough, I continue onward. Why? Because I am a survivor.

Do you feel what I'm talking about? Do you, too, have days where you feel as though you are only living to survive, but need the support of others to get through it all? Days when you wish that there was someone there to save you, rather than you saving them? Do you ever wish that the challenges in life that force you to use your survivor skills would just go away? What do those days feel like to you? How do you survive as a survivor?

My survival skills have been put to the test several times over the last four decades. For starters, my mother drank too much during my teen years and my father resorted to being angry all the time in order to cope. He took it out on me much of the time – both verbally and physically. He didn't know any better, as he had not been given the gift of survival skills, so instead he was reactive, not proactive. I, on the other hand, learned to survive in the volatile home until I could escape at the age of 18. I had plenty of opportunities to figure out how to make it through my mother's "episodes" and my father's "outbursts." As a teenager, I was mortified that my friends would find out, so I often stayed in my room or snuck out in the night to be in a safer environment. I did what I could to keep from being ostracized by my peers. I learned early on that these were "opportunities" to help me face challenges in the future and be able to survive them.

At 23 years old, I found myself surviving a bad marriage, nasty divorce, and custody battle. I eventually survived the difficult, yet rewarding privilege of raising two kids as a single mom, returning to college to finish 114 units in two years, a blended family arrangement in my mid-30's, and the passing of my father after a long illness. I survived them without resorting to drugs or alcohol as a cure-all and with the support of my family and friends. Almost everyday I survive something. I've prepared myself to be ready for anything. But am I? Probably not, but I'll never admit that. I'm up for the challenge. Bring on the opportunities in life so that I can be a better person and make a difference in the lives of others.

List 5 events in your life that you have survived:

1. ______________________________

____

2. ______________________________

____

3. ______________________________

____

4. ______________________________

____

5. ______________________________

____

Sink...

Do you ever feel like you have the weight of the world on your shoulders and you can't take one more step? Do you hear, "Calgon, take me away!!!", but you just don't have the time to stop and lay in a tub? As a woman, wife, mother, and entrepreneur, there are days when I feel as though I am sinking, sinking, sinking. I want desperately to rise above whatever is holding me down, but the pressure is too heavy. I'm unable to get up, either physically or mentally, to face even one more challenge. I find myself sinking further down. Like most days, the morning starts off well and typical. I'm walking through a jungle and conquering the elements. It's a good day and everyone had better move out of the way. I am coming through! Suddenly, the ground begins to give way. I am stuck, paralyzed by fear, as I feel the sinking ground beneath my feet. I am in quicksand and convinced that there's no way I can get out alone. I need help; I am going down fast. There are people all around me, and they do not even notice that I am in trouble. I cautiously extend my arm and hold out my hand, as I am about to do something I rarely do, and with all my might, I ask, "Can someone give me hand? Can someone please help me?" Their eyes get as big as saucers, and matter-of-factly respond, "You are a survivor. You don't need us. Come on, get out of there. You can do this! And, oh, by the way, we need *you*!" And they turn and walk away.

Somehow, I find my way out. It is a struggle, but I do it. I drag my exhausted body over to a nearby watering hole. I roll my quicksand-soaked body into the hole. I feel like I need to get cleaned up; there's too much to do to be lying around the jungle. And, anyhow, everyone is hollering for me to get moving. As I find myself in the watering hold, I begin to sink, again. My body is heavy and I don't have the energy to get up. No matter how hard I try, I am sinking…

It was 1994, and I was in the middle of a nasty custody battle. My ex-husband had kept my young children well beyond the court-ordered visitation. He was now fighting me for custody. Because he was still angry that I had filed for divorce, his goal was to keep them from me, forever. Not long after the battle began, I found myself arrested on charges of attempted kidnapping and burglary, and spent a few hours in a jail cell. Having never had a brush with the law, I was desperate and scared. The charges were entirely false, yet I had no idea how to fix the problem. My survival instincts kicked into high gear (the highest ever, I might add), and within a few months, it was all behind me. The charges were dropped, my children were returned home to me, and life became good again. I had been sinking fast, but the will power to survive and the determination to win the fight gave me the strength to focus on the goal – save myself and my children from the nightmare. I'm proud to say that I was successful and that I survived.

Swim...

I'm not a "water person." In other words, I don't really enjoy being *in* the water, except for my daily shower. I do, however, truly love being in places that have beautiful water, watching the sun set behind the ocean, and viewing from a large glass tank the incredible sea creatures among us. However, getting in it just isn't my thing. But, as my life would have it, I often find myself in situations that I don't necessarily enjoy.

Obviously we aren't talking about real water and real swimming for the purposes of this chapter, but the analogy is much the same. As a survivor, we will jump, or be thrown, into a situation that just might give us a sense that we are suddenly drowning. As we begin to flail our arms, and even panic, we quickly realize that we are on our own. We want to yell, and sometimes we do, "Throw me a life jacket!" But we *are* the life jacket. We must save ourselves. We know, instinctively, that we must get to the other side, but just how we get there will be based on how determined we are. And, as a survivor, we are the most determined of all mankind. Fortunately for us, we often see land on the other side and have acquired the ability to swiftly formulate a plan to get there before we go down. Experience has taught us well. "Swim," we tell ourselves. "Just start moving your arms forward, not upward, in a consistent and powerful motion. Don't stop."

We have swum before, and we will swim again. It feels good to know that we have the strength and endurance to face a new challenge and win the race. Sometimes we just can't stop long enough to even grasp the thought of how far we must swim, or why we are swimming at all. "How did I get in the middle of this big body of water? There are boats all around me, but no one is stopping to scoop me up and rescue me. What? You say it builds character? I'll tell you what you can do with your character-building!" But, in the meantime, I'm a survivor! I'll show them…all of them! "Watch this! Watch me survive," I scream. So, to prove I can do it, I keep swimming…

It was 1998, I was a single mother, working full-time, and told by my employer that I must get my Bachelor's degree if I was to advance any further. My time, energy and finances were low when it came to enrolling in a four-year college that would take me eight years to complete. I knew it was important for my future and the future of my kids. But I didn't have eight years. So, I found a program that would allow me to get all four years completed in 24 months. I took a double load at times and spent every weekend studying. I had to get it done and get it done right! For the entire time, I kept my head above water and focused on finishing school. I never looked back or even stopped to think about what I was doing. I just kept on swimming. Twenty-six months later, I earned my BS in Business Management & Administration, graduating with a 3.94 GPA.

Float…

Too tired to swim? Float. Because of the way our bodies are built, we have the ability to just float. If we can let go long enough to relax, we can float on our backs or on our stomachs. We can drift into a moment of oblivion. How nice for us! But as a survivor, we are trained to be on alert at all times. Not paying attention could prove fatal. Our radar must be up at all times. What will happen if we aren't prepared and something sneaks up on us? How will we know if something is headed our way if we aren't paying attention? There is a chance we will not survive an attack if we are not alert. Is floating really safe?

Honestly, if we don't float when we need to, we will likely drown. We need to take time to float when we are too tired to go any further. This is a great way to regain strength and momentum. There will be no surviving if we don't stop and re-group. Floating is all about doing what is in our own best interest. It means we step back and take time to exercise, eat healthy, drink water, take vitamins, relax, smell the roses, and enjoy life. We are so busy being strong and being in survival mode that we don't realize when we need to feed ourselves the fuel to keep going. And, before we know it, the ground below our feet begins to give way. At that moment, especially when others don't seem to understand our plight, we must turn away from the rat race and…float.

Mastering the Art of Being a Survivor

Being a survivor is not only a gift, but also a learned talent. For whatever reason, we were chosen to be survivors. And we must continue to master the art of being a survivor. It means we must not only survive the tough times, but we must be able to allow ourselves the opportunity to re-fuel, as needed. With that said, how do we master the art of survival? Here are 5 tips:

1. **Find a Strong Support Team!** Most survivors find themselves going it alone and helping non-survivors survive. But, as we grow older, we can't continue to surround ourselves only with those who need our survival skills. We must gather up a strong team of other survivors. These men and women will know when we need a break and need the time to float. They will be our eyes and ears when we can no longer fight. Ask them to help you! Lean on them!

2. **Live in the Present and Look to the Future!** As survivors, we are constantly on the lookout, so we forget to stop and live in the moment. Find activities that allow you to just focus on the moment. Activities that allow you the opportunity to just float – like golf, gardening, reading, or yoga. Whatever it is for you, do it regularly and do it often.

3. **Journal Every Day!** There's so much going on in our lives that our brains get filled to the top by day's end. Go down to the local bookstore and pick up a really nice journal. Place it by your bed and write it in every night. Even if it's just a few words, such as, "I'm too tired to write" – or if it's a novel, write your thoughts, feelings,

task list, whatever. When you download your mind at the end of each day, you allow yourself the opportunity to sleep better…and float into the night.

4. **Embrace the Opportunities to Survive!** We have been given a gift, the art of survival. We learn it through the trials and tribulations we are handed throughout our life. Some of them we bring on ourselves, but that's not a reason to regret them. Learn from them, and share your survival skills with others when they need it most. Take these opportunities to grow in mind, spirit, and body.

5. **Meditate or Pray!** Every morning I wake up and before I get out of bed, I pray, "Lord, give me a reason to get up today, give me the tools and resources to handle it, and help me appreciate the opportunity to survive it." For that reason alone, I'm never without an amazing story to tell every single day of the week! Then, at night, I pray that I will be able to let go of the day's events, survive a night of floating in and out of my dreams, and wake to enjoy another day of adventure.

If you feel as though you are sinking, reach out to your support team. If swimming is getting a little tiring, stop and float for a while. Being the best survivor you can be comes with a lot of hard work, but it also means knowing when to stop and reassess. Cheers to a successful ride aboard the ship of survivors!

"There are always survivors at a massacre. Among the victors, if nowhere else."— Lois McMaster Bujold

"We do not live to think, but, on the contrary, we think in order that we may succeed in surviving."— Jose Ortega y Gasset

ABOUT THE AUTHOR

Dr. Darlene Silvernail PhD LMHC CAP

Dr. Darlene Silvernail PhD LMHC CAP is a Corporate and Professional Trainer. She has been working in the mental health field for over twenty-three years with extensive experience developing and implementing quality assurance protocols. Dr. Silvernail has been a past nominee for the Robert Woods Foundation Award (1997) The Best Practice Award (2000) and nominated three times for the Sun Sentinel Community Leadership Award (1999-2004).

Dr. Darlene Silvernail is the President and CEO of Professional Enhancement Services and the Founder of ICU, International Coaching Unlimited with clients in the USA and abroad. She has assisted numerous companies in expanding and enhancing their businesses. Her mission is to help you reach your vision and achieve your personal, business and professional goals and to take you, your company and your employees to a higher level.

She is a member of the Professional Woman Network and has co-authored two books.: Emotional Wellness for Women Volume III and The Baby Boomers Handbook for Women.

Other Memberships

Certification Board Addiction Professional, Professional Woman Speakers Bureau, American Academy of Health, South Florida Society of Trauma Based Disorders, NAADAC and FADAA, CBAPF and NAFC, American Mental Health Counselor Assoc, Coalition for Batterer's Intervention Programs, PB County Victim Advocacy Advisory Council, Mental Health Association, Palm Beach County Domestic Violence Council and Palm Beach County Human Trafficking Committee Pride Probation Advisory Council.

Dr. Silvernail is available for seminars, workshops, keynote addresses and Corporate and/or personal coaching.

Contact:
Darlene Silvernail PhD LMHC CAP
International Coaching Unlimited
PO Box 18745
WPB Florida 33416
1-888-90-Coach
ICUCoaching@aol.com
www.ICUCoaching.com

TWO

STOP SIGNALS – ENDING ABUSIVE RELATIONSHIPS

By Dr. Darlene Silvernail

STOP!! Been there, done that! Got the t-shirt! Have you ever asked yourself how you manage to get into abusive relationships – and how hard it is to get out of them? The next few pages will highlight what to look for and how to avoid entering or re-entering an abusive relationship. If you are in an abusive relationship, this will provide you with valuable resources, safety ideas, and safety planning.

As a psychotherapist for the past twenty-four years, I have worked extensively with men who abuse and women who have suffered years of abuse. Partner abuse is not gender-specific, but this chapter is on partner abuse against women. Approximately 95% of domestic violence victims are women. (Bureau of Justice Statistics Crime Data Brief, *Intimate Partner Violence, 1993-2001*, February 2003). The most current, national studies on domestic violence suggest that 22-25% of all women will experience domestic violence at some point during their lives (www.FCADV.org).

Partner abuse, especially domestic violence, is a serious public health issue. Three women are murdered by their husbands/boyfriends in this country every day (Bureau of Justice Statistics Crime Data Brief, *Intimate Partner Violence 2001*). The health-related costs of rape, physical assault, stalking, and homicide by intimate partners exceed $5.8 billion each year. (*Costs of Intimate Partner Violence Against Women in the United States.* Atlanta, GA: Centers for Disease Control and Prevention. 2003)

Everyone knows someone impacted by partner abuse - friends, sisters, co-workers. Women stay in abusive relationships for a variety of reasons: fear for physical safety, to maintain a relationship for the children, no place to go, no economic resources. The abused hope the violence would stop. However, shame-based statements towards the victims further enforce their own feelings of being responsible for the abuse (discussed later).

Alarming Facts

- More than three women are murdered by husbands/boyfriends in this country every day. In 2000, 1,247 women were killed by an intimate partner. (Bureau of Justice Statistics Crime Data Brief, *Intimate Partner Violence, 1993-2001*, February 2003)

- Victims leave about seven times before they leave for good.

- Victims are more likely to be killed/seriously injured at time of departure. It is the most dangerous time. Any woman ready to leave must be referred to a victim advocate.

- Between 35% -56% of victims are harassed at work by their abusers. (*Understanding the Effects of Domestic Violence, Sexual Assault, and Stalking on Housing and the Workplace.* New York: Legal Momentum, 2007. http://legalmomentum.org/legalmomentum/files/statistics.pdf).
- One fourth to one half of victims lose a job due to domestic violence. (National Task Force to End Sexual and Domestic Violence Against Women. *Violence Against Women Act, 2005).*
- Fifty percent of homeless women are fleeing abuse.
- Sixty percent of battered women are beaten while pregnant.
- Domestic violence is the number one cause of emergency room visits by women.
- Psychologically abusive men are more likely to use weapons, have prior criminal arrests, abuse substances, have employment problems. (Henning & Klesges 2003).
- Ninety-five percent of men who physically abuse also psychologically abuse. (Henning, K. & Klesges, L.M. 2003. *Prevalence and Characteristics of Psychological Abuse Reported by Court-Involved Battered Women*).
- Of the battered women seeking emergency medical services, 73% have separated from the abuser.

What Is Abuse?

It is a myth that partner abuse/domestic violence is a loss of control. The truth is that violent behavior is a choice. Abusive partners use control tactics to control their victims. Partner abuse is about batterers using their control - not losing their control. Their actions are very deliberate. These behaviors are more than just an isolated incident.

Partner abuse almost always involves various forms of control: physical, emotional, psychological, sexual, economic, male privilege usage, isolation tactics, and economic tactics. (Economically, abusers attempt to control finances to prevent accessing resources. This disempowers victims, limiting them to little or no economic self-sufficiency. This includes interfering with attempts to maintain employment or education advancement.)

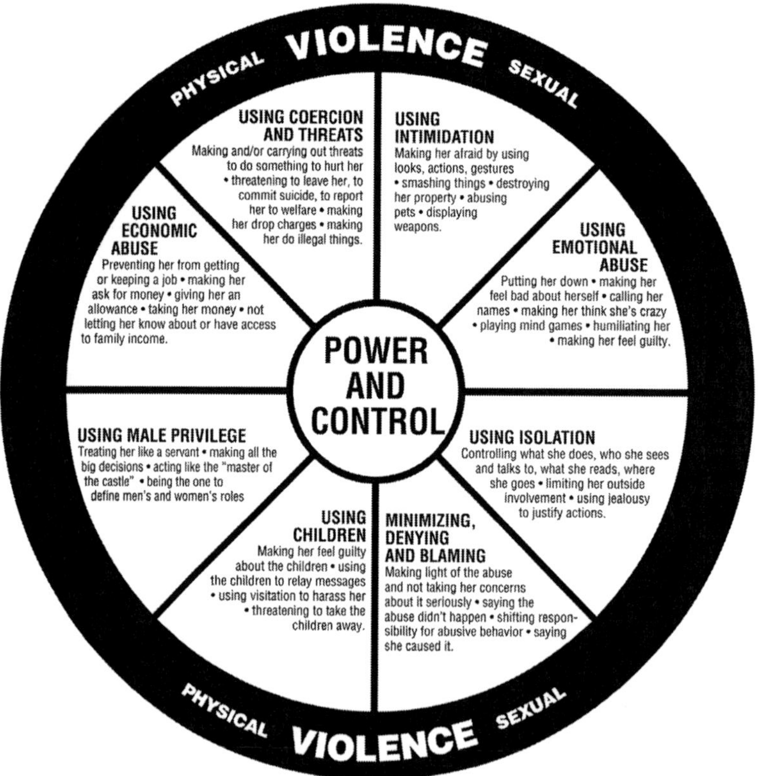

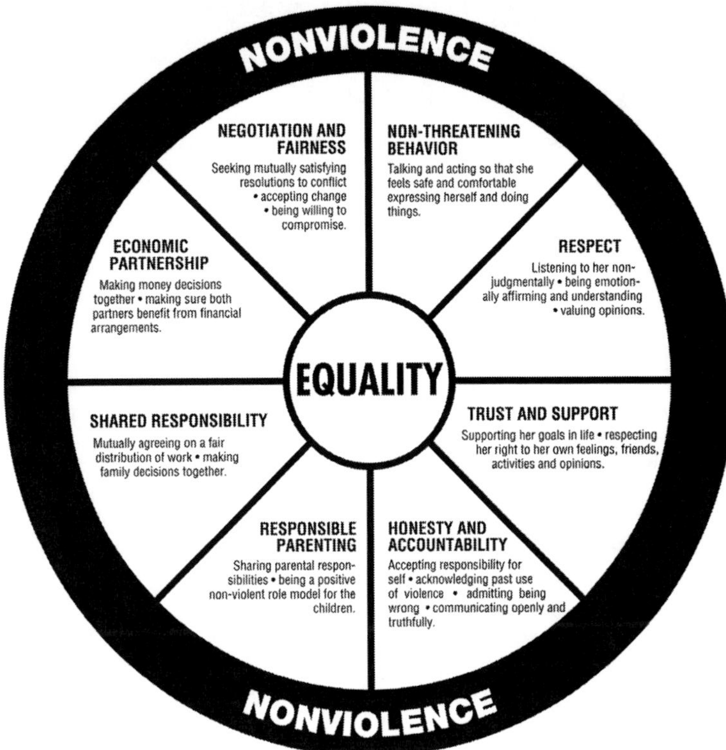

Domestic Abuse Intervention Project; 206 West Fourth Street, Duluth, Minnesota 55806 **www.duluth-model.org**

Are You In an Abusive Relationship?

Do you: Feel afraid of your partner a lot? Avoid certain topics for fear of angering your partner? Feel you can't do anything right for your partner? Believe you deserve to be hurt or mistreated? Wonder if you're the crazy one? Feel emotionally numb/helpless?

Does your partner: Humiliate, criticize, or yell at you, belittling you? Treat you so badly you're embarrassed for friends/family to see?

Ignore or put down your opinions or accomplishments? Blame you for his abusive behavior? See you as property or a sex object, rather than as a person? **Are you afraid of your partner's:** Violent behavior or threats? Controlling behavior? Rage that might destroy your belongings? **Does your partner:** Have a bad and unpredictable temper? Hurt you, or threaten to hurt/kill you? Threaten to take your children away or harm them? Threaten to commit suicide if you leave? Force you to have sex?

Warning Signs Of An Abusive Personality

Mr. Quick Involvement: Comes on very strong, claiming, "I've never felt loved like this by anyone"; pressures for exclusive commitment almost immediately; charming, attentive, but turns to demanding attention; wants to move in quickly/set up house.

Mr. Mother Seeker: Seeking parent; displays much affection; struggles with maintaining employment; with poor coping and problem solving skills, expects her to fix problems/care for him; resents woman for same traits he seeks; off balance relationship; his maladaptive way of regaining power.

Mr. Secretive: Seems very attentive; wants to learn about woman but offers little self-disclosure; may provide false last name/telephone numbers; uses avoidance to skirt issues; appears to have hidden life.

Mr. Womanizer: Cheated on others, yet you believe he changed; has history of cheating on past partners; emotionally unavailable; usually seeks women who are vulnerable; a predator; believes you are his property; this person is dangerous.

Mr. Roller Coaster: History of serious mental health issues; may exhibit signs of depression, suicidal homicidal ideation or have past attempts; has a history of non-compliance with treatment/medication. This nightmare may include the following: sudden mood swings, obsession, stalking behavior, racing thoughts, and paranoid/delusional thinking/behavior, personality disorder, history of addictions and / or impulse control disorders. (When a batterer is extremely depressed and loses hope for moving beyond depression, he's more likely to commit homicide/suicide.)

Mr. Jealousy: Excessively possessive; calls constantly/visits unexpectedly; prevents you from going to work (you might meet someone) or checks mileage on your car; may stalk; controls partner's behavior; accuses her of having affairs. Due to his intact, delusional system, this man is potentially dangerous.

Mr. Controlling: Interrogates intensely (especially if you're late); keeps all the money; insists you ask permission to go anywhere/do anything; may check mail and phone calls.

Mr. Unrealistic Expectations: Expects perfect woman to meet his every need; clinger; needs constant admiration; suffocating and draining for partner due to neediness.

Mr. Isolation: Cuts partner off from family and friends; accuses partner supporters of "causing trouble"; deprives you of phone or car; prevents you from holding a job. (Isolation: Studies indicate that batterer isolation dependence on partner correlates with the use of lethal violence.)

Mr. It's Not My Fault: Blames others for problems/mistakes; someone else's fault; has external focus of control (he is victim); world owes him something; has difficult time being accountable for his actions.

Mr. Makes Everyone Else Responsible for His Feelings: The abuser says, "You make me angry," instead of "I am angry," or "You're hurting me by not doing what I tell you." Less obvious is the claim: "You make me happy."

Mr. Hypersensitivity: Easily insulted; says his feelings are hurt but he is angry; rants about injustice of things that are part of life.

Mr. Cruelty to Animals and Children: Kills or punishes animals brutally; may expect children to do things far beyond their ability (whips a two-year-old for missing toilet seat or teases them until they cry). Sixty-five percent of partner abusers will also abuse children.

Mr. Playful: Use of force during sex; enjoys throwing/holding you down against your will during sex; finds the idea of rape exciting; forces you to perform uncomfortable sexual acts; uses pornography that depicts exploitation and abuse.

Mr. Humiliation: (Verbal abuse) Starts out attentive; begins to criticize or says blatantly cruel, hurtful things; degrades, curses, calls you ugly names; makes you feel bad about yourself or defective; sleep deprivation (waking you up with verbal abuse); attempts to break you down.

Mr. Male Privilege: May display rigid sex / gender roles: expects you to serve, obey, remain at home; "Your place is in the home," "Don't ask questions," "Be pretty and submissive"; uses **dominance** to feel in charge; makes decisions for you and expects your obedience; you are his servant/possession.

Mr. Past Battering: Admits hitting women in the past, but others made him do it; history of abusing his children/stepchildren; threats of violence ("I'll break your neck," or "I'll kill you," and then dismisses them with, "Everybody talks that way," or "I didn't really mean it."); At this point - get help or get out! His violent threats escalate; violent towards you while pregnant; has access to weapons and has threatened to use them.

Mr. Past History of Restraining Orders: Past or current history of restraining orders / injunctions for protection - and has violated the terms. BIG RED FLAG!

Mr. Party Pooper: Significant history of substance abuse; abuser justifies abuse or rationalizes behavior as result of substance use. Substance abuse escalates severity of abuse and potential lethality.

Personality Disorders

Definition: Personality disorders are "enduring patterns of perceiving, relating to, and thinking about the environment and oneself that are exhibited in a wide range of social and personal contexts" and "are inflexible and maladaptive, and cause significant functional impairment or subjective distress." (American Psychiatric Association, 2000, pg 686).

Paranoid Personality Disorder

Suspects without basis that others are exploiting, harming, or deceiving him/her; preoccupied with unjustified doubts about loyalty / trustworthiness of others; reluctant to confide in others due to fears of information being used against him/her; reads hidden demeaning or threatening meanings into benign remarks / events; persistently bears grudges – unforgiving; reacts angrily to "perceived" attacks on self; recurrent suspicions without justification of infidelities

Antisocial Personality Disorder

Difficulty conforming to social norms re: lawful behaviors; challenges law and authority; history of arrests; enjoys being deceitful, as indicated by repeated lying, aliases, conning others for personal profit / pleasure; impulsivity or failure to plan ahead; irritability and aggressiveness; reckless disregard for safety of self / others; does not display remorse or empathy; consistent irresponsibility, as indicated by repeated failure to sustain consistent work behavior or honor financial obligations.

Narcissistic Personality Disorder

Grandiose sense of self-importance; exaggerates achievements / talents; superior to others; preoccupied with fantasies of unlimited success, power, brilliance, beauty, ideal love; believes he / she is "special," unique, can only be understood / associated with other special / high status people; requests excessive admiration; high sense of entitlement –expects favorable treatment and automatic compliance; takes advantage of others for own ends; lacks empathy – unwilling to recognize / identify with feelings / needs of others.

Avoidant Personality Disorder

Social inhibitions; feeling inadequate; hypersensitive to negative evaluation; avoids occupational activities - fear of criticism, disapproval, rejection; unwilling to get involved unless certain he / she is liked; shows restraint within intimate relationships – fear of being ashamed or ridiculed; pre-occupied with being criticized/rejected; inhibited in new interpersonal situations because of inadequacy feelings; views self as socially inept, personally unappealing, inferior to others; unusually reluctant to take personal risks, or engage in new activities that may be embarrassing.

Dependent Personality Disorder

Pervasive/excessive need to be taken care of; submissive/clinging behaviors; separation fear; difficulties making everyday decisions; needs excessive amounts of advice and reassurance; needs others to assume responsibility for most major areas of their lives; difficulty with expressing disagreements, fears, loss; difficulty initiating projects or doing things on their own – lack of self-confidence; goes to excessive lengths to obtain nurturance/support from others – volunteers to do things unpleasant; feels uncomfortable or helpless when alone – exaggerated fears of being unable to care for self; URGENTLY seeks another relationship as a source of care and support when a relationship ends; unrealistically preoccupied with fears of being left to care for self.

Borderline Personality Disorder

Frantic efforts to avoid real/imagined abandonment; can't tolerate loss; unstable interpersonal relationships; patterns of alternating between idealized and devalued interpersonal relationships: unstable, intense, overwhelming; markedly and persistent unstable self-image and sense of self; highly impulsive; self-damaging behaviors such as spending, sex, substance use, reckless driving and binge eating; recurrent suicidal behaviors, gestures, threats, self-mutilations; mood reactivity: dysphoria, irritability, anxious; chronic feelings of emptiness; severe dissociative symptoms; stress-related paranoid ideation; intense anger: frequent displays of temper, rage, fights.

Histrionic Personality Disorder

Pervasive pattern of excessive emotionality; attention seeking; uncomfortable when not center of attention; often interactions include inappropriate sexual seductive or provocative behaviors; displays rapidly shifting/shallow expression of emotion; uses physical appearance to draw attention to self; style of speech – excessively impressionistic, lacking in detail; shows self-dramatization, theatrical tendencies, and exaggerated expression of emotions; easily influenced by others; considers relationships to be more intimate than they actually are.

Obsessive-Compulsive Personality Disorder

Pervasive preoccupation with orderliness, perfectionism, mental/interpersonal control at expense of flexibility, openness, efficiency; preoccupied with details, rules, order, organization, scheduling; shows perfectionism; excessively devoted to work/productivity to exclusion of leisure activities/friendship; over-conscientious, scrupulous, inflexible about matters of morality, ethics, values; unable to discard worn out/worthless objects with no sentimental value; miserly; shows rigidity & stubbornness.

The Effects of Psychological Abuse

If you experience psychological abuse, you may experience one, some, or all of the following symptoms. Women who have been in a long-time, abusive situation are more likely to develop clinical depression and post-traumatic stress. If you exhibit any of these symptoms, seek a qualified, mental health therapist.

Acute stress and effects on health - p*ost traumatic stress disorder (PTSD)*

- Depression, difficulty concentrating
- Emotional/mental impairment, suicidal thoughts/attempts
- Sleeping problems, loss of appetite, panic attacks, anxiety
- Poor work/school performance
- Self-medicating (drugs and alcohol use)

How To Help Yourself And/Or Others

Abuse is not your fault. Help yourself and others by following these important steps:

1. Avoid shame-based comments, such as, "When are you going to get it?" or comments that denote the victim is responsible for the violence. No one deserves to be abused, regardless of what they say or do.

2. Be cautious of your own beliefs/biases. Be careful your situation does not end up, "Til death do us part."

3. The choice is the victim's; shaming makes matters worse.

4. Remind her you are concerned for her safety.

5. Offer vital alternatives/safety planning, and learn your community resources - get help.

Resources:

http://www.clarkprosecutor.org/html/domviol/plan.htm

http://www.avdaonline.org/personal_safety_page/personal_plans.html

http://www.sa15.state.fl.us/SpecialPrograms/DomesticViolenceSafetyPlan.htm

http://www.avdaonline.org/internet_safety_page/computer_safety.html

Shelters – Locate one nearest you: ahttp://wadv.org/shelters.htm

America Bar Assoc on Domestic Violence	http://www.abanet.org/domviol/ http://www.abanet.org/domviol/
National Health Resource Center on Domestic Violence	888-RX-ABUSE www.endabuse.org/health
National Center for Victims of Crime **2000 M Street NW, Suite 480** **Washington, DC 20010**	800-FYI-CALL 800-211-7996 (202) 467-8700 (voice) (202) 467-8701 (fax) 1-800-211-7996 (TTY) www.ncvc.org
National Children's Alliance **National Coalition Against Domestic Violence** **P.O. Box 18749** **Denver, CO. 80218**	800-239-9950 (303) 839-1852 (voice) (303) 831-9251 (fax) www.ncadv.org
National Network to End Domestic Violence	www.nnedv.org
National Center on Domestic Violence, Trauma and Mental Health	312-726-7020 ext 10 http://www.nationalcenterdvtraumamh.org
National Domestic Violence Hotline **P.O. Box 161810, Austin, TX 78716**	800-799-7233 800-787-3224 www.ndvh.org

National Fraud Information Hotline	800-876-7060
National Organization for Victim Assistance	800-TRY-NOVA
National Resource Center on Domestic Violence **TTY Hotline**	800-537-2238 800-553-2508
National Sexual Assault	Hotline at 1-800-656-HOPE
Office for Victims of Crime	866-OVC-TTAC (866-682-8822) 866-682-8880
Pennsylvania Coalition Against Domestic Violence **National Resource Center on Domestic Violence** **6400 Flank Drive, Suite 1300** **Harrisburg, PA 17112-2778**	TOLL-FREE: (800) 932-4632 (717) 545-6400 (voice) (717) 671-8149 (fax) www.pcadv.org
Shelters – Locate one nearest you:	http://wadv.org/shelters.htm
Rape, Abuse & Incest National Network	800-656-4673
Resource Center on Domestic Violence, Child Protection and Custody	800-527-3223

Citations

American Psychiatric Association, (2000). Diagnostic and statistical manual of mental disorders (4 ed). Washington, DC: American Psychiatric Association.

Bureau of Justice Statistics Crime Data Brief, *Intimate Partner Violence, 1993-2001*, February 2003

Domestic Abuse Intervention Project; 206 West Fourth Street, Duluth, Minnesota 55806

FCASV- Florida Coalition Against Domestic Violence

Prevalence and Characteristics of Psychological Abuse Reported by Court-Involved Battered Women. *Journal of Interpersonal Violence*, 18(8), 857-871. Henning, K. & Klesges, L.M. (2003).

National Center for Injury Prevention and Control. Costs of Intimate Partner Violence Against Women in the United States. Atlanta, GA: Centers for Disease Control and Prevention; 2003

National Task Force to End Sexual and Domestic Violence Against Women. *Violence Against Women Act 2005.*

Understanding the Effects of Domestic Violence, Sexual Assault, and Stalking on Housing and the Workplace. New York: Legal Momentum, 2007

Notes:

ABOUT THE AUTHOR

ANDREA SMITH-HUDSON

Andrea Smith-Hudson is President and CEO of The Smith-Hudson Group, LLC, a company committed to International Training on customer service & professionalism. Mrs. Smith-Hudson has over 10 years of customer service experience working both in the telecommunications industry as well as the financial industry. She is on the Board of Directors of the Hanover Homecoming Foundation, a non-profit and non-governmental organization, whose founding members are expatriates and children of expatriates from Hanover Jamaica.

Mrs. Smith-Hudson has worked as a telecommunications specialist on the Call Calibration/Training Team at Verizon Communications where she enhanced customer satisfaction and quality as leader in the Global outsourcing initiative in the Philippines. She crafted techniques to identify gaps in service delivery and recommended viable solutions to senior management. As Team Coordinator, her responsibilities included pioneering work that kept the company at the edge of superior service spanning the Greater New York, Mid-Atlantic, and Potomac regions of the East Coast. Earlier she was a Coordinator for maintenance and repair of Verizon service lines where she developed a feedback tracking procedure for the customer escalations lines, later adopted and utilized throughout the Potomac region. She also supervised a professional staff of office personnel. At the start of her career she served as a Risk Associate for Capital One, the giant credit card/banking operation. As a member of the Hanover Homecoming Foundation she makes positive contributions towards the improvement of the social and economic conditions in the community of Hanover, Jamaica and assisted in establishing an education and development fund for the people of Hanover, Jamaica.

Andrea received her BS in Economics and Finance from Virginia State University, a Masters in Business Administration from Averett University, and is a certified trainer specializing in Diversity. Andrea is also a member of the Professional Woman Network (PWN).

Contact:
The Smith-Hudson Group, LLC
P.O. Box 951
Prince George, VA 23875
Email: Asmithhudson@aol.com
804-541-2629
804-541-2654(F)
www.pwnbooks.com

THREE

A LEGACY OF LOVE

By Andrea Smith Hudson

"Trust in the Lord with all your heart, and lean not on your own understanding; in all your ways acknowledge Him, and He shall direct your paths." —Proverbs 3:5

So there I was, sitting in my office trying to figure out what I would write about. Thinking about what principles or techniques I would propose in the journey towards leaving a "Legacy of Love." Then I started thinking about the legacy of those who were inspirational to me and what impact they had on my life. Martin Luther King Jr., Paul "Bono" Hewson, Bill Cosby, Oprah Winfrey, and most importantly, my parents; these extraordinary and unique individuals who dedicate or dedicated their lives to helping others despite the obstacles and challenges they had or have to endure. I started thinking about their legacy each having a diverse approach; however, their common denominator remained the same, "love." Consequently, I asked myself the questions, "What will be *my* legacy of love? And what will I leave behind?" These were difficult questions because I never thought about them before. I started to think about the impact I wanted to have on the lives of others. I remember, after completing my Black Managers Workshop at Verizon, that there was a ceremony held for all of the participants. My group leader started introducing members of his group and said, "This person has so much love she can't give it all away." Then he added, "Andrea Smith-Hudson." I remembered how I felt that day and what impact that introduction had on me. Thus, when I was asked to write this chapter, and started asking myself about my legacy, I thought about the words my group leader used to introduce me.

Ask yourself about your own legacy. What would *you* leave behind? Merriam-Webster on-line dictionary defines legacy as, "a gift by will, especially of money or other personal property." Love is defined as, "strong affection for another arising out of kinship or personal ties (maternal love for a child) and unselfish loyal and benevolent concern for the good of another." For the purpose of this chapter, we will look at legacy as a gift one leaves behind in terms of emotional or spiritual connection. Then, we will look at love as an unselfish loyal and benevolent concern for the good of another. I chose these definitions specifically because I believe the best gift one can leave behind is the gift of love. This gift does not have monetary value, but a feeling that will live inside a person for the rest of his/her life. This feeling is one of compassion, selflessness, nurturing, understanding, and forgiveness. I believe there is an emotional or spiritual legacy that can be carried on from generation to generation. An emotional and/or spiritual legacy is innate; it is how you treat people. This is more powerful than any monetary value left behind. Many people try to build an empire of monetary wealth and may work on professional accomplishments, sometimes without regard to individual's feelings. Will this be their legacy? Let it not be yours.

Exercise 1:
What would people say about you today? Write your answer in the space provided below.

____

____

____

____

____

If you don't like what people will say about you, the good thing is, you have time to change their perception of you. Always remember, *perception is reality*. If you're content with what people will say about you, then possibly, you are on your way to leaving a legacy of love.

Earlier, I asked you think about your legacy. Let's pursue this a little further, and to help you answer the questions about your legacy, I'd like you to follow these steps:

1. Visualize your desires.

2. Write it down.

3. Get cracking!

First, you must visualize your legacy desires. So please, close your eyes and relax for about a minute and then pick up the book and continue reading. Ready, Go… Place the book down and close your eyes. OK, now that you are relaxed and your mind is clear, open your eyes and write down your thoughts. What do you desire to leave for others? This will create some substance to your ideas. Use the space provided below to write your thoughts.

My Thoughts

____

____

____

____

____

You may have written about your professional and career aspirations, your accomplishments, your financial wealth, or what you're leaving behind in terms of materialistic items. Well, that's what most people do; people associate these principles with their legacy. But, please understand that a legacy of love is about how you treat others. A legacy of love is about an emotional or spiritual connection with people. A legacy of love is also about defining yourself. And lastly, a legacy of love costs nothing in monetary value. It has heart-to-heart value worth far more than money.

I read a poem on the Internet and I found it to be inspirational. The poem reads, "*Love yourself, accept yourself, believe in yourself, believe in your wishes, believe in your dreams, hopes, and desires.*" If you really dissect the words, you will see how important the principles of the poem if applied correctly, can impact your daily life.

Love Yourself.

Take time for yourself. Get your hair and nails done once in awhile; go to a spa. Eat well; good nutrition is imperative for a fruitful life. Enjoy your family and friends. This is what is most important.

Your family and friends will be the one's who feel the impact of your death. Your job will replace you. Practice work/life balance. This is not just a coined phrase, it is important for self-preservation. Go to the movies. Eat with your kids. Be kind to yourself; stop self-sabotaging by comparing yourself to others or doubting your abilities. Sometimes it's good to be still, let go and let God.

"Make the most of yourself, for that is all there is of you."
—Ralph Waldo Emerson

Accept Yourself.

Accept yourself for the person you are. Don't try to be like someone else or live up to someone else's expectations of you. Understand that as long as you do your best and give 100% every time, then you have done the best you can do. Here's something to think about: are you a person who can look into the mirror with confidence and give yourself positive affirmations? Do you think it is possible to love yourself if you cannot speak highly of yourself? Here's another important factor you should remember when it comes to accepting yourself: stop putting other people down, criticizing them or belittling them because of your own insecurities. This behavior just sets you back in your journey to becoming a better you. As women, we definitely never understand our true value or our self-worth. As a result, we think less of ourselves, we self-sabotage, and we put people down in an attempt to feel better about ourselves. You need to recognize and understand your true potential; you need to believe in yourself.

"The greatest success is successful self-acceptance." —Ben Sweet

Believe In Yourself.

Give yourself a fighting chance. Understand that *you* matter, what you do, what you say, what you feel, what you believe in; it's all relative. It is imperative that you realize you were created for a purpose. If you are not healthy, if you are not happy, you'll never give yourself the affirmations to make it day-to-day. Historically, women are more affectionate than men. It is instinctive that we tend to nurture and care for others. Try putting that much effort into nurturing and caring for yourself, and you will see how easy it will be to believe in what you can do and what you can accomplish. **You must realize that you manifest your destiny**. Giving yourself daily affirmations will help you in this endeavor.

"It's not who you are that holds you back, it's who you think you're not."
—Author Unknown

Believe In Your Wishes.

There is a saying, "Watch what you ask for, because you just might get it." So, believe in what you wish for. Remember, the Bible states, "Faith is the substance of things hoped for, the evidence of things not seen." So, continue to wish for the things you desire and believe it will come true.

Believe In Your Dreams, Hopes, and Desires.

With hard work and perseverance they will come true. Know that you can accomplish anything you set your mind to, as long as you set it as a priority. Once you have mastered loving yourself, you can master anything. Now, let's explore leaving a legacy of love in more detail.

Listed below are qualities I believe lead to a legacy of love.

Step One: Be compassionate.
Step Two: Be selfless.
Step Three: Be nurturing.
Step Four: Be understanding.
Step Five: Be forgiving.

Step One:

Be Compassionate: Most people want to be loved; in fact I believe everyone wants to be loved, despite what they say or do. If you take the time to listen beyond the words, you will recognize what people are really saying, in spite of their outward appearance or actions. Most people want to feel as if those who are around them, such as family, friends or strangers, care about them. Although life doesn't seem to be working out quite as they expected, most people choose not to give up due to their faith. Through this faith one finds compassion, and with this compassion, an innate emotional response to care. You can be compassionate by taking the time to listen, even if you think you have something more pressing to do. If you just sit back and listen, you might realize you could have saved someone's life. You could be compassionate by having "an unselfish and loyal concern for the good of another." Remember, everyone makes time when they need someone. Therefore, it starts with you; take the time to care, and to give unselfishly.

"Our lives begin to end the day we become silent about things that matter." —Martin Luther King Jr.

Step Two:

Be Selfless: "It's better to give than it is to receive"; we've heard this adage many times before. This is a profound statement. When you think you have given enough I challenge you, give more, set new boundaries. This does not always have to be of monetary value. Giving your time to share, to show you care, to help others succeed and excel can be much more rewarding than just writing a check. Now don't get me wrong, many charities need that financial support to keep them afloat, so why not give both? You only have one life to live, so why not make the best of it.

"You must be the change you wish to see in the world."
—Mahatma Gandhi

Step Three:

Be Nurturing: Foster an environment conducive to love. Think about it. Kids who grow up in a loving and caring environment are more likely to be loving and affectionate adults. You know the family that is always hugging, kissing and showing compassion to each other tends to be the ones who grow up to be just as loving and compassionate. Why is that, you may ask? Well, because their parents or guardians fostered an environment conducive to love. They nurtured their mind, bodies, and their soul. Being nurturing involves caring for others. What a difference you can make in one's life if you would take the time to not only tell people you care, but show them you care by what you do to influence change and inspire others.

Step Four:

Be Understanding: With wisdom there is knowledge, with knowledge there is understanding, and with understanding there is forgiveness. Earlier I spoke about listening not to what people say, but what they are not saying. This is imperative in our journey to leaving a "Legacy of Love." You should not assume the worst in others, but understand there is a reason why people act or respond to everyday situations the way they do. Charles Swindoll wrote a poem on Attitude and it is one of my favorite poems. The last line of the poem reads, "*Life is 10% what happens to me and 90% how I react it... we are in charge of our attitudes.*" I mention this quote to say, being understanding is about being patient enough to realize that you cannot determine what's on the inside without taking the time to peel back the layers on the outside. It is about checking your attitude and how you react to situations.

"In the final analysis, love is the only reflection of a man's worth."
—Bill Wundram

Step Five:

Be Forgiving: Start by forgiving yourself. The Bible says, when God forgives us, He "*remembers our sins no more*" (Jeremiah 31:34). That doesn't translate into God forgetting our sins; he forgave us but will never forget. The same should be expected of you. You should not forget, because then you will never experience growth. Allow yourself the same courtesy that God extended you. If God can forgive you, then you can learn to forgive yourself. Through this action you will learn how to forgive others. It will become second nature.

"To forgive is to set a prisoner free and discover the prisoner was you."
—Author Unknown

Exercise 2:
List the individuals in your life who have hurt you in one capacity or another. Then write down whether you feel the time and energy you put into not forgiving them was worth it. Ask yourself if it was worth allowing the situation to imbed itself in your heart and manifest in your spirit. After you ask yourself these questions, take steps towards healing and forgiveness in your life. You are worth this effort.

Names:	**Was It Worth the Effort?**
1. Your Name: ______________	______________________
2. ______________________	______________________
3. ______________________	______________________

In this chapter you have learned that it is important for you to work on yourself in order to leave a legacy of love. You've also learned the five steps necessary in starting this journey. The rest is up to you. You have the ability to make the necessary changes in your life to make a positive influence on someone else's life. Your inspiration can come from family members, celebrities, teachers, or anyone who dedicates their lives to helping others.

Exercise 3:
If you desire to leave a legacy of love, develop an action plan and get cracking!

- ____
- ____
- ____
- ____
- ____

Reflection

A legacy of love starts with you. Remember, God has a purpose for your life if you choose to obey, to let go, and let God work through you. The Bible says, "God is love." You are an expression of God's love. Why not show your appreciation by abiding by his teachings, and dedicate your life to helping and caring for others. This can be your legacy.

"And now these three remain: faith, hope, and love.
But the greatest of these is love."—1 Corinthians 13:13

Recommended Reading:

The Value in the Valley by Iyanla Vanzant

One Day My Soul Just Opened Up by Iyanla Vanzant

The Power of a Praying Woman by Stormie Omartian

The Purpose Driven Life by Rick Warren

ABOUT THE AUTHOR

Jane Denner

Jane Denner is the principal of Inner-States, LLC which is dedicated to the evolution of the whole person –mind, body, and spirit- substituting patterns of success for those of past failures. Emphasis is placed on nutrition and emotional awareness. Ms. Denner is a Certified Professional Consultant and Holistic Health Counselor with over thirty years of experience in the field of natural healing. She is an active member of the Professional Woman Network and serves on its International Advisory Board.

Ms. Denner uses practical exercises to demonstrate that which we hold in our minds can either hold us back or move us forward. Jane provides seminars and coaching to support and guide individuals over the obstacles they encounter on their paths. Inner-States, LLC programs help individuals navigate while focusing on nutrition, self esteem and building healthy relationships. Private one-on-one as well as small group coaching sessions, workshops and seminars for all individuals of any age are available. She is passionate about healing through physical and emotional self awareness and strongly believes in being her own example. Jane Denner is a native of Canada and resides in Massachusetts with her family.

Contact:
Inner–States LLC
P O Box 474
Concord, MA 01742
[617] 605 6205
Jane777comcast.net
www.protrain.net

FOUR

THE FOOD–MOOD CONNECTION

By Jane Denner

"Although there is a great deal of controversy among scientists about the effects of ingested food on the brain, no one denies that you can change your cognition and mood by what you eat."
—Arthur Winter: poet, author

We Are What We Eat.

We are the cumulative result of all we have eaten / ingested, internalized, breathed and experienced throughout the totality of our lives. Most importantly, there is a "cause – effect" calculus created by what we "take in" on a daily basis; we actually create our body, mind and spirit by such choices. Our physical health, and correlative emotional and spiritual well–being, is determined and defined by these choices – the "Food–Mood" matrix, as it were. While we intuitively know that "we are what we eat", it is through the empirical process of conscious observation and examination of our core experiences – how various foods actually affect our thoughts, emotions, and behaviors – that we come to understand that we effectively re-create ourselves perpetually, albeit fractionally. Of course, sometimes we can affect our mood virtually instantaneously, as with alcohol, caffeine or other drugs. And it has become axiomatic that more obvious food allergies and intolerances may well be responsible for many of the so-called "psychopathologies", particularly the affective / mood disorders which have become so prevalent.

The "body-mood" dynamic reflects, then, the biological truth of the close connection of what we "take in" and what we "put out" as thought, feeling and behavior. Our bodies are sensitive receptacles that are finely attuned to the entirety of the world we inhabit. Insufficient sunlight produces "Seasonal Affective Disorder" (SAD). Lack of exercise often results in dysthimia or more chronic depression. We can either become the beneficiaries, or the victims, of our own food choices; to benefit we must utilize our innate intuitions to recognize our own body's unique patterns – every individual has the capacity to heal / correct itself. When the mind is able to inspect, on an essentially existential or phenomenological level, the body's pain and disruption of the free flow of life force, the potential for healing and growth is established. Finding the courage to permit your pain 'to be', while holding it with compassion and love, generates the purest form of spiritual growth and awareness. Additionally, choosing to observe the natural universal laws of life also provides the body and mind with the correct fuel to function in such a singular, evolved manner.

My journey to reclaiming health began at the age of 18. I was living with my family in southern Ontario, Canada on an idyllic farm setting. At that time, I had been suffering for years with severe allergies, particularly late summer "rag weed" which left me teary, bleeding from the nose, and largely cognitively disoriented. I was also often bloated, lacking in energy and experiencing the mood swings frequently associated with affective disorders, such as bi-polarism with its manic and depressive cycles. In short, I was miserable, sick, and the conventional allopathic, western medical model offered no meaningful solutions, as the mere suppression of symptomatology without dealing with its root causes was hardly a cure. Being a curious girl with a working sense of the ironic nature of life, I could not help noticing that the animals on the farm seemed to enjoy far better health and stable moods than I. While they appeared to live in harmony with nature, human beings appeared unnatural, if not dysfunctional by comparison. Clearly, I had much work to do to catch up with the cows and horses. What was I doing wrong?

I began to observe carefully which foods made me feel better – or worse. For instance, a piece of Mom's cherry cream-cheese pound cake with a glass of milk would, within fifteen minutes, produce an almost toxic reaction, taking me to a "mucus hell" with comatose features that lasted for hours, if not longer. When I inquired about such effects of food, my primary care physician assured me that food had absolutely nothing to do with health. This was my very first clue that most doctors were not healers or nutritionists but, at best, pharmacologists with a dramatically different view of the proverbial path to health and well-being than I, and dealing primarily with treating disease rather than with proactively promoting health. Confused, scared and unhealthy, I ultimately turned inward for answers and became my own, albeit unorthodox, physician, healer, therapist and Guinea Pig, effectively becoming the embodiment of the maxim, "Physician, heal thyself."

I had noticed that the farm animals had an innate sense of what to eat and what to avoid. They intuitively knew when to fast to combat illness, or when it was the optimal time to breed. By paying close attention to the cycles of nature and the pattern habits of the animals in their daily lives, I soon recognized the laws of nature by which all of creation lives. I later recognized that I was relearning my inner knowledge. I began to apply these laws to myself, followed my instincts, and through trial and error, eventually healed my severe allergies and tortuous depression. I was ecstatic that I was able to regain my health - that the conscious and diligent application of certain well-established rules enabled me to largely control my own destiny. Since that time, I have remained the unlikely scientist and have been applying simple, natural and universal laws that pertain to all living creatures and continue to enjoy radiant physical, mental and spiritual health. I am not only witness to my own evolution as it unfolds, but have become an active participant, therein, by choosing its direction with the free exercise of my will and intention. With knowledge of these laws and the discipline to adhere to them, you too can recapture your health. It is important to remember that the human body, given half a chance, will heal itself.

The Ten Truths

Required for living and vary only in each person's capacity to use them beneficially – and work toward your potential.

Health Promoters

1. **Vigorous Exercise**

   - Requires us to breathe more deeply, and quickly expands the lungs.

- Oxygenates the body
- Builds our red blood cell count
- Keeps the lymph in free flow
- Demands more nourishment and causes the blood to circulate to satisfy this requirement
- Helps elimination of morbid debris from cells
- Boosts the endorphins in the brain that promotes happiness

2. **Physiological Rest / Fasting**

- Helps eliminative organs catch up with their tasks
- Rejuvenates our body, mind, nervous system and absorption ability
- Detoxifies for better nutritional status
- Restores the digestive organs' malnutrition of the entire body by reconstruction
- Creates glandular secretion improvement

3. **Pure Water**

- Recommend distilled water purest available
- Bathes every cell within the body and cleanses
- Water is a **carrier** and assists in cell function

- Makes up the liquid part of our blood and other body fluids
- Drink often, averaging approximately 6 to 8 glasses a day, depending on your size and activity.

4. **Pure Fresh Air**

    - Oxygen-rich air re–charges our batteries
    - Oxygen is needed for all body functions, every cell requires oxygen
    - De-carbonizes the lungs
    - Builds red blood cells
    - Vitalizes the body and mind
    - Promotes calm when breathed deeply through the nose

5. **Rest, Relaxation and Sleep**

    - Re-charges life's batteries
    - Healing takes place
    - Rest after eating
    - Sleeping on an empty stomach promotes deeper rest.

6. **Sunshine and Warmth**

    - Ultraviolet light from the sun is necessary for complete synthesis of vitamin D

- Light passing through the eyes has an effect on the nutrients in the blood
- Solar therapy for natural healing and normal human growth
- Stimulates pineal gland in brain's core promoting **well being, boosts moral**
- Bright full spectrum light improves **depression/mood swings/ SAD** condition
- Light assists in rebalancing homeostasis necessary to restore health
- Warmth of sun saves wasted body energy by conserving normal temperature

7. **Refrain from Excesses.**

   - Digesting food requires a tremendous expenditure of energy, especially overeating.
   - **All** excess is damaging; food, thoughts, work and sex, to mention a few.
   - Excess drains your energy resources.
   - The body has little storage ability; excess burdens the body's power.
   - Regulate stimulation in rest, sleep, play and eating, or else excess will drain the nervous system.

- Excess is often the starting point of imbalances, or mood swings. The body cries for help, beginning with cravings to make balance and maintain homeostasis.

8. Cultivate the Real You.

- Emotional awareness, examine your self and your thoughts.
- Determine your own positive assets.
- Align your personality with your soul.
- Be grateful for your life, your uniqueness; you are perfect just the way you are.
- Be joyful, purposeful and productive.

9. Cleanliness

- Essential to the superior life
- The skin is the largest organ of the body; daily cleansing simulates the lymph system, blood flow and flushes waste from skin surface.
- Love and honor your body, and it will respond with happiness

10. Food Tailored to Humans and Properly Combined

- Fresh raw food to sustain the life process is a biological requirement.
- Drink plenty of clean pure water.

- Eat slowly, chew thoroughly, and eat only when really hungry.
- Eat **local,** organic foods **in season,** the best quality you can find.
- Maintain normal alkalinity of the blood at 7.5 with live food, nuts, seeds, fruit, vegetables and lots of leafy **greens.**
- Eat fruit and nuts alone, not mixed with other proteins or carbohydrates.
- Honor the **circadian rhythm** of your body and eat **three** meals a day without snacking in-between. Digestion requires a lot of energy and the body requires rest in-between meals to complete its own cycle of absorption, particularly heavy proteins.
- Do not eat after 8:00 pm.
- Do not eat before 10:00 am, except fruit.

Unfortunately, we usually take no notice of the messages sent to us by our bodies until they reach such a shouting crescendo of agonizing pain that they no longer can be ignored. Interestingly, pain has become an inconvenience to us, not a necessary warning sign. In our laziness and ignorance, we routinely turn to doctors for treatment – operations, drugs etc. to mask and anesthetize these symptoms / communications. Rather than listen to what the body is clearly telling us in its perfect intelligence, the "pain–warning" has become something to eradicate, not heed.

Most of us are fear-driven, living entirely in our heads and not in our hearts. We are whipped in the emotional wind of our thoughts and fears. We are at the mercy of society's protocols and out of touch with our authentic selves. Reaching our full human potential is an evolutionary challenge, especially as we have lost much of our intuition. Even our basic, primordial five sensory-based perceptions - sight, touch, taste, hearing and smell - are failing us. However, by fostering empathy with your body and giving yourself time to re-discover its laboratory, your can participate in a continual unfolding of your own potential; there is nothing more satisfying than this process/journey. You start where you are today and go forward from there. All of our unique histories are but valuable learning experiences to ponder and process. The new paradigm – food as a dominant modality able to define an individual's variable state of health and concomitant quality of life – has emerged.

Daily Axioms for Health	**Daily Axioms against Health**
Love	Hate - Jealously
Gratitude	Blame - Judgment
Awareness of Emotions & Thoughts	Out of Control Emotions & Thoughts
Pure Air & Water	Polluted Air & Water
Sunlight	Artificial Lighting
Exercise	Sedentary Lifestyle
Sleep and Physiological Rest	Staying Up Too Late & Over-Taxing Body
Eating Green Leafy Organic Plants	Not Ingesting Green Leafy Plants
Fruits, Seeds & Nuts, Organic & in Season	Not Ingesting Fruits, Seeds or Nuts
Ingesting Organic Vegetables in Season	Not Ingesting Vegetables

What is Food?

All of life is nutrition, which can be understood in terms of primary, (basic, necessary emotions) and secondary (air, food, etc.). The weather, sun, moon physical exercise and the quality of the air we breathe, the water we drink, what we see, feel, think and experience and how we love are then all foods for our development and all centrally affect our mood. Particularly, what we eat plays an important physiological function and is perhaps one of our most intimate of personal relationships.

Consider your thoughts and their vibrational level when you think of a healthy diet. Healthy, organic whole meals will support your intentions to create a strong physical body and mind. You will discover that some foods vibrate at a higher level than others, e.g., raw organic foods as opposed to cooked, modified foods with artificial chemicals. However, even if you eat the best available food on the planet while possessing a mindset that is toxic or a heart filled with rage and recrimination, the food you are eating will turn acidic and will sustain you no better than junk foods. Ergo – junk thought / feelings = junk foods = junk health. So, when you consider a healthy diet, consider first and foremost your thoughts and intentions. The highest vibrational state is to feel love for everyone around you. Take your time; trust your body to guide you to the foods that are best suited for the unique individual that you are and the potential that you hope to realize.

Take notice of how certain foods make you feel; what are you craving?

Listen and trust your cravings, they are critical messages trying to assist you to create the balance so critical to health and happiness. Cravings are the body's response to fundamental imbalance. Our body is always trying to make us feel better by urging us to eat foods that will lessen our physical stress, boost our energy or elevate our moods. Trust your cravings - your body doesn't lie. Pick a natural healthy alternative,(such as Agave Nectar instead of processed white sugar) until you are able to deconstruct your cravings and better understand your needs.

For Example:

- Salt - can affect your mood by making you feel tense.
- Sugar - can give you a high and make you feel animated as your blood sugar rises. It can depress you when your blood sugar drops.
- Portions - eating too much can make you tired and drowsy because the blood flow is directed to the stomach for digestion and away from the brain.
- Protein - produces dopamine and norepinephrine in the brain, which brings on a more alert feeling.
- Junk food - leaves many people in a bad mood because of lack of nutrients, plus adding toxic load to the body, which it must eliminate.
- Comfort food - such as dairy, sugar, alcohol, carbohydrates sooth our feelings after a stressful day, which ironically, eventually causes more irritation for the nervous system after the initial "sedation" has worn off.
- Carbohydrates - release serotonin in the brain, which make one feel more relaxed.

- Chocolate - **only** in its natural, unprocessed raw state is good for you, and is in fact, classified as a "super food". It is rich in magnesium, the most deficient mineral on the Standard American Diet. Often it is used to relieve loneliness or depression. In its refined and processed state, it causes depression.
- Alcoholic beverages - used to release tension. Adds to our toxic load and further compromises the nervous system, liver, kidneys, spleen and dulls the brain.

The food-mood sensitivity varies from person to person. Staying in a nutritional state of balance will help stabilize your moods. Record in a journal what you crave, what and when you eat, and how you feel afterward. I encourage you to discover / experiment and decide what works best for you.

The Energetics of Food

Because everything is energy and each has its own unique vibrational resonation, each also has its own energy value, as well. Our bodies soak up the energetic traits of the foods that we eat. Your body's flexible nature will respond to the changes you make in your eating and your thinking. Remember, our thoughts have a powerful effect on all of your food and can either compliment or pervert their natural energetics. The mind has the power to render the identical food nourishing for one person and toxic for another, so intertwine your good, healing thoughts with your eating. As you make every effort to reach optimal physical, emotional, and spiritual health, choosing a diet high in vibrational energy will maximize your efforts. Give thanks for your life and the food you eat. Maintain a loving and compassionate attitude toward all of those around you.

- Never eat when you are upset; wait until you are calm.
- Challenge your anger, fear, envy and worries if they come up and choose to be peaceful.
- Focus on nourishing your body; be content while you eat.
- Be grateful for your food, chew slowly and fully, and love your body.
- Do you experience love for everyone about you without exception?
- Love is the utmost vibrational condition; filter your thoughts through love.
- Meat has a heavy vibrational quality and is theorized by many to have a cross-species transference of character traits passed onto humans when eaten in excess.
- Leafy greens have a light healing quality; eating greens rich in chlorophyll supplies our blood with oxygen and lifts the spirit.
- Root vegetables grown in the ground help to stabilize our moods and ground us emotionally.
- Be kind to yourself.

Explore how your body responds and feels after you eat certain foods. Learn to choose the foods that create the energy and the balance you are seeking in your life. Always seek to make balance. Foods that will heal one person will adversely affect another. When you start to improve your energy by challenging your fears, you will naturally become attracted to lighter vibrational foods. Remember that one man's food can truly be another man's poison.

What Should I Eat?

Start by adopting the Ten Truths of Universal Laws of Life to your regime. They are the unmovable cornerstones or our existence. Just by following them, you will notice a significant shift in you health. With regard to diet, of course, no single diet is correct for everyone. The one food most missing in our modern diet is fresh raw leafy **greens.** Adding 50% more raw greens to your diet will dramatically improve your health and functioning. Experiment with food and journal your reactions. Know your body and understand what it is telling you and asking of you. Remember your moods and emotions are the voice of your body. As there is too much to say about food in one short chapter, I am inserting a food pyramid for you to observe. Your body loves you unconditionally and will respond to your efforts to heal yourself. Trust you instincts, give yourself permission to take pleasure in a broad assortment of **wholesome** foods and enjoy your life**.**

Human Bio-Organism

The human body machine is a bio-organism that needs fresh air, sunshine and warmth, pure water, rest, relaxation, exercise, mental rest, self-control from excesses and high-quality organic food properly combined and correctly eaten. When any are neglected for any period of time, we limit our health potential and cultivate disease.

One cannot merely treat the body when there is sickness; one also must treat the mind. Realize that thought and its vibration is the source of dysfunction and illness. The body's condition is but a mirror, reflecting rather than causing the state of our health. The greatest "cost" in the spiraling/escalating health care "cost" model is actually the one that normally goes unmentioned – that is the "cost" to human beings of a diminishing quality of health and life as vast, almost obscene amounts of money are being paid to the unholy corporate alliance of the medical, pharmaceutical and denatured food industries. Sadly, the necessary purpose of the alliance is to maintain a sufficient level of disease to ensure profit levels.

Thus, while thoughts define our moods and feelings, they are, in turn, recast by the same feelings /emotions in a replenishing cycle which ultimately grows into each person's individual universe. Remember well that you are indeed (and in deed) what you "take in". If you listen to what your body tells **you** about **yourself** and you utilize the correct "fuel" in response thereto, you, Physician, will succeed in healing thyself.

AXIOM PYRAMID

For optimum growth

FULL SPECTRUM – BODY, MIND AND SOUL – NUTRIENTS

WHOLE GRAINS

PROTEINS

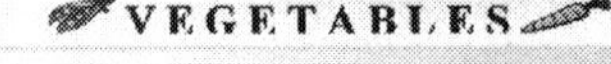

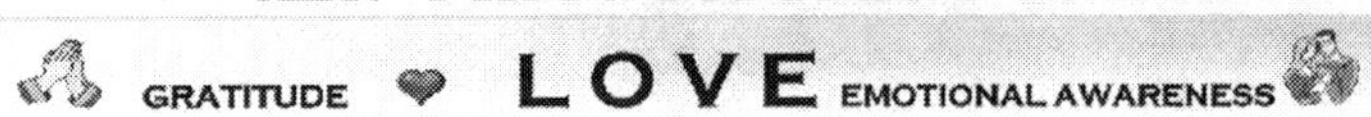

- ALL EDIBLE FOODS **ORGANIC**, PREFERABLY **RAW** FOR MAXIMUM ENZYMATIC AND NUTRITIONAL VALUE, UN-RADIATED, FREE OF ANTIBIOTICS, STEROIDS AND NON-GMO (GENETICALLTY MODIFIED ORGANISMS)

ABOUT THE AUTHOR

DONNA R. SHAW

Specializing in 'Orchestrating Dreams Into Reality', Donna R. Shaw believes success is a combination of personal empowerment and accountability.

Ms. Shaw designs and delivers seminars, workshops, and retreats focused on rebuilding and renewing women spiritually, physically and emotionally. Using a blend of high-energy, wit, and inspiration, she shares contemporary messages, interlaced with humor that is relevant and practical for today's Woman.

Prior to starting Shaw Legacy Group, Ms Shaw spent 20 years in the corporate environment strengthening her skills in management, leadership and training. She is an accomplished certified trainer on numerous topics including: visioning & goal setting, customer service, leadership development, team building and women's issues.

She is active volunteer in her community locally and abroad. She is a founding board member of Fresh Start for Women, Inc, a 501c which is a ministry of healing & renewal whose vision is for all women to live in a community free from violence. She has delivered her message of hope & inspiration through travels to West Africa, Europe and the Caribbean. She is a Lifetime Girl Scout and Mentor.

Ms Shaw is a member of the Professional Woman Network (PWN), National Association of Female Executives (NAFE), Toastmasters International and board member of the National Coalition of 100 Black Women, Inc and NAACP, Metropolitan Atlanta Chapters.

She holds a Bachelors Degree in Business Management , Masters Degree in Project Management, and Masters Degree Human Resources Management.

Contact:
Shaw Legacy Group, LLC
"Orchestrating Dreams Into Reality"
3961 Floyd Rd, Ste 300- PBM161
Austell, Ga 30106
(770) 435-9284
www.donnarshaw.com
donna@donnarshaw.com

FIVE

A COMMON THREAD: ISSUES THAT WOMEN SHARE GLOBALLY

By Donna Shaw

Do you remember the nursery rhyme we were taught as little girls to remember the seven continents; I didn't. My goddaughter, Sierra had to sing it for me.

Do you know you know your con –ti-nents…
A-sia, Afri-ca, Eu-rope, Au-stralia, North A-merica,
South A-merica and don't forget Ant-arc-ti-ca.

For most of us our world consists of our local neighborhood and communities where we live, work and play. Our lives are so full with personal and family demands we don't often have time to reflect outside of our bubble.

Did You Know…

- The World population is approx. 6.8 trillion people: 51% women to 49% men.
- The two highest IQ's ever recorded (on standardized test) belong to women.
- Women perform 66% of the world's work, but receive only 11% of the world's income.
- Women own only 1% of the world's land.
- 66% of the world's 785 million illiterate adults are women.
- Australian women have sex on the 1st date more than women of the USA or Canada.
- 55% of all college students are female.
- Women head 83% of single-parent families.
- In parts of Malaya, the women keep harems of men.
- Women hold less than 40% of leadership roles.
- 600,000 to 800,000 people, mostly women and children, are trafficked annually across national borders.
- Over half a million women in Africa & Asia die yearly of childbirth.
- Approximately 3 million women in the USA sport tattoos.

So, what do we want from this world? World peace, right? Well, for most women it's a little deeper than that. We want *"dreams to be orchestrated into reality"* by going to college, falling in love, marriage, the house with the white picket fence, the 2.5 healthy children and pets, careers, SUVs, vacations, sports cars and the list goes on and on.

I would like for you to take a journey with me for the next few moments to experience some commonalties we share as women of this world. Get ready for a reality check.

Environmental Issues

178 of the 204 member Nations to the U.N. all report extreme levels of poverty in their rural areas. This poverty is driven by the absence of the basic essentials of life: water, food and shelter. Access to clean water, nutritional food choices and a safe place to rest are needed to eradicate worldwide poverty. In my travels to West Africa (Liberia, Ghana and Nigeria), I have seen women carry their children in beautifully entwined wraps close to their bosom as they stand in the ocean, wash their clothes, and lay them upon the rocks and shanty house roofs to dry under the brilliance of the sun, very similar to how I remember my grandmother in rural South Carolina leaning over a tin tub to wash our clothes and hang them on the line. Our oceans, rivers and lakes are being used as a source for bathing, cleaning clothes and cooking. According to the World Health Organization, at least 7 million people die each year from diseases associated with dirty water, most of who are women and children. Unsanctioned chemical leakage, overuse of pesticides, nuclear waste, devastation of rain forests, melting of icebergs, and pollution are threatening the bodies and lives of women around the world.

As nurturers for our family and the land, women are the primary caregivers for Mother Earth. We plant the seeds, cultivate them and harvest them in global gardens. Do you remember the last time you ate something "directly" from a garden? Hmmmm, I know it is every two months for me, when I visit my grandparents. My 87-year-old grandfather still plants seasonal gardens and takes joy in sharing the fruits of his labor with his children and grandchildren when we come to visit. Wow, what an incredible difference to eat fresh vegetables and eat fresh meat straight from the butcher. Our lives have become so full with work, children's activities, social and civic commitments; we survive on fast foods and whatever we can cook in thirty minutes or less. We wonder why our children are obese, suffer from childhood diabetes and asthma. Why wonder, when the answers lie before us. In 2005, the U.N. recognized women's roles in preservation and generational teaching, promoting a healthy respect for the land and its value sustaining life. We must challenge ourselves to take time and care in selecting the products we are putting before our families, teach our children nutritional choices, support our local farmers market and help build community gardens in the abandoned fields in our neighborhoods. There are numerous school programs and corporations willing to sponsor our efforts. It just takes one strong woman to grab a shovel and Go Green.

The warmth and comfort of a safe home filled with love is priceless. We look forward to having a safe haven when the world has been unforgiving all day. For most of us in the U.S.A., this is a place filled with items we personally selected: our beds, our couches, our kitchen tables, our clothes, and our many, many shoes. However, there are many girls and women who do not have a warm home, so they sleep on cots or pieces of cardboard, or under trees and highways without proper clothing for the elements. On my last trip to West Africa, I visited Liberia for the first time. We were on a medical mission trip to bring supplies to the hospital, which was being rebuilt after 14 years of war had ravaged the countryside. As we drove into the city that Saturday afternoon, I was astonished at the magnitude of families, mostly women and children, living in abandoned homes, buildings, and shanty villages that had been created for safety during the war. The furnishings were barrels for tables, tin and cardboard for beds / cover, the women were cooking meals over open fires, and evening light was with kerosene lamps. Liberia does not have a functioning electric company, so if you do not have a generator for your home, you must buy kerosene in little plastic bags being sold by the children who have no school to attend.

On Sunday, we were asked to attend a Blessing ceremony by the mothers of a rural community. We participated in the most magnificent tribal ceremony; the young girls (rape survivors of the war) danced and performed, the boys danced, the women danced. The mothers and people of this remote community came together to show us the greatness of their hearts. They blessed our journey with prayer circles, presented each of us with the most beautiful handmade robes, and gave us the most Spiritual blessing of all, by renaming us after the mother who made our robe. I proudly write this as Mama Makula, Woman of Leadership and Strength, of the Fendell village, Margibi County, Liberia.

I share this story, because these are women similar to us that want their children to grow up in a safe home. These women are true survivors. They have so little but cared enough to share their most honorable of gifts with us. They are living representations of the women on every continent needing our attention, love and support. We all deserve to have the basics of water, food and shelter. Giving and sharing is something each of us can do to make a difference - one little girl, one woman at a time.

Education & Training Issues

Consider Oprah, Diane Sawyer, Condolezza Rice, Nancy Pilosi, Madam President Ellen Johnson Sirleaf, Julia Roberts, Serena and Venus Williams, Hillary Clinton, and NCAA Champion Rutgers Women's Basketball Team. Today's young girls aspire to be artists, doctors, musicians, lawyers, athletes, journalists, politicians, judges, entrepreneurs and presidents. They have role models in their lives and on TV living their dreams. It is unfortunate that, statistically, universal access to education and training for girls and women remain unequal to that of our male counterparts.

In Atlanta I participate in the National Coalition of 100 Black Women, Inc – MAC Teens on the Move, in which we mentor girls in inner-city high schools within economically depressed neighborhoods. I see and hear the hopes and dreams of our mentees and know their journey will be different than that of my very own nieces. My nieces live in the suburbs, with loving parents, individual rooms, every electronic device known to teenagers and have not a care in the world. My mentees, on the other hand, are just as beautiful, intelligent and talented, but their home lives challenge their very existence. There in single-family homes, with one parent possibly incarcerated, they live in dilapidated buildings in locations that change monthly. They fight every day to take busses, trains and walk to school, to study hard, be in the top 10% so they can be the first to attend college in their families.

High rates of poverty in the US and abroad force girls to drop out of school and expose them to potential sexual abuse. Studies in the US are revealing today's young girls in co-ed learning environments feel threatened, are low achievers in math and sciences, and have overall lower self-esteem. The shortage of teachers, especially minority females, is evident in every community further exasperating the plight of inner city young girls. All of these systematic downfalls lead to symptomatic issues in the female population. Globally, our daughters are in environments with no access to primary or secondary education. They are forced to travel miles to co-ed schools that do not want them. The societal and cultural demand for young girls to marry early, bear children, and tend the fields, produces an illiterate and vulnerable world population of females. When I traveled to the Dominica Republic, I had the opportunity to visit several schools while exploring the island's rainforest. Imagine children of all ages in one classroom, sitting on benches, sharing old books and one teacher. In reality, this was 2004. The next time you take a trip to the Caribbean or overseas, carry an extra suitcase and fill it with school supplies and learning materials for a local school (oh, and don't forget the candy). It will be the best tour you take that entire vacation.

We must reclaim our young girls. There is a direct correlation between our achievements in life as adults to the educational opportunities we have as young girls. Education is an essential human right for achieving economic independence. I encourage you to reach out and mentor a young girl outside of your environment. I often bring my nieces and mentees together so they can learn, share, and appreciate their individual God-given talents. And guess what, I learn, too.

Work Issues

Women are the backbone of societies all over the world. We spend the majority of our lives working paid jobs outside of the home and unpaid inside the home. Unemployment and underemployment are serious problems universally. The conditions, access to employment, and educational and skilled trade disparities are grossly out of line with those for men. Women in the United Stated still only make $.73 on the dollar compared to men. Women in developing countries are often forced to work for pennies or barter for food, shelter, and protection against violence. Women are not paid for equal or comparable work in any part of the world. Additionally, representation of women in positions of leadership and decision-making are less than 40% globally in private and public sectors. Take a look at the Forbes Fortune 100, or better yet 500, list, because you need a larger data pool in order to develop a reasonable statistic to show women at the helm in CEO, CIO, CFO, or any Cxx positions. Did you know there have only been three women leaders of countries, one of which was just elected in 2005, Madam President Ellen Johnson Sirleaf of Liberia. The increased visibility on the inequality of women in the global workforce has stimulated a growth in profit and non-profit organizations developing and implementing programs on education, skill training, and overall promotion of women in roles of leadership. We all know the world would be so much better, don't we ladies.

There are some good news stories. Three years ago when I became a statistic as a product of corporate downsizing, I joined the ranks of many other women as an owner of a small business. I could have chosen to transition into another corporate J-O-B, but I chose to take the path of independence. My desire to work in the community and in Africa empowering young girls and women for economic independence has opened doors to a wonderful new world. Today, women are the majority of small business owners and self-employment in informal industries. We are consultants, truck drivers, missionaries, mechanics, trainers, belly-dance instructors, computer specialists, life coaches ....we are "Doing our Own Thing and Doing it Well."

Safety Issues

Violence against girls and women, whether it is physical, emotional or sexual, has no barriers - income, class, or culture. Unfortunately, violence against women has existed throughout our history as a means of subordination. Sexual harassment, domestic violence, incest, rape, "honor" killings and wartime mutilations are happening every second of every day somewhere in the world in 2008. It's a vicious crime happening to our grandmothers, mothers, sisters, aunts, daughters, girlfriends, neighbors, church members and co-workers. The sadder statistic is, most violence against women is committed in the home by individuals we should feel safe with. In the US, 5.3 million women are abused every year and 1,232 are killed by an intimate partner. In the Middle East and African nations, women are killed legally for dishonoring their husband and family. The fear of harmful consequences for our actions keeps women from being fully engaged socially, politically and economically. It affects our work habits, family connections, personal ambitions and self-esteem.

In the Millennium Declaration created by the World Conference on Human Rights and the UN, the goal of combating and eliminating violence against women was ratified in 1993. The declaration has allowed the governing bodies to design and implement programs for education and intervention around the world. They have also been able to challenge governments to recognize these crimes, unbiased of cultural and societal demands, and prosecute through the criminal justice systems. The problem has not gone away, but the rules are being enforced with an increase of crimes being reported, prosecuted and recorded in 68 nations.

Sisters, we need to provide a positive supportive environment for each other. In Atlanta, Fresh Start for Women, Inc. (a not-for-profit organization) hosts quarterly weekend retreats and monthly workshops bringing successful Christian women and women survivors together to share their journeys. The sole mission of each session is to encourage wiser life choices through access to education and counseling. In order to begin the healing process and break the cycle of violence, we have to learn to develop healthy relationships. There are numerous non-profits and church organizations that need you. Share your story and life experiences. Make a difference.

Health Issues

Health can be summarized as a state of complete physical, mental and social well-being. Our *physical health* begins in the womb with prenatal care. All women wish to be a healthy vessel for their children. However, access to doctors and medicine is absent. Additionally, the restrictions (ritualistic & religious) and discrimination of women causes high 'female' infanticide, neglect and malnutrition. Violence against young girls and women increases our risk of sexually transmitted diseases and AIDS.

Physical health for women of the world is challenged by the varying images presented by media. Women are confused as to what represents a healthy body. Western nations are influencing women of other cultures to denounce their beliefs and become the picture perfect Barbie. Women in China are having life-altering cosmetic surgeries to have their facial features resemble Europeans. Sound familiar? What does this say about our self-image? We must learn to embrace our cultural individuality and our bodies as the temples they are. We must make nutritional and physical choices that are best for us.

Our *mental health* is challenged every day by the choices we must make to survive. Heart attacks are the leading cause of death for women globally because of the increased STRESS in our lives. Women are heads of households, working full-time jobs, and taking care of their families. For the first time in our history, our largest growing population is 60+ and needing supplemental care from their children. Women are stressed around the world. We must take the time to refill our tanks. We must learn to schedule an appointment with ourselves for much needed "me" time through pampering and support of ourselves and other women. We cannot help others if we do not first help ourselves.

Which leads us to *social health*. Society at large defines social health as access to health care and increasing prevention and awareness of the major issues afflicting us. I would like to suggest a different approach. Social health is feeding your mind, body and soul with Love, Joy, Peace, Patience, Gentleness, Goodness, Faith, Meekness, and Temperance (Gal 5:22-26). In a workshop I teach on "Envisioning U", we discuss dismantling low self-esteem, positive self-talk, the Superwoman syndrome and, "Who am I?" We end our session designing vision boards, pathway to our futures.

My favorite quote is, "Yesterday is a cancelled check, tomorrow is a promissory note, but today is blank." There are no do-overs like the childhood game of jack stones...Live Your Best Life.

Fresh Start

As you have read thus far, there are many common threads we share as women, regardless of which continent we were born on or live in. There is an ever-growing need for women to unite and connect internationally across boarders and waters to achieve equality. Make your FRESH START now…

Friendship – embrace the sister-friend relationships in your life and create new ones. Initiate connections across the waters via an on-line chat, club or blog.

Restoration – reclaim your life. Take the new improved you on a remarkable journey

Encouragement – tell your "She-story". Our testimonies are inspirations of survival and triumph for others.

Share – talents and skills are gift to be given. Volunteer, it's the best Spiritual booster.

Heritage – know your "Her-story", for it grounds your very being and molds your future.

Survival – women are natural born survivors; surround yourself with positive and uplifting people and make a difference in your life and the community.

Tireless – have continuous conviction and commitment.

Achievement – Dream It! Dare It! Do It!

Realization – *Visualize 2 Realize*; You CAN make a difference in the lives of one or thousands of young girls and women around the world.

Truth – shall set your FREE…Stand Up, Speak Up & Let Your Voice Be Heard.

Global Connection Resources:

www.un.org/womanwatch

www.care.org

www.womensissues/about.com

www.unitedway.org

www.womanink.org

www.freshstartforwomen.org

ABOUT THE AUTHOR

MICKI K. JORDAN, MLDR

Micki Kremenak Jordan is a mentor, trainer and coach. She has held a variety of corporate management positions over the past 25 years. She has participated on Visioning and Strategic Planning Teams, Leadership Teams and in Training and Development of staff.

Micki has a Bachelor of Science Degree in Sociology from the University of Iowa. After several years in the corporate world she obtained her Masters of Arts in Leadership from Bellevue University, Bellevue, NE. Micki is certified in Diversity Training, Public Speaking and Professional Coaching and holds the Certified Insurance Councilor Designation. She is a member of the Professional Woman Network (PWN) serving on their International Advisory Board and the National Association of Female Executives (NAFE).

Her passion is assisting others to recognize their true potential. She has written chapters entitled "Living Your Values" and "Mirror Image", that may be found in the PWN publications *"Women's Survival Guide for Overcoming Obstacles, Transition and Change"* and *"Women's Journey to Wellness: Mind, Body & Spirit."* She also has chapters entitled "Super Vision" in the book *"Overcoming the Superwoman Syndrome"* and "Are you a Shadow or a Light" in *"Women as Leaders: Strategies for Empowerment & Communication"*. Her latest chapter is "Macho Man: The Importance of Character" in *"The Young Man's Guide For Personal Success"*. All books are part of the PWN library.

This chapter is dedicated to her daughter, Kerri, a young woman that demonstrates *"A strong positive self image is the best possible preparation for success"* – Dr. Joyce Brothers. Kerri is comfortable with who she is and leading others by her example and by her direction. She will go as far as her dreams and aspirations may take her. Hold fast to those dreams!

Contact:
Micki K. Jordan
863 Gleamstar Ave.
Las Vegas, NV 89123
(702)463-5786
www.protrain.net
mk.jordan@yahoo.com

SIX

BEING YOU: ELIMINATING OUTSIDE INFLUENCES

By Micki Jordan

"Define your life in your own terms and live every minute consistent with the very best person you can possibly be." —Brian Tracy

Who are "YOU"? You are a composite of your genes and your environment. We cannot change our genes or our heredity; we have no control. The environment comes from the outside and ***we can control its effect.*** We are bombarded every day about how we look, what we should wear, what we eat, how we dress, act, talk and even how we think. Outside influences may come from family or friends. We are influenced by the media and products that we read, see, and hear. Among these are television, magazines and movies. The people we associate with at school, at work, or in social settings, are an influence on us. We are constantly bombarded by the world around us, and how we choose to be influenced by this "bombardment" is entirely up to us as individuals.

People Influence

Our families usually provide the first outside influences by the way they respond to us as infants and toddlers. Babies don't see themselves in either a good way or a bad way. Without really knowing it, our early behavior is molded through positive and negative responses. We all learn the rewards for acting in a manner that is acceptable to others. We also learn how to get attention for behavior that sometimes is not always positive. These early outside influences often lay the foundation for how we will continue to function and behave as we grow older.

What were some early outside influences you can remember?

1. ____
2. ____
3. ____

Designate these influences as positive (P) or negative (N) and why you feel that way.

1. ____
2. ____
3. ____

The messages we receive from those important in our development begin the formation of our self-image. If we are continually told we are pretty or cute or smart as we grow, these positives become part of the basis of our self-image. The same is true if we are told we are stupid, in the way or even clumsy; these negatives become part of our fledgling self-image. At a young age, because these messages come from those people that provide our nurturing, we believe they are speaking the truth. Brian Tracy said, "*Destructive criticism in childhood causes you to fear failure and rejection as an adult.*"

Often as we grow we are compared to other family members, brothers, sisters, cousins or others, that may have higher grades, are better athletes, or are more talented. Think of examples you might have heard growing up.

1. ____
2. ____
3. ____

Or perhaps you were the one held as the "model" for others. Either way, this can be detrimental to your self-image development.

Our playmates and peers are also early influences on our actions. The desires to be liked and accepted often cause us to behave in a manner that is not consistent with our feelings. Often times these behaviors become habit in order to elicit the desired results. As children and teens, we may strive to be like the popular kids, to look and act the way they do, in order to be accepted into their group. A big problem with being a comparison thinker is that you can always find someone better to compare yourself against.

There may also be an opposite result with a young person going to opposing extremes to attract the attention of those they want to impress. An above average student may suddenly stop studying and begin to get below average and even failing grades. The class clown may be someone that feels acting "stupid" is the only way to be noticed; outlandish or inappropriate attire becomes a billboard saying, "Look at me." Findings have shown social networks have power over how people eat, how they handle weight issues and on physical appearance.

Think of examples of opposite extremes you have observed.

1. ____
2. ____
3. ____

"Most people are other people. Their thoughts are someone else's opinion, their lives a mimicry, their passions a quotation." —Oscar Wilde

Media Influence

Our experiences in life help to shape us as individuals. However, the commercials we see on television may have the most influence over our choices and decisions. More than 98% of U.S. households have at least one television, and watching consumes an average of 30% of adult leisure hours. Our youth spend even more time in front of the screen playing video games and watching television programming. Teenagers want to look and be like the stars they see on screen.

The television ads and shows inundate our thoughts with how we should look, and what products to buy to achieve the image we want to portray. Unfortunately, it often leave us with the feeling we can never be pretty enough, or perky enough, or thin enough to reach our desired goals. The big and little screen even shows what careers we should have. I am not sure of the success one might achieve as a terminator or that we can all achieve the academic knowledge to work for the Smithsonian. In recent years we have seen women elevated to running corporations, but isn't it often at some expense to their actual psyche? Aren't these women often shown as being either different, or cold, or uncaring? What is wrong with the average, slightly overweight, soccer mom actually having some brains and business and social savvy?

Take some time on Saturday morning and watch the cartoons or dig out some of the classic Disney movies. How many of these feature a girl as the heroine or as the dominant character in the story? How many depict the female as slender and attractive? How many have characters like the kids you played with or like your children's friends?

Name some familiar cartoons or Disney movies that are a realistic comparison to our daily living? Hard to do, isn't it?

1. ______________________________
2. ______________________________
3. ______________________________

Think of the shows you watch and how they portray the role of women in society.

What are some television shows or movies that you feel are somewhat unjust to the realistic portrayal of women?

1. ______________________________
2. ______________________________
3. ______________________________

How about ones you feel depict women in a positive role?

1. ______________________________
2. ______________________________
3.,______________________________

Isn't it easier to think of those that are negative roles than those that are positive roles?

Media also comes in a printed format through the slick print of magazines and the newsprint of our local and national publications. If you were to stand in front of the woman or teen magazine sections you will see *Glamour, Cosmopolitan, Prom Cosmo, Teen, Vogue, Seventeen* and similar publications. The women shown on the covers are not the average woman; they are models, movie stars, and musical artists. Even the women shown on the covers of *Time* or *Newsweek* are usually not the one's you might meet at your local coffee shop, at the mall or in your workplace.

The articles within these publications tell us how to rid ourselves of unwanted pounds, reduce the nasty crows-feet and wrinkles, how to get the man of our dreams, why we are unhappy, and in general how to right all that is wrong with us and with our lives. No wonder we are such a negative society! We identify with the sensationalism of human problems and deficiencies. It may make us feel that we actually are okay because we don't have the issues they are writing about. It also may make us believe we might have similar issues and we maybe need to find out how to fix what is wrong with us (even if we aren't sure what is wrong!).

"We are the product of editing, rather than authorship."—George Wald

Being You

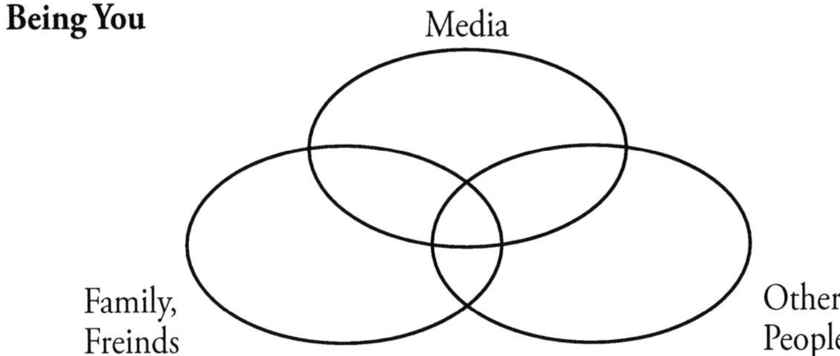

The above Venn Diagram depicts the cross over of outside influences and the roles that others play in the development of our lives. Be aware, no one person or group of people can influence all or most of any individual's behavior. Our thoughts and actions are part of our sense of identity. This sense of identity becomes our self-concept. Our self-concept comes from:

1. Other people's opinions and judgments about us.
2. Our comparisons and perceptions of the ways we are different from and similar to other people.

A very important component of our self-concept is our self-esteem or our self-perception. Our self-esteem has been shown to be directly affected by whether 1) and/or 2) above is viewed as positive or negative. Brian Tracy said, *"Self-confident people do not compare themselves to others. They only compare themselves with the very best they can be."*

No one can define who you will be. Your self-concept, self-esteem, and self-perception become part of your belief system. Your entire personality is held together by these beliefs. They reside in your subconscious mind and are often not easily changed once they have been developed. There is no set definition for your beliefs and how you use them. Nancy Sim, in her *A Creed To Live By* stated, *"Don't underestimate your worth by comparing yourself to others. It is because we are different that each of us is special."* She also said, *"Don't set your goals by what other people deem important. Only you know what is best for you."*

How does one become their own person? We are constantly being bombarded by, and some times sabotaged by, other people's opinions and advice of who we should be and how we should act. Every time we turn on the television or read a magazine, we are reminded of how we should look or how we can become better or more successful. The important thing is to *"Be yourself; everyone else is already taken."*—Oscar Wilde. The following are steps you can take to BEING YOU:

1. You have to find yourself. If you don't know, understand or accept yourself, you can't be yourself.

2. Stop listening and caring about the perceptions of others; it doesn't matter what they think. What matters is that you are comfortable with yourself.

3. Be honest and open with yourself and others. We all have our flaws; we aren't perfect in everything we do and say. Life is a constant learning experience. Admit your mistakes and grow from them.

4. Stop worrying about what might be; the world won't come to an end because you mess up. Relax and enjoy the ride with the ups and downs.

5. Learn how to express yourself as an individual. Be proud of who you are and what you are becoming.

6. Celebrate your accomplishments in life. To quote Brian Tracy, *"You are nature's greatest miracle. There never has been and never will be anyone just like you!"*

7. Above all, believe in YOU. Believe in who you are and stop trying to be someone you are not. You will never be happy trying to be someone else. Be proud of the way you are, and accept yourself for who you are - flaws included. Just BE YOU.

Be Yourself

By Ellen Bailey

Why would you want to be someone else,
When you could be better by being yourself?
Why pretend to be someone you are not,
When you have something they haven't got?

Cheating yourself of the life you have to live
Deprives others of that only you can give.
You have much more to offer by being just you
Than walking around in someone else's shoes.

Trying to live the life of another is a mistake.
It is a masquerade; nothing more than a fake.
Be yourself and let your qualities show through.
Others will love you more for being just you.

Remember that God loves you just as you are.
To Him you are already a bright shining star.
Family and friends will love you more, too
If you spend time practicing just being you.

ABOUT THE AUTHOR

SHARYN LYNN YONKMAN

Sharyn Lynn Yonkman is the founder and principal consultant for Lynn Consulting Group, a personal and professional development training organization. Lynn Consulting specializes in career advancement skills for the professional woman, helping her in achieving personal excellence. As a passionate advocate of women's Self-empowerment and life balance issues, Sharyn offers special expertise in dealing with transition and change in the workplace, as well as programs designed for those of the baby boomer generation.

As former CFO of several high profile retail and hospitality companies, Ms. Yonkman has gained valuable in depth financial and managerial experience in the corporate community providing the knowledge for cost effective solutions for todays business challenges. Programs available include: Interactive Sensitivity and Diversity Training: Superior Customer Service in Retail and Hospitality; and Handling Conflict Fear and Transition.

One on one individual life balance coaching is available in addition to group sessions. Highly customized curriculum is offered to meet your specific organizational needs. Ms. Yonkman is a Co-author of *Remarkable Women*, an anthology project with Marci Shimoff of "*The Secret*", and actress Jennifer O'Neil. Additionally, she is an author in several of the PWP library books, including *Becoming The Professional Woman* in which she addresses overcoming fear ; *Overcoming the Superwoman Syndrome,; You're on Stage! Image Etiquette, Branding & Style; A Woman's Survival guide for Overcoming Obstacles, Transition and Change,* and *Beyond the Body! Developing Inner Beauty.* She is currently completing a self-help book for baby boomer women facing the challenges of moving from the first act of life to the second, and would love to hear input from her fellow boomers on how they feel. Please contact her at the info provided below.

Author, trainer, motivational speaker, and life balance coach, Ms. Yonkman is available internationally to help the individual or organization with their professional and personal developmental needs.

Contact:
PO Box 1266
Ventura, Ca 93002
805.677.3117
www.protrain.net
Lynnconsult@ yahoo.com

SEVEN

THE SELF-FULFILLING PROPHECY AND THE NEGATIVE MIND

By Sharyn Lynn Yonkman

"You create your own universe as you go along." —Winston Churchill

Much is written about the perils of negativity within the PWP library (and elsewhere), but this particular chapter's focus is on the self-fulfilling tendencies negative thinking has, courtesy of the Law of Attraction. This prophecy is based on the law that thoughts become things, and if we hold negative thoughts and beliefs, those will be our experiences. To put it simply, we are the ones that create our reality, for good or ill. I can hear the moans of some upon reading this, insisting that they are not responsible for their current circumstances, since they never thought of, nor wanted a particular event. But, please take a leap of faith and stay with me for the next few pages. I, too, spent most of my life staunchly defending myself that I was not a pessimist but a realist. The more I focused on "the way things really were", the more of it I eventually got. It turned out that I created my reality with my negative (realistic?) thoughts, and this mindset cost me dearly.

The purpose of writing this chapter is to help you avoid similar results. For those of you already onboard and understanding the Law of Attraction, I hope this chapter will serve as a refresher course by adding some yet unrealized insights and tools. For the naysayers out there, I ask only why not give this a chance? You are already here and have nothing to lose and much to gain.

The Law of Attraction – The Essentials

"All that we are is a result of what we have thought."
—Buddha, 563BCE-483BCE

We cannot escape the laws of metaphysics. Our thoughts are a powerful source of energy in the universe behaving like magnets. Basically, thoughts become things and like attracts like.

What you think about and focus on most will eventually appear in some form in your life experiences. Everything exists because of the energy of attention. As one places attention (thought) on something, it becomes more powerful and draws like energy to it. Conversely, things we do not give attention (thoughts) to are either never created or perish from the lack of attention.

The mind is neutral energy. The way you think, the choices you make, determines whether the results are positive and therefore beneficial, or negative and harmful. A simple thought is not so simple, for left unchecked, the energy of negativity will attract more of itself to whatever you are creating.

Self-fulfilling defined:
Brought about or proved true because of having been expected or predicted

"Heavy thoughts bring on physical maladies."
—Martin Luther, 1483-1546

I Invited This?

Thoughts are extremely powerful, much more powerful than most people give them credit for. When you think about what you don't want, you are posting the invitation, via the Law of Attraction, to bring that experience into your life, and then are upset when the universe RSVP's.

Few of us would agree to the notion that we brought about our current (unwanted) situation, but that is exactly what happened. What you give thought to is what you invite into your experience, for thoughts grow and gain power. Most people spend the majority of their time thinking about what they don't want, and then are surprised and upset when it keeps showing up over and over in their life.

EXERCISE:
What are your predominant thoughts? Take time right now to jot them down in the spaces below. Write down the first few things that come to mind. Analyze how you are spending your time and your power. You may be getting negative situations by default.

____

____

____

____

Admittedly, it is very difficult to *not* focus on a bad situation while mired in it, but the longer you stay focused on the negative the more power it will gain. If you continually focus on the pain or LACK in your life, you will get more of it.

Going Down?

Your classic *downward spiral* is a disturbing example of the Law of Attraction in action. It all begins with a little negative thought, which in turn becomes more thoughts that gather and attract even more. Dwelling on the negative simply contributes to its power.

The more you think negatively, the worse you feel. When you are thinking negatively and feeling unhappy, you cannot attract happy. It defies law (of attraction). Holding negative thoughts in your life, along with their inevitable negative expectations, tend to create self-fulfilling prophecies. If your thoughts reflect the attitude, “I can’t possibly do that”, chances are that prediction will become a reality. If you have mainly negative expectations, you will probably find life more difficult and will always be awaiting the next bad thing to happen.

Dwelling upon one's scarcity of anything brings on more of the same. Habitually thinking about negative thoughts also tends to pull you down into depression, escalating the decline. Your thoughts, and ultimately experiences, continue to spiral downward.

Let's look at the following example. Suppose you want a new car, but you believe you cannot afford the one you want, so you begin to feel badly about yourself. Your thoughts become negative and before long feelings of depression set in. One bad thought leads to another: you do not make enough money; you will never make enough to afford this car; you probably will never have another car, and so on the downward spiral to despair and ultimately hopelessness.

If you say there are no customers, no good men available, no good jobs, etc., there will not be any new customers, quality dates or career opportunities. You will attract what you focus on and what you expect.

"What you resist persists."—Carl Jung 1875-1961

The good news is that it takes many negative thoughts, with persistent focus on them for a sustained period of time, to bring about something bad. However, if you persist, in time it will appear.

How To Withdraw Your Invite (or better yet, never send it)

The remedy is very simple:

- Spend more time focusing on what you really want in your life.
- Spend less time thinking about what you do not want.

Letting go of the negative, while embracing the positive sounds like a simplistic statement, yet the difficulty involved in accomplishing this can be significant.

The following is an exercise to complete to help you start to do just that. You need to know what you want so that you can focus upon it.

Exercise: Your Personal Top-Ten List

In the spaces below, list the 10 things you want most in life. Being clear on what you want will make it much easier to focus on. You need to know what you want so that you can consistently focus upon it.

1. ______________________________
2. ______________________________
3. ______________________________
4. ______________________________
5. ______________________________
6. ______________________________
7. ______________________________
8. ______________________________
9. ______________________________
10______________________________

The Law of Attraction does not understand nor recognize the concept of not. For example, you should not say, "I do not want to be tired and sick." Instead, you should say, "I want energized, good health." Rather than saying, "I do not want to lose my job," tell yourself, "I want to enjoy a long and happy tenure at my place of employment." Do not think, "I don't want there to be a traffic jam." Instead think, "I want free flowing traffic." See the difference?

Watch for these Warning words and phrases in your thoughts and speech:
Can't | not able to | too hard | futile | hopeless | don't have | I'll fail | not important

Remember, there is no excluding your thoughts, even if you say no to them. Even if you say STOP to a bad thought, it will continue to grow for the simple reason that you are still focusing on it and giving it attention. It's not likely you will <u>never</u> have a bad thought, but if you are aware and mindful of them, you can quickly withdraw your attention from the unwanted thought. Simply focus on what you really want instead and eventually, as you think less about the unwanted, it will lose power.

Don't bother to try to erase the past (negative) thoughts. Your time is better spent merely focused in the present (positive).

Essential Element - EXPECTATIONS

Viewing life as having limitless opportunities opens the doors for those opportunities to materialize. It focuses our minds on possibilities, rather than limitations. You are far more powerful than you could ever dream. When you focus on what it is you really want, and then believe and expect for it to happen, the energy of expectation will bring you the wanted results that much sooner.

Expectation is a potent attraction force. It is not enough to simply focus on what you want. The next most important step is that you must expect your want to become a reality. You must believe that your want will manifest into your experience. Visualization is a great tool to enforce your belief and strengthen your expectation. Expect what you want, see it already in your life, believe it is coming. Hand and hand with the power of expectation, creating from a point of happiness and sense of gratitude for wherever you are now, is essential. Always create from a feeling of joy and gratitude. Find ways to place yourself in a happy state of mind when setting your attention on what it is you want.

Thoughts influence our emotions and cause responses in the body. Think of something you love and notice how you feel. Think of something you hate and notice that feeling, as well. The positive thoughts, such as joy and fulfillment, have positive effects on your emotions, such as enthusiasm, calmness, etc. Negative thoughts, such as unworthiness and fear, produce negative results, such as anxiety and anger.

EXERCISE: **Creating your happiness/gratitude touchstones**. Take some time to think about the things that truly make you happy. For example: a certain song / pets/ playing with children / walking in nature, etc.
List them below.

____

____

____

____

Now that you have this list at the ready, you can use these touchstones to bring you to a place of joy and gratitude at any time. Starting from this place, a place of gratitude and happiness, your creation process will be that much more powerful and will produce the desired results much quicker.

The Choice is Yours.

Okay, now for the good news or bad news - depending upon how you feel about the responsibility associated with free choice. You get to choose your thoughts. Now this may be something that some of you might argue or struggle with, but the unvarnished truth is that we can choose how we think. We have the awesome power to decide how we want to see any situation, how we want to react and how we want to feel. You can choose to create more to feel negatively about, or choose to create more to be happy and grateful for. Positive thoughts give you limitless possibilities, while negative thoughts severely limit your potentiality.

Remember, the way to more happiness is not to focus on your current lack of it, but to focus on happiness, and all that may mean to you, instead.

No More Negative Nelly

As I confessed to you in the opening paragraph of this piece, I am a recovering Negative Nelly myself. I say in recovery, for it is a work in progress every day for me to renew my mind, but an assignment I look forward to completing, for I now realize the benefits of this important work. It is a perilous and very slippery slope back to the valley of "I didn't ask for this" and I would like to take this opportunity to express my gratitude to the like-minded people in my life that help me keep on track, for they make the work easier, more rewarding and fun.

Yes, fun. Although it is work, and sometimes very hard work, I want you to know that this process can also be fun. It is exciting to see your expectations come to fruition, and there is a delightful sense of wonderment on what will happen next, what great surprise is right around the corner.

I highly recommend your seeking out the fellowship of those individuals who are on the same wavelength. You will be doubly blessed and you can reinforce and cheerlead one another on. Support is superb, so invite those like-minded people into your life and avoid those who are not. Why not put an open invitation to the universe for all the things you really want, and happily await the positive response?

Finally, I would like to invite you to reach out to me with any questions or comments you may have concerning the content of this chapter. I would be happy to share my personal experiences regarding this most important subject and provide any further guidance that I can.

Thank you for spending your valuable time with me. I hope you will start letting the Law of Attraction work in your favor, for your greatest good.

I wish you all the best.

Notes:

ABOUT THE AUTHOR

LaWanda S Dudley

LaWanda S Dudley is Founder and the Chief Executive Officer, of The SmithDudley Group, an organization specializing in empowerment seminars for women, young adults, and youth. She has more than ten years of professional experience. As a former Flight Attendant, she traveled and explored different cultures and is committed to educating individuals on the importance of diverse corporate cultures, business etiquette, professional image and maintaining a positive attitude. The SmithDudley Group was founded in 2005, created to motivate, inspire, encourage, and empower individuals to make positive changes in their life.

Ms. Dudley was educated in a universal setting; experiencing the unique challenges faced by today's women, young adults, and youth. Her determination to make a difference motivated her desire to fulfill the need for empowering and building the self esteem necessary to achieve greater mental, physical, spiritual and emotional health.

Ms. Dudley has a BS in Management and is currently pursuing a MS in Counseling/Psychology. In addition to working as a volunteer in her community, she has facilitated workshops on Leadership, Professional/Teen Image, Perception and Self-Esteem. Ms. Dudley is an active member of The Professional Woman Network International Speakers Bureau.

Contact
LaWanda S Dudley
The SmithDudley Group, LLC
P. O. Box 610353
Birmingham, AL 35261
(205) 337-2428
lawanda@thesmithdudleygroup.com

EIGHT

UNMASK! REVEALING THE REAL SELF

By LaWanda S. Dudley

What does unmask really mean?

According to Webster's Dictionary:

- Unmask is defined as to disclose the true character.
- Real is defined as not imaginary, fictional, or pretend.
- Self is defined as the essential qualities distinguishing one individual from another personality or character.

Revealing the true self is a challenge that requires extreme discipline; after completion, you will have created a sense of peace. This experience will motivate you to be all you can to your real self. If self is real, then everything else is whole. Wearing a mask can feel like you have on blinders; your inner vision of self is in darkness, and your real self needs to be brought to the light. When the light is shining, you will become thankful for who you truly are.

Grasping the thought of identifying your real self can be overwhelming. You feel you are limited to the undersized choices of socially expected behaviors and personalities, although the belief doesn't portray your real self. You are unsure about the real self from the distraction caused by the reality that society periodically keeps you from acknowledging the absolute difficult strengths of each day, while you continue trying to improve life. Your real self exists, even if you decide to acknowledge it or not. It is hidden under your insecurities and learned behaviors. Appreciating your power to celebrate the real self is living a life of complete fulfillment.

The Mask that covers up your Real Self has been developing throughout your childhood. Your emotions and ideas were furthermore unavoidable articulations of your real self. The behaviors were not created overnight and will not disappear immediately. You played dress-up as a child and pretended to live in a make believe world. This pretend world has developed a false image of the real self. The real self is the place hidden deep within; it is there were your true feelings, dreams, values and beliefs are located. When you can be your real self, you make decisions in life that are satisfying to you, and are not concerned about what others think.

If you're living behind a mask, it is not too late to remove it. Getting free from the mask by meditating can force you into your uniqueness. In order to discover your role in life, it is important to be comfortable with your real self; learning how to accept you, regardless of the consequences. I would suggest meditating daily for 20 minutes silently, taking walks in the park, and concentrating on thankfulness. Don't think about making a to-do list.

I know you are busy with the daily routines of life, but I am a witness of how these exercises can change your life. If you have difficulties finding time to spend alone, try rising a few minutes early in the morning or listening to a good inspirational book on audio to smooth the ride to and from work. Also, visit your local library or bookstore to purchase literature on dealing with the real self. When I first started removing the mask in my life, I would sit in my room for hours listening to inspirational music and reading my Bible. It created a peace and a calmness that I learned to practice in my everyday life. Experiencing the real you will allow you to be at peace and in love with your self. There is a sense of confident, empowering, competent feelings when you are being your real self.

Let's Reveal the Real You!

When was the last time you made a decision and didn't concern yourself with the opinions from others or what they thought about you? During this decision process how did you feel?

- Trust yourself by listening to your heart and don't doubt the energy you are feeling. Many times we question what we feel in our hearts and start to doubt ourselves.

- Always maintain Integrity by telling the Truth about how you feel. Recognize whatever you maybe experiencing and embrace it. Don't try to figure everything out all the time.

- Enjoy everyday, and be thankful. Focus on giving value to what you are working on and not what others make, think or say.

- Don't be afraid to take some time out for you. It is ok to say no to others, especially when you are not respecting your goals and values.

Questions to Ask Yourself:
Who Am I? Why am I here?

____

____

____

What do I truly value within myself? Why?

____

____

____

What values motivate my daily life?

____

____

____

What makes my life meaningful?

____

____

____

Taking off the mask is a process that will take time, but don't get discouraged and give up. Remember, it was not created overnight. Visualize how the average woman applies facial make-up: cleanse, moisturize, anti-aging, foundation, eyes shadows, lips, and cheeks and then finishing powder. You add all the ingredients to make a "perfect" look, but it took some time and patience. When removing the make-up, you don't think about the time required to create your "perfect" face. It is important to understand that removing the mask to reveal your real self will not happen automatically. The best way to overcome the unmasking process is to not set a completion timeline, but to continue making progress and to make sure you continue finding out the real you. Not questioning the path, but focusing on your individual destiny. I truly believe each of us is assigned our own individual destiny. Therefore, it is crucial for you to learn how to love and accept all the imperfections about you. Be patient, kind and respectful to you!

Write down all the physical dislikes about you. After you complete a list, replace the word dislike with the word love. For example: I dislike my flabby arms. I love my flabby arms. Many times we focus on our physical attractions, without realizing these attractions don't make us happy, complete, satisfy us nor does it provide real self-love.

I Dislike	I Love

Remove the mask, as my mother would say. "Grow up, life is too exciting to be worried about making others happy. Celebrate you; embrace who you truly are and allow the radiant light to shine through. For God created you, and there aren't any mistakes in his creations."

I hope you will unmask and continue to reveal your real self, realizing that we are to focus on the importance of greater spiritual, mental and physical healing. It will allow us to be better women, which will create great mothers, daughters, wives, sisters and friends.

Pain

Sometimes it feels like rain.
It makes you feel upset,
Especially when you didn't expect to be a reject.
The thing about it is,
I look inside, and examine myself,
Trying to learn, so I can turn this thing around.
It doesn't matter what I found,
This energy I have to make a turnaround.
God has given me all I need
To fulfill a life I can succeed.
By LaWanda Dudley

Notes:

ABOUT THE AUTHOR

Phyllis Avery

Phyllis Avery, President of The Avery Group, is a Certified Diversity Trainer with special emphasis in Women's Issues and a member of the Professional Woman Network (PWN), an international consulting organization specializing in professional and career development. She is a mentor for several small business women in the Greensboro NC area.

Mrs Avery is a Qualified Practioner of the Myers Brigg and Strong Career Interest Inventory. She holds a B.S. in Industrial Organizational Psychology from High Point University.

Mrs. Avery serves on the Board of Director for Beauty 4 Ashes. Professional affiliations include: member of NAFE (National Association of Female Executives), Psi Chi and SIOP (Society for Industrial Organizational Psychologist) and the Greensboro Chamber of Commerce.

Client List

Rockingham Community College , Small Business Center , Wentworth, NC
Kollege for Kids , Rockingham Community College, Wentworth, NC
Women of Seasons. www.womenofseasons.com
Tom A. Finch YMCA, Thomasville, N.C.
House of Jkare www.houseofjkare.com
Beauty 4 Ashes International www.beauty4ashesintl.org
Pleasure Chateau www.pleasurechateu.com
Malik Davis Creations

Phyllis is available for speaking engagements, workshop facilitation, and small business consulting.

She wishes to thank her mother for the love, teaching and encouragement, and also her best and closest friend, Jkare, her sisters, and Constance (who is like a sister) are to be thanked for their love, support and commitment.

Contact:
336. 616. 8159
P O Box 19621
Greensboro NC 27419
www.averyprofessional.net
info@averyprofessional.net

NINE

OVERCOMING THE GOOD LITTLE GIRL SYNDROME

By Phyllis Avery

"What you think of me is none of my business. What is most important is what I think about myself." —Dr. Wayne Dyer

One year ago today I lost my father; I had always wondered how it felt to lose the person that you loved the most. Oh, I had heard stories of indescribable, inconsolable grief but had never experienced it. My daddy was the love of my life, my hero, my cheerleader; he was the man whose opinion I most solicited and respected. His unexpected death on the morning of February 25, 2007 brought about a time of introspection and self-reflection for me. As I thought about the life that I had lived as an adult, I realized that the unbearable loss that I felt was not the worse that I had experienced. No, the most profound loss that I had experienced was the loss of self.

I had become so preoccupied with the expectations, needs, wants, and desires of others (and just fitting in) that I did not know or even recognize when the "real me" left the building. Women oftentimes confuse the roles that they play in their day-to-day activities with labels that they consider being "self". It is very easy to test this theory: just call up one of your girlfriends, sisters or mothers and ask them to define themselves. You will hear responses like: I am a teacher, I am a mother, I am a sister, I am a friend, etc. Some of the women that you speak to may define themselves by the cars that they drive, or the houses in which they live. As young boys and men are taught to be aggressive and to take action to get what they want, many girls and women are taught to be quiet, be small, behave and not cause any problems or make any waves.

What is a Good Girl?

We begin to create labels at an early age. Think about the messages that you heard as a small child of what constituted being a "good little girl." These messages often start out as parents try to teach their young children what they *don't* want them to become. I was raised in an all-girl household with three sisters, and if your parents were like mine, they wanted to raise their female children to **not** become "bad girls". My parents felt as if they had to forbid all traces of bad ways of thinking, feeling and acting. As is the case for most of our parents, my parents used "bad little girls" or "bad girl" behavior as the anti- models and tried to raise me and my siblings to be the opposite.

Our minds have a way of holding onto labels and definitions and acting them out. Take a moment to review some of the descriptive words that are used to label "bad girl" behavior. I encourage you to take a moment to recollect some of the examples that were cited to you as a young girl.

Good little girls are:

- Not negative
- Not self-centered
- Not angry
- Not rebellious
- Not selfish
- Not a talk-backer
- Not dishonest
- Not loud

Did you notice that most of these examples require contrasts? Well, most parents also point out what "bad girls" are like. The following is a list of typical bad girl messages that a child hears.

Bad little girls:

- Fight
- Swear
- Are dirty
- Talk back
- Cheat
- Skip school
- Are noisy
- Lie

Research indicates that some female children hear these statements about what a "good little girl" shouldn't do and learn that it is extremely important to cooperate in trying to be "good" and not to be "bad". Well, the problem is that the childhood message that people are either "good" or "bad" carries over into adult life. One of the toughest things to do when we become adult women is to reject those messages that we heard as a child. Otherwise, these messages usually show up as behaviors in relationships and other interactions with people.

Our "good little girl" behaviors may also derive from what we were taught as children regarding respect and authority. Consider this, as children we often learn to place more value in what others think, especially authority figures such as doctors, lawyers, police officers, older siblings etc. It seems that authority has two basic sources: fear and respect. Using a scale from 0 to 10 (0 being not at all and 10 being the most), on the continuum below we can see that the total source of a person's authority could be thought of as equal to the combination of how much they are feared plus how much they are respected.

Source of Authority
Fear Respect
0 1 2 3 4 5 6 7 8 9 10
Fear + Respect = Total Source of Authority

For example, in a dysfunctional family a child might fear their parents (Fear = 8) and respect them (Respect = 2), for a total of 10. In a healthier family, the authority base might be more like Fear 1, Respect 9, again for a total of 10.

Authority Figure	Fear +	Respect =	Total
(Example) My Manager at Work	2	6	8

Unfortunately children are sometimes taught to fear authorities rather than respect them. As a result, the person who is taught to fear authority figures may always defer to their opinions. Conversely, if we respect the authority then we have the ability to disagree with them.

Looking Glass

If you want to know if you have fallen victim to any of these patterns of behavior, review the following actions:

Women who are experiencing "the good little girl syndrome" tend to:

- Smile when they are really upset
- Not show true emotions when they are angry
- Smile and compliment people to their faces, but say critical things behind their backs
- Warn others about "bad people" or people who are "bad for them"
- Not be able to accept compliments
- Worry about others thinking that they are selfish or tough
- Try to appear "small" when they enter a room i.e. sit with their ankles crossed, hands folded, taking up as little room as possible
- At work the woman who is struggling with "good girl syndrome" may exhibit these behaviors:
- Will not openly express criticism.
- In group meetings she will smile and go along with the manager and when asked to express a contrary opinion will decline to do so. But as soon as the meeting is over she is the first one to complain.
- When entering a meeting, they may quietly slink into the room rather than walking in with confidence.

- They are motivated by things outside of themselves.

In dating relationships the "good little girl's" main concern is:

- How much does he like me?
- Focus on pleasing him.
- She has set herself up to fail in every relationship because there is absolutely no way to satisfy every person.

Double AA's included

Have you ever purchased a product that needed batteries? Better yet, have you ever purchased a product that needed batteries, and much to your excitement, discovered that the batteries were included in the product packaging? Whew, what a good feeling – especially when you had purchased that coveted birthday or Christmas present that required batteries to operate. Well, acknowledgement and approval can give us the same feeling of relief and excitement. Think about the last time that someone acknowledged something nice that you did for him or her or seemed to approve of something that you were wearing. How did the person express the acknowledgement or approval? Did they do it privately or in front of others? Let me make a vital point here. It does feel good to get acknowledgment and approval from other people. However, the problem comes when acknowledgment and approval is the motivating force of your life. Think about that famous little pink battery-operated bunny that we have become so familiar with on television commercials. The little bunny is motivated by those Double AA's that he needs in order to operate – when he gets those Double AA's he keeps going and going and.... . It's the same reaction that those of us who are susceptible to "good little girl" syndrome give to what we deem as approved behavior. We keep going, and going and ......

It's a losing situation to be constantly striving for approval based upon other people's standards and expectations. In my personal journey of looking for self, I realized that I habitually gave into other people because I couldn't stand the thought of upsetting them. I put my needs to one side because I enjoyed everyone else's happiness. There is such an epidemic of people-pleasing type behaviors that in early spring 2007 Dr. Robin Smith appeared on Oprah and discussed these behaviors and how to stop seeking the approval of others. I am going to share some of the steps that I went through in an attempt to recover from "good little girl" behaviors.

Life Doesn't Frighten Me.

Dr. Maya Angelou completed a beautiful poem that was featured in a children's book entitled, "*Life Doesn't Frighten Me.*" In the poem she highlights the courage that exists within each of us, and she discusses the fact that, in order to overcome fear, we must have faith in ourselves. Look at the fears that are surrounding you regarding this "good little girl" behavior. Are you afraid to change because you feel that no one will like you or might leave you? Do you fear that you will be left alone if you don't do or say the right thing?

"Even the fear of death is nothing compared to the fear of not having lived authentically and fully."—Frances Moore Lappe

Live Authentically.

Stop basing your self-worth on how much you do for other people. It is one thing to want to help others, but you should do it because you want to do it, not because you feel like it is something that you should do because you don't want to disappoint another person. Learn to trust your own actions and choices; know they are the right ones for you in your life. Remove your mask and be true to yourself. You don't have to live for anyone else's approval.

Start With a Small Thing and Then Work Your Way Up.

Learn how to say no without making up excuses. "No thank you – I don't have time today." Really successful people are not afraid to operate outside of their comfort zone. Stop fearing that someone else is going to judge you. Stop caring about what other people think of you. One of the reasons that we place a lot of value in the approval of others is that some people tend to confuse attention with love. We also confuse disappointment with a loss of love.

Self-Acknowledgement

Remember the Double AA analogy we discussed earlier? I am going to teach you another way to get that same motivating charge through self-acknowledgement. Self-acknowledgment is the belief in your own authority. It is the way that you talk to yourself about your attempt to reach your goals. "Self-talk" (as those of us in the psychology world call it) is what you tell yourself about events; it is talking to yourself in your mind. If you were acknowledgement-deprived as a child and experienced constant criticism, you are more apt to talk to yourself in a critical way as an adult. Berating yourself turns off motivation and makes you feel small and unworthy. Acknowledgement is powerful and it is also free! Self-depreciating self-talk is not humility, it is self-abusive and the impact of negative self-talk about your achievements or accomplishments is far greater than you probably realize. Negative self-talk is a bad habit, but you can successfully change it. Catch yourself doing something right. Most of us tend to focus upon things that we have done poorly or failed to do; this hampers your motivation and makes you feel depressed and demoralized. Instead, train yourself to focus upon what is right, positive and good about your efforts. If you need a scriptural reference to help you with this exercise, consider Philippians 4:8. *"Finally, brothers, whatever is true, whatever is noble, whatever is right, whatever is pure, whatever is lovely, whatever is admirable–if anything is excellent or praiseworthy, think about such things."* – (NIV) and Proverbs 18:21, *"Death and life are in the power of the tongue: and they that love it shall eat the fruit thereof."*

Shake Up Your World – Just Stop!

"Stop trying to be so small. Stop thinking that your presence is bothering other people."—Ann Vertel (Business Success Coach).

Shake up your world and the world of those around you. Stop justifying everything that you do, think, feel or believe. You don't owe anyone an explanation of who you are.

Stop saying I am sorry and apologizing for your actions. Are you in the habit of apologizing for everything? "I am sorry - this is not what I ordered." Why are you apologizing for the mistakes of others? Conclude this mission by taking charge of who you are. Do not continue to accept the unsolicited opinions of others. Become fully present in your life – don't disappear like I did. Stop trying to fit in. You don't have to be the good little girl any longer.

ABOUT THE AUTHOR

Alesia Bryant

Alesia Bryant holds a B.A. in Economics from Spellman College in Atlanta, Georgia and a M.S. in Management from Troy State University. She is currently completing her PhD.

Ms. Bryant has worked in Human Resources for over 16 years with the Federal Government. She is a member of the Atlanta Metro HR Professionals Council. She also has a strong background in runway modeling and is the former winner of "Ms. United States Woman Supermodel" with style competition.

Contact:
Bryant & Associates Consulting
P.O. Box 918
Atlanta, GA 30301
404.308.1377
AlesiaBryant@aol.com

TEN

THE CREATIVE SELF: DESIGNING THE LIFE OF YOUR DREAMS

By Alesia Bryant

You are a beautiful and wonderful miracle, a unique and awesome creation, and I am delighted to have you as a student because I know that we are going to have a wonderful time together learning how to explore your creative self and design the life of Your Dreams. I am going to teach you how to create a strategic plan and design the life that you want. You will learn about a very important Partnership that you will need to recognize. This Partnership will be a key component as you work the plan for your life. You will learn about critical life elements and how they play a role in understanding the life that you were born to live. I will teach you about learning curves and how they shape the foundations for your life. You will learn about the 45-Degree

Dedication Line and the importance of "stick-to-itiveness". You will complete a self-assessment that will help you with creating the DNA for your life.

Everything around you started as an idea in someone's mind; then it became reality through creation. Creation is a part of life and at the very core of existence. "In the beginning, God created the heavens and the earth. And the earth was without form and was dark." Then God created what he desired. The Infinite Power that started it all used His power and created the world. And, that same Powerful Spirit flows within you, as well. As an extension of the universe and all that is within, you have the same creative spirit that flows through all living creatures. You have the ability within yourself to create anything that you desire. You can create the life of your dreams. I am so excited about having this opportunity to teach you and I know that you are going to be splendid!

A Strategy for Designing the Life of Your Dreams!

If you want to have the best design for your life, then the key is not in *you* creating that life by yourself. It's about working with God and creating that Life, together with Him. My dear, this has been a tried, true and fail-proof system throughout the ages and this will be your strategy. When you put forth a true and real desire to do His will, then He will create a life for you that you would never have believed would be possible. He will create a life for you that transcends the Spiritual existence and is awesome. Believe me, you'll see as everything begins to take shape and form; you will be left saying, wow! So, from this point forward you are entering into a Partnership with God to design your new and amazing life.

Critical Life Elements: Hobbies and Interests

Your hobbies and interests are important in the design of your life because they are connected to the higher purposes of your life. It's true. The reason you like these activities is because they come from your soul. I remember when I had interest in modeling and pageant competition, and I absolutely loved collecting books. Plus, I loved being a part of certain businesses and partnerships. However, it wasn't until I had actually gone through the process of The Creative Self: Designing the Life of *My* Dreams that I realized how connected my interests were to my higher purpose. It was really amazing how it all came together. My collection of books became my arsenal of knowledge that would be the foundation for being equipped to live my purpose. Modeling and pageants were critical keys to who I really was and how I wanted to present myself outwardly; business ideas and partnerships would be the elements that would provide the strong financial support needed to maintain and live my life and purpose.

Learning Curves

We all have learning curves. These learning curves represent the timeframe it takes for you to learn and get the life experiences you will need to support your designed life. It's your preparation time. Learning curves can expand to various degrees. Embrace your learning curves. Get as much as you can from them. This is your time to complete your education, work, learn and understand money management, time management, or whatever you need. It's a time to get your credentials and it is also the time for making mistakes and learning from those mistakes. Imagine a game where your opponent knows everything about the game. He is a certified expert, but really wants you to win.

So, He plays with you, tossing out various moves, just to see what you will do. And, the moves your opponent makes are designed to set you up to win easily. There is one catch: with each move you make, there are consequences that you have to address. These consequences can be in the form of going back to school, taking on a second job, working harder, whatever you need that will create a learning experience and give you credentials which will make you qualified to live your dream life and higher purpose. Anyone can describe a life they believe they want to have; however, there may be skills, educational requirements, financial backings that are necessary to be successful in that life. Your success in accomplishing those critical life elements will have an impact on your designed life. They give you the credentials and tools needed to support it.

God is very thorough. When you are in partnership with God to create the life of your dreams, He will make you and mold you. He will teach you and listen to you. He wants you to represent Him well and to do that, you have to be properly prepared. Once your preparation period or learning curve is completed, you will then walk into your life, the life that you created in partnership with God.

The 45-Degree Dedication Line

As you begin to create the life of your dreams, it is important to realize that you will be at a 45-degree angle starting point. The starting point is point B, also called Base. The horizontal line of the angle represents time, and is called BC, meaning Base to Change. The vertical line represents the life of your dreams that you will get in partnership with God, considering your hobbies, interests, education, work and other critical life elements. This line is called BA, meaning

Base to Awareness. Your learning curve is in the middle of the two lines. As a student of creating the life of your dreams, you must realize that your learning curve can expand from a short period of time to years. Your time frame is based upon your own personal life environments and experiences, As you are working through your creative self and designing your life, you will utilize time to make it through your learning curve. At the end of this time, you will be at change, or point C. However, at the same time, you will be going higher towards your new life, until you reach point A. At point A, you reach Awareness and are ready to walk into your designed life. As you work through your learning curves, you also become closer to living your dream life. Stick to it. Be dedicated, have faith and trust your Partner. It will happen for you. Be committed to go the distance of your dedication line. The best is yet to follow.

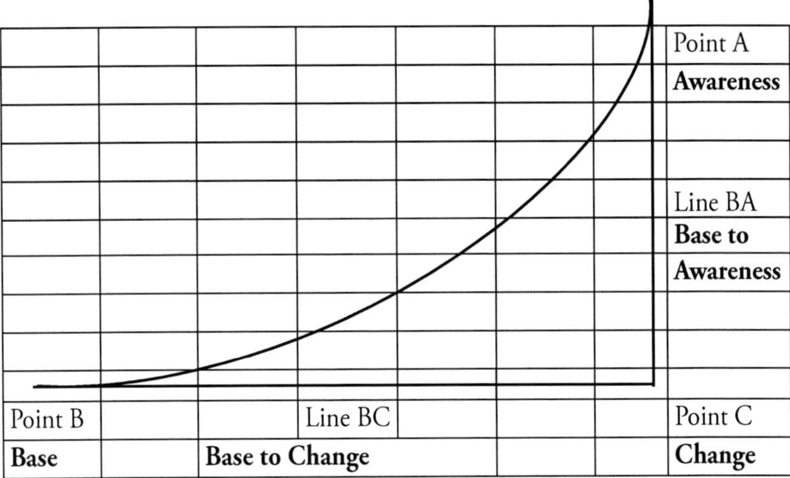

The Power of Surrendering

Faith is believing in that which you cannot necessarily see, but which you know is true and real. As you begin to work your 45-Degree

Dedication Line, you may have to step out on Faith in some instances, knowing that a particular way is the path that you need to take. However, keep in mind that making decisions and surrendering based upon Faith have results that are positive. They make you a better person, more complete, and gives you Peace because these Faithful insights are God's actions in your partnership. He is making a move. Next, it is your turn. By surrendering to God, you are putting your trust in His suggestion. Pretty soon, you will begin to see that the Faith-filled action created an experience that you will need in the new life that is being designed especially for you.

Insights and Intuitions

Pay attention to insights and intuitions, especially those that come back to you over and over with the same thought. These can be notes from your Partner, handwritten notes that are true and important. Keep in mind that God knows what is best for you, but you are working together in a Partnership to create the life of your dreams, so you will have to do your part, as in any other type of business venture. Creating the life of your dreams is an adventure, and it's *strategic*. You will have actions to take. And, sometimes your Partner will leave messages and tell you what to do, or give you information. Don't lose the notes by ignoring your intuition or forgetting critical insights. Your dreams and wants are important to your Partner. He wants you to be happy, but he also wants you to be a reflection of His desire for you, which is a far better than you and I could ever hope to imagine.

Self-Assessment

In this section, I want you to take a complete inventory of yourself. This will help you with creating the DNA for your life. How much do you really know about yourself? How in-tune are you with your inner self? On the following pages you will find a series of questions that you are to answer. The answers to the questions will help you to become more in-tune with yourself. This is your self-assessment and analysis. This is a secret and personal book. No one has to read it but you. In your journal you will write down personal feelings and thoughts. Afterwards, you will put all your information together and decide the most appropriate object for your life DNA.

Let's Get Started

On the very first page of your journal, paste a recent photo of yourself. Write underneath your name, age and the date. Turn the page and you are ready to begin Part 1. You may write the question in the journal if you prefer, or you can simply answer the questions. If you answer the questions only, be sure to answer in a complete sentence. By answering in complete sentences, you can look back after a period of time and still understand what you wrote. Go beyond yes or no responses. Really put heart and thought into your answers and write them down. Take as much time as you need to answer the questions. There is no rush. Just remember to be completely honest with yourself.

Exercise:
Personal Analysis Questions

1. Describe yourself in detail by writing your own personal advertisement.

2. What are your hobbies?

3. What are your interests?

4. If you could change places with anyone in the world, would you? Why? If yes, who would it be and why?

5. If money were not an issue, what type of life would you have?

6. Are you happy? Why?

7. Are you a spiritual person?

8. Are you a leader or a follower? Why?

9. Do you believe life is what you make it, and that you have the power to be whatever you want to be? If not, why not? If so, how far are you willing to go to get what you want?

10. Do you let minor obstacles get in your way and stop you from accomplishing your goals?

11. Are you easily frustrated and do you let small things bother you? Why?

12. Do you do your absolute best in all situations, for example school, work, parenting? If not, why?

13. Are you an organized person?

14. Are you content with your educational level?

15. Have you accomplished all that you want to accomplish in life? If not, what is missing?

16. Do you worry unnecessarily about anything? If so, why?

17. Do you give into peer or group pressures? If so, why?

18. Write an overall view of how you see yourself. Who are you?

Once you have completed this self-assessment, go back and read over everything. This information will be used to create the DNA for your life.

Three Steps to Creating the DNA For Your Life

Creating the object that represents your life DNA should be a playful act. Be happy, be free, and let your imagination take over. Be clear on what you are creating before you begin. Think about your hobbies and your interests. Go back and look at your self-assessment. Think about something that you have always wanted that is significant to you. Do not try and create the life of your Dreams. This exercise is not for you to do that type of creating. If you do, you will place limitations on your life. Only your Partner has the insight and knows it all to create the best life for you. Your role for this exercise is to create the *starting seed.* Your life will grow in some form or fashion from this seed or DNA. This is why you will create something that you want that reflects your hobbies and interests and those things that make you happy and give you a sense of well-being.

Step 1: Sit or lie in a comfortable spot, close your eyes and relax. If you prefer, you may have on soft and light music. This should be music that places you in a relaxing state of mind. There should be no singing, only music, and the music must be low and in the background.

Step 2. Imagine standing in an open field. This is a field with beautiful green grass all around. Imagine a fresh smell in the air and the beauty of a warm spring morning. No one is in sight. The sky is clear and blue. Imagine breathing in the crisp spring air. Breathe in and out. At a point when you are ready, imagine that you begin to grow taller.

Pretty soon you are so tall that you are looking over all the buildings and houses around. Continue to grow so that you are overlooking the tallest trees and mountains. Pretty soon you are among the pure white clouds. The clouds are all around, and amid the clouds you spot your canvas.

Step 3: As an artist starting from scratch with a blank canvas, so shall you be. Go to your canvas and create what you want. This should be one single object. After you have created the object, imagine going down, down, down, overlooking everything that you saw when you where growing tall. When you reach your normal height and are back at the field, breathe in and breathe out 3 times, then open your eyes and reflect on what you created.

Your Support System

Friends and family provide you with a support system for your life. These are the people that will encourage you, be there for you, and motivate you to be your best. Seek out those friends who are in line with your desired life. If you are still within your learning curve, they can provide you with the energy and inspiration to continue through the challenges. Relationships can be a really inspiring element because that special person can provide an abundance of energy and motivation for you. Children can be your strongest supporters because they want you to succeed. Just as we want to be proud of them and their accomplishments, they also want to be proud of us and our accomplishments. By creating and designing the life of your dreams, you also set a standard and example for your children and others that are touched by your life.

Designing the life of your dreams is going to be a process of thinking about what you want - with no limitations - and God transforming it into a bigger and better experience. It's about surrendering to God and trusting, no matter the circumstances. It's about having the desire to put Him first and allowing Him to take over and make you, mold you, and turn you into that lovely gem that is at the very heart of your being. You are His Partner in the design of your life. I have really enjoyed this time with you and wish you much success and happiness in your quest to create the Life of your Dreams!

ABOUT THE AUTHOR

AHMON`DRA (BRENDA) MCCLENDON

Ahmon`dra, President of Brilliance Inc., is an international speaker, facilitator, motivator and author. She imprints an indelible impression upon your heart and makes you smile, laugh, cry and contemplate the deeper issues of life. She arouses in each listener a passion to commit to his or her higher purpose with her grace, power and spirit.

With twenty plus years in the human services arena and an MSW from San Francisco State University, Ahmon`dra has developed a highly successful program called P.L.A.N.E. – "Passionately Living A New Existence." She has spoken to thousands of young adults in North America, Europe and Africa on how to create a powerful future by staying devoted to their dreams, trusting their intuition, boldly taking risks and asking for what they want.

She is a Certified Facilitator for Motivating the Teen Spirit Inc. a teen empowerment program that conducts transformational workshops, and leads the international program, Core Value Training as a Senior Instructor. Ahmon`dra is a recipient of the "Speaking with an Active Voice" grant sponsored by the American Medical Women's Association and Pharmacia Corporation.

A contributing author to the best selling book *Chicken Soup For the African-American Soul*, she was featured as a keynote speaker for The Monster Diversity 2003 Leadership Program in the United States.

Passion and magnificence exude from her presence with an amazing energy of wisdom, healing & love as she creates, flies and soars! Get clear on your life and passions with the energy and excitement of Ahmon`dra

Contact
Ahmon`dra (Brenda) McClendon
Brilliance, Inc.
484 Lakepark Ave pmb 485
Oakland, California 94610
ahmondra@brillianceincorp.com
www.protrain.net

ELEVEN

WOMEN AND ADDICTIONS

By Ahmondra McClendon

Addiction is on the rise in the lives of women. Many are suffering in silence with a serious problem. In an attempt to maintain control and meet their ever-increasing responsibilities, women have unknowingly developed dysfunctional behaviors. Left unchecked, these behaviors have evolved into full-blown addictions.

Drugs, alcohol, gambling, smoking and sex used to be the most common addictions, but other behaviors such as eating, shopping, watching TV, exercising and socializing are now on the list. These behaviors are harmless if used occasionally to relieve stress or anxiety. However, when they are relied upon for **comfort,** occasional use turns into obsessive use. The result is a total loss of control. The journey into addiction can be quick and unexpected, whereas the trip out can be long and arduous.

For twenty plus years, I existed inside a prison of drug and alcohol addiction. To the outside world, I appeared happy, successful and accomplished. Behind closed doors, I was scared, miserable and confused. I was out of control and I lived in constant terror that this horrible secret would be exposed. I struggled to find answers. How could I be strong and powerful in some areas, yet so weak and helpless here? Why did I allow this to happen? Each day I labored under the crushing weight of my addiction until I found the help I needed to break free.

In this chapter, it is my intention to give the reader information to help clarify addiction. Utilizing my experiences from 22 years of active addiction and 21 years of unbroken sobriety I will:

- Show the link between stress and self-medicating behaviors
- Explain the cycle of addiction
- Outline the process of recovery
- Define relapse prevention

Addiction - The Link between Stress and Self-medicating Behaviors

Any environment saturated with high tension generates pressure. When this pressure is not released, it creates emotional stress. Allowed to accumulate, emotional stress turns into internalized pain. Internalized pain causes dis-ease and agitation in the body. To get relief, behaviors such as eating, shopping, drinking, smoking, etc. are used. With excessive use, these self-medicating behaviors may turn into addictions.

Identify Areas of Stress

High Tension = **Pressure = Emotional Stress** = Internalized Pain = Self-medicating

1. List the pressures in your life that have caused emotional stress. For example, the domestic violence (pressure) in my home caused fear, uncertainty, and anger (emotional stress). These feelings created internalized pain (agitation, dis-ease).

____

____

____

____

2. Explain how internalized pain (feelings caused by emotional stress) has affected your life.

   Example:

   - The fear prevented me from trusting myself and others.
   - The uncertainty created a state of hyper-vigilance. (I always looked for something bad to happen.)
   - The anger developed into an uncontrollable temper.

____

____

____

Identify Self-Medicating Behaviors

High Tension = Pressure = Emotional Stress = **Internalized Pain = Self-medicating**

1. List the behaviors used to self-medicate (relieve internalized pain).

Example:

- I took tranquilizers to soothe my feeling of fear.
- I drank alcohol to ease my feelings of uncertainty.
- I shopped to placate my anger.

____

____

____

The Cycle of Addiction

Pain triggers an automatic response in the body for relief. When relief comes, it is accepted, no matter what form it takes. Because the body remembers the effect, it will demand that same relief anytime pain is present.

The moment we experience internalized (emotional stress) pain, we feel the urge to relieve it. We use what gives the most comfort, and we keep using it (regardless of the consequences) in an attempt to free ourselves from the pain. Since the pain is not eliminated but only masked, our attempts to gain lasting relief are in vain. The more we use, the more we need, until we find ourselves caught in the trap of addiction. Addiction is, "The condition of being habitually or compulsively occupied with or involved in something."

Identify Active Addictions or Potential Addictions

List all compulsive, obsessive behaviors.

Example:

- I eat compulsively and I am obsessed with food.
- I drink compulsively.
- I shop compulsively and obsess over the money I spend.

___

___

___

2. List the impact these behaviors have on your life.
   Example:
   - I have gained over 150 lbs. Because I am ashamed of my weight, I don't socialize. I stay home and eat.
   - I isolate myself to keep others from knowing how much I drink.
   - I have trouble paying my bills and I am in debt over my head.

___

___

___

3. List the feelings associated with these behaviors.
   Example:
   - I feel depressed and lonely.
   - I feel afraid.
   - I feel angry and frustrated.

___

____

____

4. Describe how the <u>feelings reinforce</u> the <u>behaviors</u> and how the <u>behaviors increase</u> the depth of the <u>feelings.</u>
   Example:

   - The more I feel depressed, the more I eat. The more I eat, the more weight I gain, and the deeper I go into depression and despair.

   - The more I drink, the more frustrated I get. The more frustrated I get, the angrier I get with myself, and the more my anger turns into self-hatred.

____

____

____

Recovery

<u>The Process</u>

Recovery is a process, not an event. It will not happen once and be over. In truth, it is a life-long commitment that requires courage and patience. The journey of recovery is personal and begins when you are ready. The first step is to ***STOP*** active addiction.

When you stop self-medicating, the floodgates to your emotions open and the internalized pain pours out. You must commit to <u>feel the pain</u> and go through it <u>no matter what</u> otherwise, you succumb to the pain and seek relief (begin self-medicating).

Identifying the Three D's

1. Make a clear DECLARATION about your situation.
   Example:

   - I am addicted to prescription drugs and my life is in shambles.
   - I am addicted to taking care of others so they will love me, because I don't love myself.

   ___
   ___
   ___

2. Make a list of what you DESIRE to have in your life.
   Example:

   - I desire to take care of me first, say no to others when I want to, and not feel afraid that they won't love me.
   - I desire to live without having to depend on pills for comfort.

   ___
   ___
   ___

3. List a specific outcome (related to the desire) you DESERVE and put a date to when you will receive it.

   Example:

   - I deserve to take a vacation and I will sign up for a singles cruise in August.

- I deserve to have fun, so I will sign up for a dance class on 6/1/08 and attend without taking pills to build up my courage.

____

____

____

4. Identify a source of support for your particular addiction. Example:

    - I will attend a meeting for co-dependency.
    - I will follow through on my doctor's recommendations for my pill addiction.

____

____

____

Relapse Prevention

Relapse prevention is a series of actions specifically designed to keep the addict from lapsing back into active addiction. When active addiction is stopped, the most difficult task is to ***stay stopped***. Understanding what triggers addiction can prevent it from activating. Any feelings, condition, or incident that triggers (stimulates) internalized pain can instigate self-medicating behaviors. Self-medicating is the beginning of a lapse back into active addiction.

The Cycle of Relapse

Trigger (losing temper) / **stimulates** / internalized pain (anger) / **starts** / self-medicating behavior (relapse) / **activates** / obsessive, compulsive behaviors (active addiction)

<u>The Process of Relapse Prevention</u>

Identifying a trigger can disrupted the cycle of relapse.
Example:

What develops, when trigger is activated (losing temper)

- A perceived threat (someone screaming) activates the flow of adrenalin in the body. Breathing becomes shallow and temper is triggered.
- Hearing ceases (no reasoning is occurring, only reacting), body feels discomfort, and readies for defensive action. Shallow breathing increases and anger surfaces (internalized pain).
- Reactions start, voice raises in pitch, body goes into fight / flight response, and full force of anger hits (pain increases).
- Self-medicating behavior (drinking) starts to bring anger (internalized pain) under control and comfort back into the body.

What develops when relapse prevention is in place (temper held in check)?

- At the first sign of threat, take a deep breath, relax muscles, be conscious of the adrenalin being released, and notice irritation (temper being triggered).

- Concentrate on what is being said. Keep taking long slow breaths, keep muscles relaxed, and use reasoning to decipher what is real and what is perception (delay anger from emerging). Stay present to the other person's communication and body language.

- Begin to formulate a response (not a reaction) by analyzing the situation and deciding what outcome you want. Continue to breathe deeply, keep your body relaxed, and remain in control by staying present.

- Respond to the situation. Talk in a non-accusatory tone, speaking clearly and slowly. Keep your body relaxed and allow the other person to have their anger and opinion. Don't push your agenda and don't make them wrong. When acceptable, excuse yourself from the situation. If the verbal attack continues, do nothing. Keep breathing and listening but don't speak. When appropriate, walk away quietly. The most important issue is that you maintain your composure, stay conscious, and don't allow your emotions to trigger your temper and unleash your anger. Stay in control of your reactions.

Relapse Prevention Strategy

- Using the above examples, identify a trigger (something that creates emotional pain or stimulates negative feelings) and outline what happens when it is activated.

____

____

____

- Make a second outline and develop the necessary steps for a relapse prevention (keeping trigger from activating) strategy.

____

____

____

- Do this exercise for each trigger (anger, rejection, etc.), creating a comprehensive program for relapse prevention.

____

____

____

Remember to S.T.O.P. - *Stay Tuned on Prevention!*

- Be alert and stay focused on what is happening in and around your immediate environment (identify pressure).
- Understand and use techniques to handle triggers (negative feelings that stimulate internalized pain).
- Develop strategies to cope with stress (situations outside of your control).

Create a *New Life* Free of Addictions

It doesn't matter if you are walking on the path of addiction or heading toward it. You have the power to change direction. Don't be afraid and don't hesitate. If I could stop an active addiction after 22 years and then stay stopped for 21 years, YOU CAN TOO!

Take that first step and start on a new path to **LIFE!**

Author's note: Please contact a physician or addictions counselor to assist you with overcoming addictions and chemical dependencies. This chapter was written from my own personal experience in hopes that my journey to recovery will help you. However, it is highly recommended to also seek the advice from a professional health specialist.

Resources:

National Mental Health Association
2001 N. Beauregard Street - 12th Floor
Alexandria, VA 22311
703-684-7722 or 800-969-6642
www.nmha.org

Society for Women's Health Research
1828 L Street, NW, Suite 625
Washington, DC 20036
202-223-8224
www.womens-health.org

The National Women's Health Information Center
A service of the Office on Women's Health in the U.S. Department of Health and Human Services
800-994-WOMAN
www.WomensHealth.gov

Notes:

ABOUT THE AUTHOR

Essie Nail

Essie Nail is the founder and President of Essie Nail & Associates, an organization dedicated to the training and development of women. Her mission is to assist women *ascend to higher heights in their personal and professional growth.*

She holds a Bachelor of Arts degree in Journalism with a minor in Marketing from Georgia State University. She is a Customer Service Professional, a Certified Trainer of Women's Issues and Diversity, Certified in Faith Based Counseling and Ministerial Education, and soon to be a Certified Life Coach.

Essie Nail & Associates designs workshops and seminars that specialize in promoting the emotional, physical, and spiritual well being of women, along with personal and professional success coaching. The training is offered to a wide range of women and encompasses corporate, religious, and community groups.

Ms. Nail is a member of the International Professional Woman Network (PWN), and Women Impacting Norfolk Southern Corporation (WINS). She is an active member of the Church of Acts in Atlanta, GA where she has served as New Member Coordinator, Co-Leader of the teen ministry, and is currently serving as Intercessory Prayer Coordinator.

Contact:
Essie Nail & Associates
P.O. Box 561
Union City, GA 30291
(770) 969-2578
essienail@yahoo.com

TWELVE

THE GLUE THAT BINDS: UNDERSTANDING SISTERHOOD AND FRIENDSHIP

By Essie Nail

"The bond that links your true family is not one of blood but of respect and joy in each other's life. Rarely do members of one family grow up under the same roof." —Richard Bach

How simple and beautiful is Richard Bach's quote. If not for malevolent forces at work in so many female relationships, I could just borrow this as my definitive statement regarding sisterhood and cheerfully move on. Instead of moving on however, imagine with me one circle of girlfriends, perhaps on a girl's night out, indulging in a good laugh at such a sweet sentiment. The discussion would inevitably touch on how women sometimes betray and batter one another under the very guise of friendship. This recall might also conjure up images of how females call one another unbecoming names, give or receive the proverbial evil eye, or dare to aim that *you must be out of your mind* stare at a target in the middle of another's back. Now is this what sisterhood is about?

On the other hand, your eyes might get misty thinking of a day you sat on a 'pity pot' and could not rise; a sister pulled you up. And then there are the times you laughed outwardly but secretly cried within; a sister recognized your pain and hugged you until you were calm. Is this sisterhood?

Whether observing malevolent or good forces, understanding sisterhood and the glue that binds is necessary to tip the scales permanently toward the good. Webster's Dictionary defines a sister as *being a female person having the same parents or one parent in common; a woman or girl allied to another or others by race, creed, or a common interest; membership in a society, and more.* To understand the deeper relationship that is alluded to in Richard Bach's quote however, we must examine the heights and depths of the female soul and explore the sister-friend connection.

It is my belief that there is within us something comparable to an adhesive substance; super glue (if you will) that not only binds friends together, but also serves as a gateway into a higher realm of spirituality. This super glue will bind two or more friends tightly and permanently. It is strong enough to withstand controversy, heartache and pain, disappointments and any other strong force designed to cause separation. Determining what ingredients make up this powerful adhesive and how to live by their principles will transform ordinary relationships into life giving, life building, and mutually beneficial friendships that define true sisterhood. My research uncovered several components that I think personify this super glue. I will list these ingredients and give some practical applications.

Ingredients of the super glue of sisterhood:

- Showing acceptance without qualification
- Knowing that sometimes there are no easy solutions
- Examining yourself before looking for perfection in others
- Learning to listen without always offering a solution
- Not always asking to be heard; be willing to listen
- Practicing forgiveness
- Cultivating peace and harmony
- Maintaining an attitude of gratitude
- Ridding yourself of tools of destruction - envy, hostility, lying
- Getting in touch with your spiritual side
- Loving at all times
- Being a friend

There are no overnight solutions or quick fixes to enhance understanding. Applying these ingredients is a one-day-at-a-time process that ultimately has the potential to harness and heal some deep-seated emotions stirring within females. This glue will act as a bonding agent sister to sister. The application is more than a notion but quite doable. There will be times, for example, when you will feel as if a friend has literally ripped your heart from your chest. The pain runs so deep nothing and no one could possibly help, or so you think. This is the time to apply the glue of *sometimes there are no easy solutions* to this broken place.

If you are quiet and remain still long enough, you might also be able to picture in your mind's eye another friend who has become somewhat sullen and is entirely non-responsive towards you. She is so tight lipped that the strongest attempts have not succeeded in getting her to open up. You have done nothing to warrant this attitude as far as you know, but the situation continues. It is time to apply the glue of *peace and harmony*. Be patient with the sister.

What about the friend who displays such wonderful insight, a person of exceptional intelligence? Unfortunately, she never shows up for an engagement on time, and when she finally arrives without an apology, she points out that your dress is too tight, really ugly, or out of style. You know this friend; she is perfect and appears to feel a little sorry for anyone who is not her. Apply the glue of *practicing forgiveness* and add a dash of *showing acceptance without qualification*.

At this juncture, I have a question. Has a friend ever committed an act or said something so painful that you considered it unforgivable, and even today hold on to it? Write this act in the space provided below, or if this scenario does not apply, give an act that you might feel is unforgivable. But be sure that you are relating the issue to someone you consider a friend.

____

____

____

____

Now ask yourself, is this incident more important than health, peace, well-being, or life itself? If it cannot get pass this simple test, let it go. It probably is not worth losing your friendship over. Life does go on, but the quality of your life depends on you. It is time to apply the glue of *love at all times*.

What type of people would choose friends referred to thus far, you might ask? I request that you reserve judgment. After compiling data, observing, and using personal experience, the overwhelming conclusion is simply that people are people. There are different educational levels, varying degrees of integrity, honesty, wisdom, understanding, and insight. People are young, they are old, have great vision, and yes some have a certain naiveté. But universally, everyone wants to be loved, to be happy and to be accepted. A true sisterhood provides all of these things and more. It can include women, men, children, any religious group and fraternity of any kind. This type of friendship connection transcends gender, race or religious affiliation. I believe it is safe to assert that any broken place among any group could use this glue that binds.

Amazingly, all of the ingredients that make up the super glue of sisterhood are already on the inside of you. You do not have to go here and there searching. I have already identified some of them. Use and develop the ingredients and nourish them. For just as a tiny mustard seed falls into fertile soil, and grows and produces a great plant that becomes a shelter for the birds, you will not only grow and flourish yourself, but will help provide shelter for another sister in the midst of her storm. This is an application of the glue of *examine yourself.*

I feel compelled in this writing to share with you, the reader, something that is occurring in my life. It is ironic that I should be writing regarding emotional wellness in women at a time I am experiencing such tumultuous emotional flux. I find myself applying the glue of understanding each day in order to make it through. The reason being, my mother is seriously ill, having become barely recognizable as the vibrant person that I once knew. She all too often does not recognize me. I am actively applying super adhesive to this situation. I have welcomed my sisterhood into the situation for support. I believe it is important to include trusted sisters in difficult times.

However, because there will probably be instances when no one is available, in that midnight hour so to speak, it is necessary to learn to apply the aforementioned ingredients to your own broken places. Today I applied the glue *maintain an attitude of gratitude*. What are you grateful for? Write at least three things for which you are grateful today, especially if you are in some kind of turmoil or confusion. Focusing on gratitude will help to lift you mentally and emotionally.

I am grateful for:

____

____

____

It is one thing to *know* about applying glue to achieve sisterhood, yet another to *actually apply it.* There is a vital area to consider. Although you are probably comfortable with the people in your inner circle, beware of whom you bond with. It is imperative that you choose your friends wisely, however, not looking for perfect people. Do you know someone who tries to encourage and to motivate you? Is there someone who is *willing to listen and not always wanting to be heard*? Is your associate concerned with your well-being, and is that person there for you in times of trouble? Do you have a friend that you can laugh with and have fun? If you have found such a friend, bind with that person and apply the glue; *be a friend.*

You have applied the super glue to many broken places, and by now should be walking away from the shadows of emotionalism and hurt and fast approaching understanding. It is time to go deeper. As I previously stated, I am convinced that a true understanding of sisterhood and the glue that binds can serve as a gateway to a supernatural realm called spirituality. A very real clue here is that by definition, a gateway can be opened or closed. You are looking to open a door to your higher or spiritual self that was previously closed or partially closed.

In this computer age, yet a new definition for a gateway has emerged. A gateway enables communication between computer networks that use different communications protocols, also called a router. The sisterhood gateway is communication between the mind and the spiritual nature - different protocols or formats, yet still able to communicate.

Spirituality as defined by Webster's Dictionary is: *breath of life.* For the sake of this writing, I will make a distinction between spirituality and religion. While religion is grounded in tradition, codes of behavior, rituals and beliefs, spirituality deals with more inherent qualities such as consciousness, love, essence, serenity, trust, and wisdom. Spiritually as defined here provides an open door or gateway to a Higher Power, God, or whatever you recognize your breath of life to be. Breath of life or spirituality similar to the wind denotes a divine force that, although invisible and immaterial, is also a force so powerful that a person's inner being can shift and move. This is an application of *getting in touch with your spiritual side.*

As with all the aspects of understanding sisterhood, spiritually is reached by diligence and a sincere desire to ascend to a higher state. Learn to set aside time to review; come away from your everyday activity, especially matters that clutter your mind. Look at your pain and learn from it. Look at what is working for you and what is not. Take the time to relax. What is your favorite relaxation technique? Meditate, listen to music, and dance. Remember, life is about both joy and pain. The spiritual gateway will slowly open as you focus. Concentrate on your essence, *gratitude, forgiveness, peace, acceptance, self-examination, love, and a listening ear.* Your life and the lives in which you are linked or bound will transcend. Your new reality rises above your human or self-centered nature to a higher spiritual nature.

In the face of abusive relationships, divorce, blended families (remarriage with two families coming together), gender discrimination, violence and the list goes on, it is more important than ever to bring light into our lives. Spiritually is that light and it lights from the inside out. Old attitudes and actions begin to fade as spiritual forces along with the other glues of understanding become active. Imagine no more *tools of destruction,* envy is gone; backstabbing is indulged in no more; condemnation has all but vanished. Friends are being forged (glued) together into a sisterhood. But it will be up to you to put in the necessary work to gain it, maintain it, and practice to prevent losing it.

Applying the glue that binds brings understanding, and understanding brings unity. Unity seals this bond that holds friends fast to one another. *"The bond that links your true family is not one of blood, but of respect and joy in each other's life. Rarely do members of one family grow up under the same roof."* Richard Bach's quote has become more than just another sweet sentiment.

May I share my conclusion with you poetically? I feel that poetry lends itself to expression that is higher than nature, or facts, or history. Man-made objects and ideas can be visualized with a new mentality, out of the box, not charted and bold, truths that are matched somehow to a higher spiritual actuality.

Experience Sisterhood

Sister, step up and take charge of your reins
Of change, of hope, of love against undue pain.
Expand your mind as you learn a positive vent,
Even as life's negative elements urge you to relent.
Sister, forgive, forget, show gratitude and gain
A peace and harmony as acceptance sustains.
Look to solutions worked out for the best,
For the common good is your new request.
Do not decline, but ascend to heavenly places.
Wipe out tools of destruction, leaving no traces.
Replace the bad with good, for your change has come.
Sister, lift up your soul to a higher Power. Shalom.

—Essie Nail

ABOUT THE AUTHOR

Sharon M. Hudson

Dr. Sharon M. Hudson is a corporate trainer and an Adjunct Professor. She facilitates education and training via face-to-face, blended courses and online. She provides coaching to employees and students to increase their knowledge, competencies, and skills to ensure their marketability in this fast-changing environment.

She has participated in an international exchange of information with a focus on the adult learner with universities and social service organizations in South Africa. She has her own business, Hudson Institute for Excellence, with a focus on Coaching, Diversity and Women's Issues, and Leadership.

Dr. Hudson's formal education includes a Baccalaureate degree in Liberal Arts, a Master of Arts degree in Communication, Governors State University, and a Doctorate in Adult Continuing Education, Northern Illinois University.

She is a member of Professional Woman Network, National Association of Female Executives, American Association of University Women, and the American Society for Training and Development.

Contact
Dr. Sharon M. Hudson
Hudson Institute for Excellence
15774 S. LaGrange Road #250
Orland Park, IL 60462
(708) 227-3737
sharon@hudsoninstitute4excellence.com
www.hudsoninstitute4excellence.com
www.protrain.net

THIRTEEN

THE POWER TO CHANGE: OVERCOMING THE NEGATIVE ATTITUDE

By Dr. Sharon M. Hudson

Green, reddish, orange, brown, or a combination of these; they appear at certain intervals. To see them all together is a heavenly sight. They are leaves during the fall season. The seasons change each year to give us variations of beauty from God. We have no control over this process. The change comes automatically.

Just as the seasons change, life does as well. Change comes when you least expect it or upon occasion when you know change is coming. You may purposely cause change. You accept or reject change. You like it or dislike it. Change occurs in your personal life and professional life. Can you avoid it? No. Can you manage it? If you choose to.

Webster's dictionary defines change as: *"to make or become different, to replace with another."* To add to this definition, change is external, inevitable, natural, constant, and unpredictable. Often, based on my experience, when change is being discussed, the word transition is not mentioned. Webster's dictionary defines transition as: *"a passage from one state, place, stage, or subject to another; change."* To add to this definition, a transition is internal.

As you can see, these words have similar meanings, but they are different. Change is an event that occurs that you may or may not have control over. For example, the seasons change with no input or influence from man. This is an external event. I like the changing of the seasons, but I don't particularly care for the cold. How do I transition from the hot weather to cold weather? How do I make that passage? For now, I bundle up as much as I can to keep warm. This is an internal event.

Think about how technology has advanced so much and so fast. It seems as though by the time you purchase a software program and become familiar with how to use it, another software program has been developed that's better and quicker. These technological changes are inevitable. You can't stop them. Each day you wake up you get a little older. You cannot avoid it. There are techniques available to try to help you keep that youthful look or body. No matter what you do, those techniques do not stop you from aging. This change is inevitable.

Using the example of the different seasons, you can see how change is natural and constant. We know at certain times of the year this change will occur and we adapt to it as best we can. We adapt to change differently. If you don't like the cold, you might decide to move to a location that doesn't get too cold.

Buying a new car, starting a new relationship or job, and going back to school are exciting events. Do you know in the beginning of these events how they will turn out? When you purchase a new car you do not anticipate having any problems with it. Starting a new relationship or job, you do not know the outcome of either event. Going back to school may not be what you expected it to be. These events do not come with predictions of how they will turn out. Even though you can't predict what will happen, you do not eliminate these events from your life. You expect and hope for the best and transition into the new.

Think about the first transition you made – from your mother's womb into this world. The process of developing in your mother's womb had to end in order for you to enter this world. Even though the process ended, a new process began. Transitions are about endings and beginnings.

You may or may not be able to control change. You can, however, manage the transition. The literature on this topic states that transitions basically mean something is ending, then you're in a state of neutrality, and then something else starts a new beginning.

Multiple changes and transitions can occur simultaneously. For example, you just got married, purchased a new home, and getting ready to start a new job. The changes include a husband, new home, and new job. The transitions include going from being single to married, moving out of an apartment/condo into a house, and leaving one job for another (or maybe this is your first job). These are all exciting, new changes that you are transitioning into. In each scenario, something is ending while something else is beginning. How do you respond to change? How do you handle transitions? During transitions, you have to let go of what is familiar to you. The emotional experiences during this time include loneliness, fear, hurt, uncertainty, resistance, helplessness, devastation, worry, or feeling stuck, attacked, tired, sad, or wanting to give up.

In handling transitions, you have a choice. You can choose to stay in your comfort zone or you can forge ahead into the unknown. Stepping out of your comfort zone helps you grow as a person.

To survive transitions in life: be open to change, obtain information to help you process what is happening, transform your thought process to accept/experience the new before automatically rejecting it, and adopt the change.

What changes/transitions have you made as of today?

____

What changes/transitions, if any, are you going to make?

____

What changes/transitions, if any, do you need to make?

____

When responding to change, several questions may surface. They are:

1. What am I giving up or losing?
2. Am I doing the right thing?
3. What if it doesn't work out?

Think about a recent or pending change in your life. Answer the questions above. This will help with the transitions.

Surviving changes is mostly made up of your thoughts about the change. You can survive the changes and make the transitions a smoother process. Remember, at each step God is with you!

The Power to Change

I pray for everyone to have a connection with God. I want everyone to be at peace, healthy, happy, and have the finances they need to take care of themselves and their family. I realize I cannot make this happen for everyone. It's unfortunate that we have so much pain, suffering, and evil in the world. It's unfortunate that you have experienced really difficult situations in your life. In the midst of this, you can be positive and have positive events happening in your life. It starts with you.

As an individual, you have the power to make a positive change. Not the world but yourself. How? By simply making a conscious choice to change your thinking, act on it, and stick to it. God has given you free will to make that decision to choose good or evil.

Don't allow anyone to cause you to lose focus on being positive. Identify what's going to help you focus on the positive and bring you joy! For example, posting inspirational quotes where you can see them in the areas you spend the most time in. Don't get me wrong. I'm not saying this is easy. I know it's not. But you can do it!

"These things I have spoken unto you, that my joy might remain in you, and that your joy might be full." —John 15:11

- The power of positive thinking will help reduce stress, which helps to maintain your health. Your positive attitude will project to others, increase self-esteem and confidence, and attract other positive people in your life.

- The power of positive thinking increases your confidence. Confidence makes you feel good about yourself and is obtained through faith in the word of God. Faith, prayer, and the belief in God can help you change your situation. God will help you change your life for the better and lift you out of a negative situation.

- The power of positive thinking will eliminate negative thinking, which is self-defeating.

- The power of positive thinking will loosen your hold on complaining. You will start to see more positive than negative.

- The power of positive thinking will reduce those negative self-fulfilling prophecies. You will begin to think more positively about yourself.

With all of this power, how could you not want to change?

The "Whys" of a Negative Attitude

Situations arise that can disrupt your life. For example, the loss of a loved one can cause great emotional pain. How do you cope with this? Why do you have to experience this? To cope with this pain, you sometimes seek help from family, maybe a counselor, your pastor, or you may try to deal with it alone. Whatever you do, it's difficult. To understand "why" this painful event happened can possibly help you better cope with the pain. Do you always know why? No. How can you find out? Good question. Can you recover from this? Yes.

I know it is difficult to believe, especially while going through emotional pain, but your pain and healing process enables you to help someone else that is experiencing emotional pain. **Your pain heals others.**

Some of the reasons for a negative attitude include the following:

- The environment you grew up in was negative
- Great emotional pain
- Placing your trust in the wrong people, putting people in place of God
- Health, family, financial, or employment concerns
- You have been told too many times (even as a child) you will not amount to anything

Have you ever noticed how many negative statements you hear in one day? Have you ever noticed how many negative statements you make to yourself and others? Is your attitude mostly positive or negative? Is your outlook on life mostly positive or negative? Think about how often you have heard the following negative statements.

- It won't work.
- This is too difficult for me to do.
- I can't.
- It can't be done.

Do you have a negative attitude? If so, why?

____

Let's examine another scenario. By the time a young girl reaches womanhood, she may have already faced difficult situations to cause her to feel victimized or defeated. For example, too many young girls are sexually assaulted or physically, emotionally, and mentally abused. This treatment lowers their expectations of others and life. It also lowers their expectations of how they should be treated, reduces their self-esteem, could possibly cause them to lead a passive life and continue to be mistreated by others and even mistreat themselves, causes them to not have any goals in life, creates an uncaring attitude, leads to hurt feelings and resentment, robs them of peace and joy, or could lead to worry, hopelessness, and substance abuse.

Under these circumstances, anyone can understand why this young woman is so negative. Does she have to remain negative for the rest of her life? No. Can she reduce or eliminate feeling victimized or defeated? Yes. For anyone facing so many trials, turning to God will give you peace.

"Peace I leave with you, my peace I give unto you: not as the world giveth, give I unto you. Let not your heart be troubled, neither let it be afraid."
—John 14:27

Steps to Overcoming a Negative Attitude

Overcoming a negative attitude can be really difficult, depending upon your circumstances. It is okay to have ill feelings. That's normal and part of the healing process. The key is not to dwell on the ill feelings.

Overcoming a negative attitude leads to emotional wellness. The benefit of emotional wellness is ***greater quality of life***. You can achieve this by taking the following steps:

1. Pull out your Bible. It is critical that you increase your knowledge of God's word. Be prayerful. Keep God with you at all times.

2. Trust God. Trust yourself. Know that what God has for you is yours!

3. Expect kindness/favor from God. *"Wait on the Lord: be of good courage, and he shall strengthen thine heart: wait, I say, on the Lord."* —Psalm 27:14

4. Don't seek the approval of other people. Seek God's approval. Not everyone cares for Jesus. *"If the world hate you, ye know that it hated me before it hated you."*—John 15:18

5. For every negative thought you have, substitute it with two positive thoughts.

6. Decide to be happy and act on it. Bring joy to your life and the lives of others.

7. Develop positive, supporting relationships. As much as possible, keep positive people around you to uplift and encourage you.

8. Let go of the negative attitude to achieve success. You should be the one defining what success means to you.

9. Develop a positive attitude toward yourself.

10. Know that you can overcome difficult situations with prayer, will power, and a positive attitude.

11. Laugh. Have fun. Participate in activities that you enjoy.

12. Save. Save. Save. Because worries about money, or lack of, can cause you to be negative, position yourself to be financially fit.

"The God of my rock, in Him will I trust; he is my shield, and the horn of my salvation, my high tower, and my refuge, my savior; thou savest me from violence."—II Samuel 22:3

Make the right choice. Choose to have a greater quality of life by choosing to have a positive attitude. Know that you will face trials and tribulations but these events should not dictate you being a negative person. Invite God into your life forever. Through the word of God you can maintain a positive attitude and release the negative.

Notes:

ABOUT THE AUTHOR

Dr. Stem Mahlatini-Marks

Dr. Mahlatini is President and CEO of Global Coaching & Consulting Services, LLC (GC&C), a service that focuses on inspiring, and empowering people to lead stress free lives by stabilizing the mind, body and spirit through counseling and coaching. GC&C's services also include a focus on promoting eldercare work/balance. GC& C provides specialized trainings to employers and community organizations on developing innovative, cost-effective approaches to preventing and resolving eldercare/work conflicts. Dr. Mahlatini is an Independent Licensed Psychotherapist who conducts individual, family, group-counseling services to clients of diverse backgrounds from ages 8-99. In addition, She conducts workshops and seminars throughout the United States and abroad. Dr. Mahlatini's passion is to empower and inspire youth and adults in overcoming obstacles that hinder their everyday success through her counseling and coaching services.

Her knowledge of business and mental health counseling is supported by her fifteen years of experience working in corporations, hospitals, nursing homes and as an Employee Assistance Professional. Dr. Mahlatini's work includes working with adolescents involved with the department of Juvenile Justice, critically ill patients as a heart transplant social worker, elderly patients as a consultant and therapist, Superintendent and Quality Assurance Manager with the Department of Juvenile Justice as well as a middle school teacher. She has been a trainer and consultant in all the positions she has held, experience which has been a blessing and motivator in presenting seminars in her own practice.

The oldest of seven, Dr. Mahlatini was born in Zimbabwe and came to the United States in 1986 to pursue her education in Boston Massachusetts. She received an Associate's Degree in Business from Middlesex Community College, Bachelors Degree in Business from University of Massachusetts Lowell, a Masters Degree in Social Work from Boston University and Doctor of Education Degree from Nova Southeastern University. Her accolades and one of her lifelong dreams include Co-author of four upcoming PWN books. Dr. Mahlatini truly believes that she is at the onset of an annointed journey that will take her globally where she is destined to impact many lives young and old.

Dr. Mahlatini-Marks is married to her husband, Harold "Tim" Marks, the love of her life and has continued support from her parents, Benjamin and Idah Mahlatini in Zimbabwe, as well as siblings and in laws around the world. With an exuberant passion and dedication to empowering, inspiring as well as helping other people excel, Dr. Mahlatini-Marks is available as a youth consultant, mgt consultant, key note and conference speaker to small & large organizations, leadership teams, hospitals, professional associations, civic & public organizations, school systems & youth groups on a local, national and international basis.

Contact:
Global Coaching & Consulting Services, LLC
75 Fox Ridge Court Suite C
Debary, FL 32713
Telephone: (813)431-5154
Email: Drmahlatini@globalcoachconsulting.com
Website: www.Globalcoachconsulting.com

FOURTEEN

CELEBRATION OF LIVING A JOYFUL LIFE

By Dr. Stem Mahlatini-Marks

As I celebrate life and celebrate my journey as an author and life-career coach, I often reflect on the words of my mother, "Experience is the best teacher." In those moments of reflection, I acknowledge and thank my higher power, my Lord and Savior for being my guide. I also thank my parents, Benjamin and Idah Mahlatini for their blessings on my journey to the United States in pursuit of the life that I am now celebrating. My mother's tenacity during adversity is unparalleled; she is the main reason I celebrate a joyful living today. Because of this reflection, I have grown into a more grounded human being. I also believe and know that God's presence is my protection. Whatever happens, I will never go down because God will be carrying me in the hollow of His hands. I now strive to think only peaceful thoughts because I know that God will take care of the rest.

What then is a celebration of life? It means taking one step forward in peace and equanimity. MY purpose therefore, is to be useful, responsible, and to stand for something that makes a difference in my life and in the lives of others. As Leo Rosten stated, "I cannot believe that the purpose of life is to be "happy". I think the purpose is to be useful, to be responsible, and to be compassionate. Above all, it is to matter, to count, to stand for something, and to have made some difference that you lived at all." In life anything is possible; therefore, if you dream big you can become Big. Celebrating a joyful life means reflecting on the trail that you have blazed, learning from the challenges and the adversities. Use the lessons learned as motivation and inspiration to run faster and climb higher than you have ever run and climbed before. In other words, you must grow from your past, not live in your past.

Remember that everything that happens to you in life happens for a reason. Your job is to do all that you can to find and identify that reason and use it to your advantage. Use those life's lessons to make life livelier. Remember, too, that celebrating a joyful life means that you must accept your life as a journey. No matter what challenges you face, you must commit to staying on path until you reach your destination. Along the way, remember to laugh, and acknowledge that the world is full of loving and caring people who are on a similar journey as you.

Amidst the challenges of life, you must never be afraid of life and what it throws your way. There is always support. So remember that in life's every pinch you must always give your best, to make your life more lively and enjoyable. To lead a joyful life means that you must find and appreciate that the most beautiful and peaceful place is within you.

When you find that place, you will come to appreciate the beauty that surrounds you.

In this chapter, I will now share with you the six themes of creating a joyful life.

Achieve More In Your Lifetime.

You must have heard this before: setting goals could make a serious difference in your life. But, it won't hurt to hear it one more time. When you set and measure your goals, you will be able to see the road that you have traveled. The process of achieving goals, however, builds your confidence and increases your self-belief that you have the ability to go higher by setting more challenging goals. One way you would be able to do that is through improved communication.

Learn to become a sponge, and soak up as much as you can whenever you are in the presence of someone who knows more than you do. On the other hand, be willing to share as much as you can whenever you are in the presence of someone who knows less than you do.

Help them become as confident and knowledgeable as you are. When you are open to learning and receiving, your life improves; hence, you achieve more in your life. Keeping track of how you are changing on a daily basis is a tool that empowers you and gives you the self-satisfaction and courage to celebrate a joyful life. Use the following as a guideline to track your improvements:

Today I opened myself to learning:

____

Today I opened myself to sharing:

____

Today I opened myself to receiveing:

____

Improve Your Overall Performances In Life.

There are times when pain, struggle, and frustration bring out creativity in some people. Other times, pain, struggle and frustration have stifled the creativity in others. Keep in mind, however, that millions of people in the world are struggling or frustrated. But that's not you. Amidst you struggles, you can always find a way to pull yourself out, dust yourself off, and smile. Remember, the answers that you seek are inside you. In fact, the answers are in the problems that are challenging you at this moment. So make time for yourself and never cease in your search for avenues to improve the quality of your life, your overall performance, and ultimately the lives of those around you.

Think back to an experience that you have had, something terrible that you struggled to get over. Complete the following:

My experience was:

____

____

____

Now that I've looked back, my lesson was:

____

____

____

You can duplicate the sentences above as many times as you want and recall experiences that have shaped who you are. Remember, some experiences will be negative. If you haven't come to a place where you can see the lessons, feel free to talk to a professional who could assist you.

Increase Your Motivation to Achieve the Most Out of Life.

We have been told that financial stability and a contented feeling in work and business are necessary to leading a joyful life. We've also been told that to achieve more in life means that you should be a doer, a competitor, and one who makes things happen. But, I believe that the will to win and the need to achieve in everything you do could be critical in life. Being focused and persistent could help move you from last to first in all that you do, and it could ease the burden of the struggle. If you are to achieve the most out of life, you, therefore, must worker harder, and become a believer in your own abilities. For most, having your own business could be the ultimate achievement for financial independence. No doubt, to become a business owner, however, is a huge undertaking. But it is not beyond you; if that's your goal, you can do it, but that must be your motivation.

Motivation means being happy and enthusiastic about your life, your career, your family and friends. The happier you become, the more energetic you feel. For life-energy to move in your direction, commitment to self-motivation is essential. If you observe, the life you are leading right now demands a certain level of commitment, commitment to your work, family, and your friends. The more committed you are, the greater the level of achievement, and the greater the possibility that you would lead the most peaceful life possible.

Whatever you are committed to strengthens you. If you are committed to your family, then there will be greater family support.

If you are committed to society, society will do more to support you. If you are committed to starting a business, then your commitment will show and pay off in the end. In the long run, commitment always brings comfort. So, make a commitment to creating a better world, to a safer society, to a successful life, a contented family, and healthier society. If you do, the results will return to you a hundredfold.

Reflect on the achievements that you have enjoyed in your life and complete the following sentences. Remember that each step counts. So, celebrate your achievements, big or small; every task you complete is an achievement in itself. Remember also, that the small steps lead to the big victories, so make the steps count.

My achievements are:

1. ____
2. ____
3. ____
4. ____
5. ____

Don't forget that recognizing your achievements daily will empower and encourage you to do more for yourself. So, record your achievements every day.

Today my achievement was:

____

Increase Your Pride and Satisfaction In Your Achievements.

Pride and dignity are words that we use to describe our personal satisfaction, values, and self-worth. To some people, pride projects a negative impression. Here, pride and dignity mean some things that are wholesome and positive. Remember, there is nothing wrong in feeling a sense of pride when you achieve some thing beyond your wildest imagination.

In such situations, you have every right to be elated and proud. Culturally, however, some of us are not supposed to be overzealous with our achievements. But pride and overzealousness are not the same. It is, however, different if we allow our pride to be projected as egotism. Accomplishing something that matters to you through your own efforts, determination, diligence and dedication, and without putting others down is a reflection of your pride.

Expressing your pride also means acknowledging your own worthiness, while defining your self-worth. Acknowledging your self-worth allows you to feel dignified in the face of attempted humiliation. Having a proper sense of pride allows you to continue to walk tall, while brushing aside the insults. To enable you to feel proud, you must know what's important to you, but appreciate the values in others. Set your own standards of what you will or will not accept and do only what is right. Despite the indignations that you have suffered, you have the right to celebrate the achievements that you secured and the courage that you have conjured, while learning from the mistakes and failures of the past. Your future does not have to be the extension of your past failures and mistakes. Never judge yourself too harshly. In other words, always take pride in yourself. You cannot get to the celebration phase without stating what your goals are and what you want to achieve. Setting simple short-term goals is more effective than setting long-term and cumbersome goals.

Plan to Eliminate Attitudes That Hold You Back and Cause Unhappiness.

One of the quickest ways to spread the luminous rays of happiness over your life is to directly confront the negative attitudes that darken your doorstep. Emotions like jealousy can destroy the joys of your successes or the success of others. If your friend succeeds, celebrate his/her victory as your own. If your enemy succeeds, celebrate his/her success.

Celebrate their success because doing otherwise could be self-defeating. Jealousy is pointless, and merely extends an enemy's power over you. In family, personal or professional relationships, do not let your jealousy create situations or circumstances that prevent you from enjoying the relationship you have.

Realize that only you can control the outcome of your life. You might not control every situation, but you do control your reaction to those situations. Instead of passing the buck, take responsibility for every failure and learn and grow from them. Remember, perfection is rarely attainable and seldom necessary. You're a human being, not a robot. Use the 80/20 rule whenever appropriate. That rule states that 20% of your activities produce 80% of your results. You can apply that rule to every aspect of your business and life.

Learn to let go of the things that are unclear or the things that do not feel right to you. Remind yourself that there are more positive forces in the world than there negative ones. Consequently, your fixation must be on the positive forces and not on the negative ones. Be mindful though, that winners focus their energy only on the things that can go right, not on the things that can go wrong. Always focus on the positive.

Inject meaning into your life by following your passion. Unhappiness is both self-defined and self-imposed. Pay attention to how you feel and what your mind is thinking. If you understand the sources of your unhappiness, your fears, your uneasiness, you can take the necessary steps to climb out of the hole of despair and into the sunlight of a joyful life.

Complete the following:

The one thing that holds me back is:

____

____

I can take the following step(s) to overcome my holdback:

____

____

____

In conclusion, I would be doing you a disservice if I did not address breathing as part of our overall wellness. After all, it is the focus of this book. Learning something about your breathing is very important. Your breathing can teach you an enormous lesson. It relates directly to your mind and your emotions. So, when you feel stressed, helpless, anxious, or even joyful and excited over the challenges of life, monitor your breathing.

The first thing you did when we came into this planet was breathe, and then you cried. The last thing you'll do when you leave this planet is breathe. In between life and death, we are breathing in and out. Unfortunately, we have learned little about breathing! If you don't have Breath, you don't have life. You will know life better and expand your wellness when you know how to breathe deeply and monitor this on a conscious level.

Breathe deeply; breathe fully. Relax your body and mind. Open your heart up to all that is good.

May your life be a journey filled with much joy.

Notes:

ABOUT THE AUTHOR

LEANNE NORWOOD

Leanne Norwood is president and founder of Synergy Consulting Group; an organization specializing in improving and enhancing the lives and images of their clients.

Leanne is certified in areas such as self-esteem, image and branding, coaching, and marketing strategies. She's an active member of Professional Woman Network offering training and educational seminars worldwide. The workshops and seminars consist of topics such as: Women a Journey to Wellness; Branding and Image; Leadership & Empowerment Skills; Professional Woman Coaching Institute; and Professional Presentation Skills.

Leanne Norwood is President and Founder of Supermom Network which is dedicated to the improvement and well-being of today's moms. She has written several newspaper articles on the issues and challenges today's mothers face, and is in the process of taking this organization globally with inspirational articles, specialized gift items and several books.

Leanne has a diverse financial background consisting of more than twenty years in the financial arena. She is a public speaker, a real estate investor, expert in foreclosure investing, and has written and published '*Real Estate Wealth Toolkit*'.

She is president of the local chapter of Business Network International. Leanne teaches self-esteem awareness to women's abuse shelters in hopes that women will change self destructive patterns of abuse. Her passion is helping others understand and improve their thought process so they can become all they were meant to be.

She attended both Rochester Institute of Technology and the University of Houston where she studied Management Technology and Marketing. Leanne has several awards and honors for her contributions as well as her talents. Her third book '*Emotional Wellness for Women Volume II* and fourth book '*Baby Boomer's*' will be published in 2008.

Contact
Leanne Norwood
(865)680-4410
leannenorwoodz6@yahoo.com

FIFTEEN

PRIORITIES: WHAT IS REALLY IMPORTANT?

By Leanne Norwood

As women, we juggle multiple roles: wife, mother, worker, caretaker, chauffeur, mediator, counselor and more. Our lives have become so full of tasks and responsibilities that it is often hard to get clear on our own priorities and what really matters to us. Most of us feel that something is lacking in our lives, but don't take the time or effort to find out what that is. The very idea of living a balanced life seems like an oxymoron.

Do you find yourself saying, "There's just no way for my life to be balanced. I don't think it can be." "It feels like I'm on the fast track to nowhere and I can't get off." "I wish I knew what I wanted in life." "I think it's been so long since I've thought about it, that I don't think I can find it anymore." "What is this all about anyway?" "My life is out of control 24 hours a day, 7 days a week, and 365 days a year and then another year starts it all over again." "My life is just not fulfilling; it's not even enjoyable." I could go on and on with more statements like these or I can tell you it's time to **stop the chaos**! It's time we realize that the only way for our lives to change is for us to stop what isn't working and find what does. If we don't take the time to fix the problem (and we all know this fast-paced life is a problem), then we might find ourselves at the end of our lives wondering what the purpose was. Let's face it, we will all come to the end of our road some day. The question we can't control is when our road will end. The question we can control is what kind of road we will travel. Was it a road filled with regret and disappointment, or was it a road filled with wonderful memories, love, and caring relationships? Was it a road worth traveling? How will it be for you and me?

If someone were to look at how we spend our time, would they be able to accurately assess what we value the most? If not, it's time to take a careful look at how we prioritize our lives. People seem to take different approaches to prioritizing, but the key is to start. It can be a tough battle, to be sure. But even the toughest struggle begins with a single step!

So, do you want to continue to live your life on the wrong road, or do you want to take the time to make the corrections now and live your life as if it matters? Are you ready to live life as if it is limited, and as if it is precious and irreplaceable? We have the choice, and for those who choose to live with purpose, love and wonderful memories, read on! I have included some simple steps to help you find your priorities, find what matters to you, and live as God intended: joyfully, purposefully, abundantly and spiritually.

Step 1: Write your obituary based upon your life to date. Yes, I said to write your obituary so you can see in print how you have been *living up until now*. Your obituary is a notice of your death, often with an account of your life and work. It should reflect what you have achieved and how you are remembered. This can be a sobering experience, but it will give you insight on the areas of your life that you need to change and areas that you are doing well in. At some point, we will all have an obituary and now, more than later, would be the time to insure the lasting memories of a fulfilled life.

Mine would read something like this:

"Good mother, hard worker, didn't know how to rest.
Would have liked to have seen her smile."

As you can see, I have some work to do to correct mine. Here is what I am correcting mine to:

"Great mom. Lived life with gusto. Will miss her love, her smile and her gentleness. She was an inspiration and a blessing to know.
She is now happily with God, her Father."

Your obituary now: ______________________________

____

____

____

What you would like your obituary to read in the future:

____

____

____

Doing this exercise will make you truly understand where you are and where you need to go. Change the direction of your road while you still have a road to travel.

Step 2: Write a personal mission statement defining who you are, what you're all about, and why you're here. The main objective of a personal mission statement is to understand what's important to you. It is your master plan to keep you focused on the important areas of your life, and to keep you on the right road to a life of wellness. Here are some questions to help with your mission statement. Please be honest with your answers and write them with no editing or worrying if they are wrong.

- I would like my life to be different in this way:

____

- To change this I will:

____

- I do not like these things in my life:

____

- To change these I will:

____

- The most important people in my life are:

____

- To spend more time with them and change this, I will:

____

- There is no time for me. To change this I will:

____

- If something catastrophic happened to me today, would I have any regrets about the way I have lived my life?

____

- To change this I will:

____

- Success to me means:

____

- To be successful, I will:

____

- A life of purpose means:

____

- To have this I will:

____

Write your personal mission statement:

____

____

____

____

So, now you are becoming clear about changes you need to make to truly live, not just survive. Here comes the hard part! It's time for you to put action behind the words. Wishing is not enough. Planning is not going to make your life better, and putting your answers in a drawer for another day will surely not change your life's direction. The only way to change where you are today to where you want to be tomorrow is with action. Action is where many of us lose the desire, give up on the dream, and stay in an unbalanced, unhealthy life. One of my favorite scriptures addressing the need for action is, "*For unto whomsoever much is given, much shall be required.*"—Luke 12:48. God is clearly telling us that we can have the life we want, provided we take the steps and have the faith to get it. It is not up to Him, our children, boss, or spouse. It is up to us. Action, action, action causes change, change, change!

This leads us to step 3, which is the action step.

Step 3: Put a timeline to the changes that you will make. You need a clearly defined time to complete each change. Statements like, "Someday", "Maybe tomorrow", "I'll get to it as soon as I get a chance" are not going to get you on the right road to a life of balance and wellness. Here is a sample of a chart you can use to list the changes you want to make and the dates to accomplish these changes.

A Change I Want to Make:	Date to Start:	Date to Complete:
What I Need to Do To Accomplish This:		

You will want to make several copies of this for each change and then monitor your progress to keep you on track. Remember, nothing happens until you make it happen. This is your life we are talking about here, not just a list of items in a workbook or journal. It is up to you to create the life you want and no one but you have responsibility for that.

Step 4: Keep a "What Not To Do List". That's right; I said what NOT to do. We have all, probably numerous times, written out the dreaded "what to do" lists. Usually they are long, mind boggling, and simply unattainable by even the greatest multi-tasker to date. Even if we could attain everything on the list, it would have been at a great cost to our personal lives, relationships, and most likely our sanity and health.

I like to have a "What Not To Do" list to remind me of the things that are not a priority. Check these against your "to do" list to be sure they aren't on it. If they are, quickly eliminate it from your things to do. Just think of how good you will feel when you can take your "to do" list and scratch off all those chores simply because they're on your "what not to do" list. So have fun, relax, and enjoy getting your life back in balance.

Here's how to make this work for you:

1. List all the things that are not a priority, but you think you should do anyway.

___

___

___

2. List all the things that are not important and you shouldn't spend time doing.

___

___

___

3. List all the things you can delegate to someone else. The key here is to ask someone else to do a task. As women, we tend to think it is up to us, and take on many tasks we can assign elsewhere.

___

___

___

4. List all the things you do because you can't say no. Now learn quickly how to say no.

___

___

___

5. List all the things you do to avoid doing what you should be doing.

____

____

____

Many of us have seen our "to do" list grow and grow because we can't say no or because we take on the tasks ourselves for various reasons. Sometimes it is out of guilt, frustration with others, or from a lack of cooperation or possibly a job done poorly by someone else. Whatever the reason, we need to learn to stop doing everything ourselves as if we have an endless supply of time, energy and resources. I, for one, have experienced a definite shortage of all of the above.

It is important to remember that your time is important, your life is important, and you really do matter. It's time to take charge of your time, your life and your future. Live by your "What Not To Do" list as if it were your second Bible.

Exercise:

Complete the following "What Not to Do List":

"What Not To Do List"

1. ____________________________________
2. ____________________________________
3. ____________________________________
4. ____________________________________
5. ____________________________________
6. ____________________________________
7. ____________________________________
8. ____________________________________
9. ____________________________________
10. ___________________________________

Step 5: Simplify. I think this is one of the most important steps you can take to have the life you are wishing for. We have become a society that wants "stuff". We have become so driven by our *wants* rather than our *needs* that we are completely unbalanced in several areas. Not the least of these are:

- Health and fitness
- Finances
- Spirituality
- Relationships
- Work vs. play

The wanting of "stuff" has become a time-and-a-half job and we are still not keeping up to other people's "stuff", which forces us to work even more. It is this insatiable need to own things that has created havoc in our lives. Simplifying or living with less clutter and toys takes effort, work, determination and self-control. It is not always easy to scale back, now that we have spent years learning to spend. This may be a good time to remind you of why you are reading this book right now. Possibly, it is because the lifestyle you have been living is no longer working and you are looking for answers. Simplifying is one of those answers that will have immediate results and usually immediate gratification. Here are some steps you can take to start to de-clutter your life:

1. **Get organized.** Try to get your home and work lives organized so you are not losing valuable time trying to find what you want when

you want it. Usually this causes much stress as well, so getting organized can have a two-fold benefit.

2. **Prioritize your day and your activities.** Do what is important and stop doing all those little jobs that really don't make a difference. Most of us spend our days appearing to be "busy", but at the end of it, little has changed or been accomplished. This leaves us with a sense of failure and a defeated attitude. Learn to do what is important and what is meaningful and stop doing the little things just to avoid the big things.

3. **Allow time for yourself when simplifying your life.** You matter to yourself, to your loved ones, and to the world, and it is unhealthy to feel otherwise. Always "write yourself in" on your daily schedule and give yourself "me" time. You need to rejuvenate, refuel and re-motivate on a daily basis. Even superwoman took off her cape now and then!

4. **Eliminate the people in your life that drain your energy, emotions and time.** Often we allow negative people to control our days and zap our life force without questioning why. Many of these people can be tactfully removed from our lives with little resistance. Say no if you need to. Walk away if you can. Do what needs to be done to eliminate them from your life.

5. **Get closer to God.** He has all your answers and is eager to share with you how to have a balanced and spiritual life. Seek Him first for guidance, wisdom and strength. He is the epitome of simplicity and a faithful role model. As He said: "*Come unto me, all that are labor and heavy laden, and I will give you rest.*"—Matthew 11:28

We have discussed the steps to follow to re-create your life. What will you do now with what you've read? Do you use it or discard it? Who is responsible for your life and your choices? Only you can make the changes to have a life of balance and wellness. You hold the answers in your notes; you have the map to a new road. I pray for your journey to be successful, joyful and spiritual. Enjoy your journey!

Notes:

ABOUT THE AUTHOR

Tynisha Gardner

Tynisha Gardner is an Entrepreneur, Certified Professional and Youth Development Trainer and Motivational Speaker. Her expertise includes but not limited to Life Coaching, Self-Empowerment and Journalism. She has a bachelors of Science in Business Administration with a concentration in Management. Currently she is obtaining her Masters of Science in Organizational Leadership. Through her unique style to reach women of all ages, Tynisha serves graciously in her community, mentoring young-single moms and speaking to all women through conferences in both the natural and spiritual realms. Topics expounded on are; Self-esteem, Self-worth, Personal Growth, Achievement, Parenting, Marriage, Education, and much more. Tynisha teaches how keeping a life journal is the tool needed to being a better you and overcoming negative past experiences.

As an Entrepreneur of Sisters Holding Sisters NFP, her uprising projects consists of an international self-empowerment program that mentors to women from different ethnic backgrounds, ages, and living environment. Tynisha's international vision stands on the mission to "Empower through the unity of all women." Her professional experience is tailored with management, staffing, public relations and politics. Through out the 10 years in the professional layout, she continues to excel in leadership, being sought out after to implement new communication procedures, continual company growth and networking. Tynisha's diverse background has put her in the presence of many prestigious professionals. Intentions of her life journal is to leave behind a legacy.

Contact:
"Inspiring All"
Tynisha D. Gardner
3605 N. Spitz Drive # 202
Waukegan, IL 60087
(847) 596–1234
Tgardner31@yahoo.com

SIXTEEN

THE HIDDEN SECRET: OVERCOMING SHAME

By Tynisha Gardner

It's more than breaking the heel of your shoe right before an important engagement, or smeared makeup after a bountiful cry; shame is more than a moment. For some it alters lifestyles, goals and dreams. It can be humiliation that lingers on, preventing you from living a full, healthy and empowered life. Shame is the past that never stays hidden, whether it brings public exposure or self-destruction; it is the shadow that trails your every footstep. As women, we have allowed it to affect the way we communicate with others, express our emotions, and determine how we act in relationships. During difficult times, you might find it convenient to wear it as a shield, hiding you from the challenges of life. The twist of this emotional state is that we go on blaming ourselves for what has happened, causing scars and illnesses. Our self-esteem becomes lower than a barometer on a cold winter day and our expectations of life are meaningless. If you are not careful, you can allow shame to operate like a curse, stopping you from receiving that promotion that you earned last year, being fearful of falling in love with the man who loves you for you the good and bad about you, and forgetting to be there for your kids when they need you the most. Your opinion of yourself is worthless; you become limited to any accomplishments or achievements, the thought of "less than" becomes embedded in your mind. Life to you is normal, but the fact of the matter is, you may not be aware of the impact that shame has on you because you refuse to diagnosis it, treat it and cure it. Stop and take the time to really concentrate on being whole; you'll find that the equation is simple: add up the bad, multiply it by the good, and subtract the negative. In this chapter you will find a shorter way to solving your equation and have a long-term answer.

There are three easy steps to overcoming shame:

1. Exposing your Shame
2. Understanding your Shame
3. Accepting your Shame

All these steps may be achieved through the pages of a life journal. The good thing about keeping a journal is that you don't have to be a creative writer to essay the events of your life. Over time your thoughts become a story, telling about the life that once was and is still to come. You don't have to overload yourself or make it a chore when it comes to journaling. You'll be surprised by how much you can say in just a minute or two. Some of the greatest novels and movies have stemmed from a journal. The focus is not to publish or direct your life; however, the reward can be the best seller for personal empowerment. In just a minute, you will be given the opportunity to start the pages of your life journal.

The first step to recovery is confronting the facts. What is the shame in your life that has you bound?

____

____

____

____

____

When answering this question, you are pulling out the root of this seed, revealing the one thing that has held your mind captive. This will require you to remember the pain and face the truth. Like any program, you must start here first. The hardest part is always taking the first step. For some, you might have to relive the moment when you were violated, view the pictures from the domestic violence report, or release the anger that you have carried around for so long. You must know that this process is not to torture you, but to heal you. There is no trick to this treatment; through the uproar of your emotions, you must do your best to focus on the outcome, a new you! Having to confront your shame may also require you to expose others who were involved, stirring up feelings of disappointment or hatred.

List the names of the person(s) that were involved in this shameful event of your life.

1. ______________________________________
2. ______________________________________

3. ______________________________
4. ______________________________
5. ______________________________

This second part of that question is preparing you to express your feelings to any people who played a role in this experience. It is likely that you have not been able to have a decent conversation or healthy relationship with this person at all. Buried feelings may give the impression that you have forgotten what happened and have forgiven. In reality, you may clench your teeth at the sight of this person's presence, or tremble at the sound of their voice.

As you continue to revisit this trying time in your life, you will eventually have a sigh of relief. In the end, you will vaguely remember the level of pain that was caused, like the woman who pushes for hours during labor, but once she gives birth, all that matter is the gift she holds in her hands. At the end of this chapter, you will birth destiny and continue to reap the benefits of it. The duration of your labor is determined by the level of your shame, and how much it has consumed your life. Are you willing to endure this pain to work through the healing process? Every victory deserves a good fight. The battle is not learning to control your emotions; it is you believing that you have value. The motive of shame is to get you to believe that what has happened is because your life has no value. Let us work now to establish the fact that no matter what has happened to you in the past, your life has value!

I use to blame my father for leaving before I got the chance to be daddy's little girl; I also blamed my mother for her having to work third shift and always needing to sleep. I thought that people were handpicked to live happy and prospering lives. I didn't understand why we had to struggle, and that the red sign on the door meant we had to move because we were behind on the rent. I remember a time when my mother packed a suitcase with my favorite clothes and keepsakes. She wrote a letter to the family saying she couldn't take care of us anymore and that she was leaving. Today I can imagine the shame she felt, thinking she couldn't take care of her three kids. Over the years, I watched how she surrendered to the pattern of failed relationships and bad choices. For a while I was convinced that my life would mirror hers. But I realized that my marriage didn't have to be like my parents'. We don't have to be limited by the past!

Earlier, you identified a situation that brought you shame, but now there is a need for understanding. For every question we need an explanation. The "Why" question. Why did this happen? We think if we are given an explanation, we will understand why it took place, but really it only probes for more questions to be answered. Understanding of the shame that was caused doesn't answer the why; it answers the when.

When in your life were you most vulnerable? Provide details.

____

____

____

____

____

____

____

____

When did you get to the place when you let shame take control of you?

____

____

____

____

____

____

When did you stop living?

____

____

____

____

____

____

This set of questions requires you to be honest with yourself. You may need to answer these questions in separate sessions. The attempt is not to discredit you, but to give you a clearer picture of how your life was transformed by a single experience that has caused a lifetime of hurt. You might have gotten the job of your dreams, but you continue to look over your shoulder at your shame. Your peers accept you, but you can't let go of what happened last summer. It is when you begin to be truthful about the role you took on that you stop being angry at yourself and leave the shadows behind that follow you. Because it's been you who has carried this shame and torment, and it is also you who can *release yourself from it.* You have the authority to put an end to this misery. Sometimes we become our own enemy, holding on to the past and letting go of the possibilities. When you understand, you can accept what has happened and move forward in your life.

Through life experiences, it has taught me there is a lesson to be learned in every situation. No matter how much weight it holds, there's a meaning behind it. I didn't want to be a single mother at the age of 20, but at that time I was given the opportunity to love myself, gain personal growth, and love my child. You probably wouldn't have chosen to grow up in a foster home, or mismanage your finances, or even have that affair that destroyed your marriage, but somewhere your consequences delivered a message. You may not like what happened, but at some point you have to accept it. Accepting your shame allows you to understand; it puts you on the road to recovery and strengthens the inner you. Our thoughts and feelings shape the way we think, which triggers the way we act. When you know that you are more than a helpless victim, you can overcome some of life's biggest challenges. Accept that you have experienced a life- changing encounter, but don't accept that you can't overcome it and do great things in life.

Take a moment to reflect on what has happened in your life and journal what is it you can now accept. What have you learned?

____

____

____

____

____

____

____

____

____

We don't always get to choose the path we start out on, but one thing's for certain, we can influence the end results. Since I grew up with no direction of a future, I relied on the will to be somebody. I realized that there were no short cuts to take to have a better life. I needed to face what had taken place, understand and accept it. The continual push to keep these secrets buried in the back of my mind brought me more grief than the experiences themselves. There were many times when no one was available to vent with, so I would stand in front of a mirror and just blurt out my feelings, crying until my knees became weak. On the days when I couldn't utter a word, I would just write! It seemed to be just a temporary fix, but I found that I became stronger by expressing my feelings. The anger and hurt that I harbored decreased over time. I became even more determined to turn my life around. One of the best life lessons you can learn is when you forgive yourself. It makes it easier for you to forgive others.

The secret to overcoming shame lies within the pages of your journal. Your words are your release from self-bondage. As you continue to address what has happened, understand it and accept it, piece by piece you remove the bandages and start the process of healing. It is when you go to the depths that you come out with gold! I hope that as you have faced your secret shame during this chapter, you realize that you can rise above and release these "skeletons in your closet". Hopefully, your shoulders are much lighter than yesterday. You don't need to carry the bricks of shame on your shoulders any longer. I encourage you to hope for tomorrow while you live for today. Release the past. Whatever happened in your life is behind you now. You have faced it head-on. Hold your head high. You are worthy of joy, peace, and self-forgiveness. The shame is no longer hidden. It has been released.

Notes:

ABOUT THE AUTHOR

VENITA S. MURRAY

In 2006, Venita S. Murray launched Professional Image Consulting Group to teach women and young women the subject of image as a means to eliminate the barriers to personal and professional success. After achieving a sixty pound weight loss, she had a deep passion to educate women that "When your image improves your performance improves".

She is President & CEO of her Chicago- based company; she envisioned her business as an opportunity to help women develop better wellness habits through an overall mind, body & spirit connection. Professional Image Consulting provides consulting services and seminars designed to develop overall appearance, build confidence, and enhance personal & professional development.

She is currently attending Roosevelt University where she is candidate for Master's Degree in Professional Communication. She is a member of the Professional Woman Network and holds several certifications: Certified Wellness Consultant, Certified Professional Speaker and a Certified Image & Brand Consultant.

Contact:
Professional Image Consulting Group
P.O. Box 39234
Chicago IL 60639
312-458-9235
venitamurray@sbcglobal.net
www.proimageconsulting.net

SEVENTEEN

GOOD ENOUGH: OVERCOMING THE NEED FOR APPROVAL

By Venita S. Murray

Our lives are our own. It is not for someone else to dictate to us how we should live. All that awaits those who allow themselves to be continually swayed by what other people say or do is unhappiness. We simply need to have the self-belief to be able to say, "*This is right. This is the path I will follow. I am content. Happiness is born from inner fortitude.*"—Daisaku Ikeda

I am glad you are reading this book because it means you are a person of action and you are ready to create some changes in your life. Being emotional for women is a big part of our lives, whether those emotions are positive or negative.

Part of the reason we suffer so much emotionally is because we live our lives according to what others say we should think, be, and do.

When we buy into this, it causes major suffering because we are going against what are our own beliefs are. It is the purpose of this chapter to provide the confidence to make your own decisions and truly believe they are *good enough.*

The treasure house within you is good enough. You have to reach deep inside of YOU to extract all that you need to live life happily, joyously and abundantly. Many people are closed off to their own potential and will constantly seek approval from others. We have to use caution when seeking advice from others, especially the individuals who are *not living their own life* to its fullest potential. People don't realize that they need to live their own advice, but they will be quick to tell you what you should and should not do. Why do we not know that we are good enough to make our own choices and decisions? Why do we feel the need to tell all our dreams, hopes and fears to everyone just so they can tear them down with what they think we should do? And most importantly, why do we listen or feel we need their approval to fulfill our destiny? Have you heard the saying, "Misery loves company"? It's true, and unfortunately some of us have had to learn this the hard way.

The need for approval comes from a deeply rooted belief of not being worthy. The very belief of unworthiness sends out signals to search for the seal of approval. Symptoms of this dependency are all around us, but we call these symptoms a way of life. For example, these symptoms show up from small statements such as, "Do you think I will get the promotion?" "Do you think I look okay?" "Do you think I will be approved for that business loan?" "Do you think I'm too fat?" Think for a moment when you catch yourself making any of the above-mentioned statements. Are you acting out of the need for approval? You must dig deep to come up with your own answer.

There are two types of approval which most of us seek, approval for our actions from others and approval from within ourselves. Both are equally important. Peers can be a tremendous help in tough situations, but if bowing down to peer pressure means that you are betraying your own personal beliefs and values, then that becomes a negative force.

That is when the need for approval from within you should step in. It will often be your subconscious mind that will tell you that what you are doing is wrong. The need for approval from your peers or elders is fine, as long as it does not become the sole objective of your existence. Every action should not depend upon approval from others. You should not feel disempowered if your suggestion of work has not met with approval or praise. Stop looking for affirmation from others. You must have faith in what you are doing and trust yourself in a tough situation. You have to respect yourself before you can expect respect from others, and then the need for approval won't matter so much.

How Does the Need for Approval Manifest Itself?

People Who Have a Need for Approval:

- Work hard at being good: at their job, in their home life, with their spouse, as a parent, and as an adult child with their own parents.
- Depend upon others to give them a sense of self-worth.
- Are poor at problem solving.
- Work hard at keeping "peace at any price" in a relationship.
- Avoid conflict because of the fear that the "other" will not approve their point of view.

- Have a problem in letting others know how they feel about things.
- Lack self-confidence in their skills, abilities, and knowledge. They tend to see themselves as "incompetent."
- Do anything to avoid hurting the feelings of others, even if it means swallowing their own feelings or denying the reality of things.

People Who Have a Need for Approval Have:

- Low self-esteem due to (1) lack of positive feedback as a child, (2) lack of sense of worth due to no reinforcement as a child, (3) sense of rejection and emotional abandonment as a child, (4) sense of neglect as a child
- Deny that there are any problems in their families of origin or in their current nuclear families, yet they cannot get enough affirmation of self worth
- Never become emotionally independent enough to positively affirm themselves
- Dependent personalities and a need for other's affirmation

How to Overcome the Constant Need for Approval:

- Step 1: Identify and refute the irrational belief that the approval of others is necessary to feel good about yourself.
- Step 2: Identify your fear of rejection, neglect, abandonment, disapproval, and look for the origins of the fears. Identify rational means to desensitize yourself to these fears.

- Step 3: Develop an inventory of the positive attributes you possess.
- Step 4: Develop a list of positive affirmation self-talk scripts you can affirm on a regular basis.
- Step 5: Reflect on your feelings about conflict events. Do not avoid conflict situations, but use positive assertiveness to maintain your position and protect your rights. Emphasize how you feel about the issue by using "I" statements.
- Step 6: Answer the question, "What do I gain if I am agreeable and pleasing to everyone in my life and never take a "stand" on how I really feel about things?"

Start to put these steps into practice on a daily basis because this is a process and will take at least 21 consecutive days for this new behavior to become a habit. Ask yourself daily what *you* really want to do, rather than what others would like you to do. And keep asking yourself, from time to time, "Do I keep doing this or refusing to do that because I really want it that way? Or do I, once again, insist on trying to please others?" Take risks, commit yourself, and don't desperately avoid making mistakes. Do not be needlessly foolhardy, but convince yourself that if you fail to achieve something and people criticize you, it is their problem, not yours. As long as you learn by your mistakes and failures, does it make that much difference what they think?

Steps For Taking Control of Your Mind:

1. Speak affirmatively and with a deep sense of authority to the irrational.

2. Be aware of emotions generated in your deeper subconscious. You can say, "Be still. Be quiet, I am in control. You must obey me. You're under my command."

3. Beware of what goes into your mind. "Garbage in - Garbage out."

4. Read good books that will develop your mind.

5. Surround yourself with positive people who will encourage you.

6. Meditate daily.

7. Never say, "I can't."

8. Overcome fear by saying, "I can do all things through the power of God."

9. Don't let others do your thinking for you. Choose your own thoughts and make your own decisions.

10. Believe in good fortune, divine guidance, right actions, and all the blessings of life.

11. Create tranquility, harmony, love and health by allowing life to be a prayer.

12. Maintain clean thoughts, heart, and feelings at all costs.

13. Listen inwardly for total guidance every step of the way.

14. Pray daily for universal peace for yourself, for family and the world.

15. Give selfless service to someone less fortunate than yourself.

16. Create your own personal sanctuary in your home.

Values

Values are what really matter to each of us. They are the ideas and beliefs we hold as special. Caring for others, for example, is a value; so is the freedom to express our opinions. Most of us learned our values and morals at home, at church or at school. What are your personal values?

Exercise:

1. What are your family values?

____

____

____

2. What are your values in a relationship?

____

____

____

3. What do you value in life?

____

____

____

4. What do you value about yourself?

____

____

____

Whatever one's values, when we take them to heart and implement them in the smallest details of our lives, great accomplishment and success are sure to follow. The key point to keep in mind about values is that implementing them energizes everything concerned.

For an individual, committing to and applying values releases fresh energies, which will attract success, achievement, and a sense of well-being.

Below are positive affirmations that you can recite daily to build your self-esteem and confidence. Say these out loud:

- There are beautiful things happening in my life daily.
- Change is a blessing I am working toward.
- Belief in self is a step toward personal growth.
- I will let others know who I am.
- There are opportunities in life to be tried.
- God does not make junk.
- There is nothing I cannot handle.

The daily use of "I" statements is another form of self-affirmation designed to counter negative self-concept. It can result in a positive attitude, optimism, and motivate you toward emotional growth and progress. Examples include:

- I am the best friend I have.
- I owe no one explanations for my behavior, which is legally, morally, and ethically correct.

- I love myself for who I am.
- I like the way I handle problems.
- I am a rich treasure ready to be found.
- I am courageous.
- I am strong.
- I will gain emotional strength each day.

By taking a personal positive inventory of your attributes, strengths, talents, and competencies, you build your self-esteem and embed this into your subconscious. Soon you will manifest these feelings of self-worth and self-love.

Conclusion

Learn to love and respect yourself and people will respect you, too. Whatever you release into the universe will come back to you in the same form. Know in your heart that you are capable of making the right decisions for your life and do not need your decisions approved by anyone. Always keep yourself in the company of good people and engage in activities that will help you feel positive about yourself. Understand that no one can make you feel inferior without your permission. Say "Welcome" to the new you and "Good Bye" to the old you. If you believe in yourself and almighty God, you can truly overcome the need for approval. *You are good enough.*

Recommended Reading

Your Erroneous Zone by Dr. Wayne Dyer

The Power of Now by Eckhart Tolle

Women & Self-Esteem by Linda Sandford & Mary Donovan

Breaking the Pattern by Charles Stuart Platking

All About Love by Susan Taylor

Notes:

ABOUT THE AUTHOR

LOUGENIA J. RUCKER

Lougenia J. Rucker is President and CEO of LJR Training and Consulting, LLC dedicated to providing empowering and life-changing services, innovative programs and training for businesses, churches, organizations and women/youth groups. Lougenia is an entrepreneur & an award-winning business owner. She is passionate about empowering others to grasp their identity, gifts, talents and fulfill their purpose with joy and prosperity! Her professional background includes 25+ years in human services with expertise in non-profit administration, corporate healthcare management, childcare development & elderly care.

Lougenia earned a MA in Public Administration & a BS in Social Welfare. She is a Certified Wellness Trainer with an emphasis on stress management & holistic wellness. She is a Consultant & Trainer specializing on women issues, personal empowerment, leadership skills & entrepreneurship. She is a member of the Professional Women Network-an international consulting organization and eWomen Network-an international businesswomen's network. She is a contributing author for PWN Publishing book: *Emotional Wellness III* to be released May'08.

Ambassador Lougenia is a certified *Daughter of the King Ambassador* of the DOK Ministries, for the Philadelphia region, assisting women & youth to discover a path of personal empowerment. Overcoming personal health challenges led her to become a healthcare advocate, dedicated to helping women learn how to love themselves & to dedicate time to self-care & sacred pampering. In support of this mission, she facilitates Pampering Parties designed to create space for women to experience the importance of taking time to restore, recharged & rejuvenate. She facilitates seminars & workshops as a part of her *Women's Wholeness, Wellness and Wealth* Events. Lougenia is a licensed and ordained minister. She is the Director/Founder of *Youth Empowerment Service,* a non-profit group, dedicated to engaging youth to identify their potential, talents and purpose.

Lougenia is available as a consultant, trainer, inspirational and keynote speaker.

Contact:
Lougenia J. Rucker
Lrucker54@aol.com
215.806.4356
lougeniai@LJRtrainingandconsulting.com
www.LJRtrainingandconsulting.com
P. O. Box 26544 • Philadelphia, PA 19141

EIGHTEEN

STEPS TO EMOTIONAL RECOVERY

By Lougenia J. Rucker

Any significant loss can trigger stress, anxiety, negative emotional feelings and physical discomfort. Experiencing these feelings and discomforts over a period of time can lead to physical complications and even serious health conditions. But if you will allow your pain to be a catalyst for change, renewal and rebirth, you can then allow yourself to reflect search within and heal. Look within and to do the soul searching that will connect you to the core of your values, personal beliefs, and convictions of the unique person you really are.

Go gently within as you endure the temporary dark nights, and in doing so, you will (sometimes unknowingly) begin the restorative healing process. Identify your fears and strengths, face the unknown, and accept the wrong choices and decisions as learning experiences.

Encourage yourself, and be kind to yourself. Allow yourself to be refashioned and repositioned to move forward in a new beginning, a new season, new chapter, new day and a new level of life. Embrace a fruitful, productive and creative life characterized by a purpose driven life, sense of wellbeing, and healthy lifestyle. Allow yourself to be filled with peace and joy, which will lead to the flexibility to accept and endure life's sudden and unexpected challenges.

By initially taking one step at a time, and then larger steps, supported with friends, along with courage, faith and perseverance - you will eventually transition to the bright morning glory side of change, growth, acceptance, gratitude, self-love, self-care, personal empowerment and an abundant life designed by God!

"Weeping endures for a night but JOY comes in the morning".
—Psalms 30:5

There are many ways to take an active role with recovering from physical and/or emotional loss, limitations, restrictions, instability and a disorderly state of being. I will share with you some of my practical tips, safe and natural healing steps of renewing the mind, regaining a sense of self-worth, recapturing life and sense of purpose, and restoring a balanced lifestyle and a sense of well-being.

My Personal Journey

My emotional recovery began unplanned and unexpectedly. My well-organized professional life started spinning out of control and balance as I moved unconsciously into a mid-life personal and family crises. I was thrust into a full-time role of a personal caregiver for my disabled mother while I worked full-time as a corporate manager. My schedule became increasingly more hectic with continual stress, tremendous caregiver responsibilities, added professional responsibilities tagged along with my first management promotion, hormonal imbalance, personal health crises and weight gain. I suffered the end of a golden-like marriage, loss of my physical wellbeing, loss of a rewarding career, and then the ultimate loss of my dear and precious mother.

At the end of this chaotic, overwhelming and crisis-driven time of my life, I experienced feelings of guilt, oppression and depression, loss of appetite, isolation and loneliness, anger and frustration. I was burned out and physically exhausted. Sometimes, I was unable to focus and fully complete any project. At other times, I was having trouble with short-term memory. Some days, I wanted to stay in bed all day, and yet had trouble sleeping at night. I had no hope for tomorrow, and no sense of direction.

But every now and then, as I struggled with doing the right things for myself, I could feel a ray of light and a sense of hope. There were feelings of comfort and support when I would reflect upon happy times, or received an encouraging card, letter, motivating email or inspiring phone call from a caring friend or family member. Often times I would cry myself to sleep. But one day I had a wake-up call. After having a routine medical check-up, to my surprise, the doctor informed me that my blood sugar level was borderline *diabetes* and my blood pressure numbers were high. I knew very well what all of this could mean for me and I was in a state of unbelief. He immediately enrolled me into a four-week pre-diabetic course. I attended every week, but was still upset and angry. But the most interesting thing about it all – I did not recognize who I was really angry with. During a time when I was writing in my journal, I realized that I was angry with myself. At the end of the program and at the prompting of one of my dear friends, I suddenly realized that I did not want any chronic health conditions that could lead to major complications, disabilities and ultimately death. I took ownership. I accepted the fact that I was the only person who could change my present condition. So, I initiated changes in my eating habits and food selections. I enrolled in a fitness center and began to learn how to take care of ME.

Getting in Touch with Ourselves

Once we get in touch with ourselves and our feelings associated with the loss and pain, we can then begin to move forward. This journey of restoring balance and emotional wellness involves recognizing our current conditions and changes associated with it, identifying our fears, and stepping out in faith. We must accept those things that we cannot change, accept and love ourselves and God, eliminate uncomfortable symptoms, while yet preventing disease and increasing the overall positive quality of our lives.

Some of the initial integrated steps and holistic healing tools for my emotional recovery journey included:

- A closer walk with God by increasing my time spent in fellowship with Him and studying the Word of God. Recognition that God was working everything out for my good, and if there was something taken away, then there will be something, even greater added to my life. Acceptance that God would provide and protect me, as I trusted in Him!

- A mental acceptance of what I could not change and a quality decision to move forward!

- Daily prayer, meditation and/or reading of personal inspirational books.

- Identification, gratitude and appreciation for the friends/family, the happy times, the accomplishments, the gifts, the talents, the abilities and the power to change!
- Conviction, courage, compassion and activating a sense of hope and expectation.
- Acts of self-love and self-care.
- Positive self-talk, affirmations, journaling and lots of laughter!
- Creation of healthy and peaceful internal and external environments.
- A supportive, loving emotional network of family and friends.
- Life-generating activities, including exercise, nutritional meals and supplements, teleseminars and training, mini trips and personal retreats!

Life is designed to keep moving forward until it reaches its destiny. It will always move forward seeking wholeness, balance, growth, satisfaction and purpose. Every woman is uniquely designed by God and has an inherent self-healing internal process to overcome every loss and suffering. A natural self-healing, emotional recovery, process takes time and love. It requires a gentle and compassionate search for inner truth, acceptance, expression of appreciation and love, and the responsibility of growth and expansion. Next, we will look at three primary steps to emotional recover.

Emotional Recovery: STEP 1 - Look and Listen!

Researchers have found that there is a connection between the mind-body-spirit. What we *believe* affects the way we *feel* = which affects what we *think* = which affects what we *do* = which affects our *physical health* = which affects our overall *quality of life*.

Emotions and issues such as stress, tension, strain, anxiety, worry, hostility, sadness, anger, isolation, and unresolved emotional issues will negatively affect our health. However, there is an intricate healing power to be discovered as we go deeper into the awareness of ourselves and how we relate to others. We can change and control our emotional wellbeing.

Exercise:

What situations or people have caused the following feelings within you?

- *Sadness* ______________________________
- *Loneliness* ______________________________
- *Anger* ______________________________
- *Frustration* ______________________________
- *Hostility* ______________________________
- *Depression* ______________________________
- *Resentment* ______________________________
- *Confusion* ______________________________
- *Guilt* ______________________________
- *Low self-esteem* ______________________________
- *Pain* ______________________________
- *Fear* ______________________________
- *Betrayal* ______________________________
- *Bitterness* ______________________________
- *Disbelief/Distrust* ______________________________
- *Disappointment* ______________________________

"You cannot conquer what you do not confront."—Paula White

We must understand and accept that disappointment, death, pain and loss are a part of life. However, it is amazing how God will use the pain and all that is associated with it, for *Purpose*. With time, the pain will begin to heal, our thoughts will begin to adjust and change, our perspectives will begin to expand, our feelings will begin to modify and shift, our circumstances will revise, and new relationships and new opportunities will begin to develop.

Although the pain of my divorce was major and it hit the core of my soul, the passing of my mother was both emotionally and physically debilitating for me. But, I have experienced the love of God and I have witnessed, first hand, that broken hearts do heal. It may takes months or even years to heal, but there is hope, peace and even joy to be found in the morning.

Phase 1 – Identification – (Self-Knowledge)

Our first response is nearly always a series of negative emotions when dealing with death, divorce or loss of any kind. Identification is the first step in the recovery process. Here are some holistic tips and recommendations:

- Take time to grieve your loss and give yourself permission to cry.
- Identify your feelings, become aware of your inner emotional needs, and seek wise counsel or help.
- With time, take the courage to look into the mirror and take a good look at yourself; sort out your feelings. Journal what you see and what you feel.

- Observe, listen to your body, and identify any stress symptoms, including headaches, back pain, indigestion, compulsive eating, inability to get things done, grinding teeth, crying, nervousness, fears, trouble thinking clearly, lack of creativity and forgetfulness.

- Take the courage and the risk to face your feelings with loving compassion towards yourself and seek wise counsel. Ask God to heal your broken heart.

- Find constructive ways to vent anger through physical exercise or sports.

- Journal and express your feeling with details. Once you write out your feelings, you will begin to feel a sense of relief.

Emotional Recovery; STEP 2 - Learn!

Recovery is a process involving identification and acceptance. When you can *locate* where you are, then the healing process can begin. Accept your feelings, needs and agree with yourself that you will learn to handle your feelings in a positive way and not with destructive behaviors. Do not ignore your feelings or put on a mask to cover up your true feelings. We must learn to accept those things that we cannot change, but pursue those things that we desire to change and *must* change.

Phase 2 – Acceptance (Self-Care)

The second phase of our healing or recovery process is to learn that feelings and emotions are temporary and they are subject to change. The recovery time can be improved and enhanced by learning new habits replaced by new thoughts. New thoughts and desires can be inspired by new learning opportunities and experiences. Here are some holistic tips and recommendations:

- Change "stinking thinking" by renewing, nurturing and nourishing your mind and emotions with prayer, drinking plenty of water, getting plenty of rest, eating nutritional meals and taking appropriate supplements, listening to inspirational music and motivational CDs/DVDs, joining a support group, or taking a course and learning something new.
- Identify the obstacles that hinder you (people, problems, places, positions). Begin to make corrective adjustments.
- Learn how to manage your emotions and take charge of your emotional wellness by being proactive with a wellness and self-care plan of action, including massages, pampering treatments and other alternative health therapies. (I joined a fitness club for the first time in my life, as well as a support group. I treat myself to professional massages, and facials and I maintain a weekly in-home spa treatment night to help rejuvenate my body and to retain my emotional wellness.)
- Press, persevere and pursue: do not let despair or depression take over. I made a decision and a commitment to myself to become engaged again in the game of life. It did not come easily. It was one of the greatest battles of the mind – to move forward. So, I started off slowly, but yet committed to one moment at a time, one step at a time, one day at a time.

- Learn how to get unstuck and to let go by making a decision to live free of guilt, shame and condemnation, so that you can gracefully transition to the next season of your life. Do not be hard on yourself to make quick changes. It will be easier on you to be patient and kind to yourself while you make changes. Do not forget to reward and celebrate yourself.

- Learn to allow *time* to do its part. Create a sacred space so that your emotions will begin to recover and to heal. From time to time, I get completely away from it ALL.

Emotional Recovery; STEP 3 – Love!

The final step is LOVE - most powerful force in the universe. Love is kind and compassionate. Love forgives and heals all hurts. Love empowers you to rise above all hurts, longsufferings and rejections.

Love settles all bad debts. Love transitions you back onto the main road of life.

Love is the glue to emotional recovery, but you must first love yourself before you can truly love others. Here are some holistic loving ways and means to realize a self-care and self-love lifestyle:

Phase 3 – Transformation (Self-Love)

- Give thanks with a grateful heart for every step of recovering and every day of new beginnings.

- Create a spirit of expectation reflecting hope and belief in possibilities.

- Empower yourself with a circle of supportive, caring and supportive network of friends and family.
- Do not take yourself so seriously; learn to laugh at yourself.
- Forgive yourself.
- Honor and value yourself with positive self-talk, positive affirmations; create dream boards or write a loving poem about you.
- Love yourself by taking the time to reflect and take the responsibility to LEARN THE LESSONS!
- Step out of your comfort zone and experience new opportunities for growth and development.
- Actively participate in life-coaching sessions.
- Attend workshops, seminars, and conferences. Enroll in an adult learning course.
- Growth opportunities – arise and take small risks, create a healthy and peaceful home environment, seek new friendships that are in alignment with your new state of mind.
- Pursue your passion or a new career.
- Love others – we love and serve our own needs so that we can give, serve and love others. One of the greatest joys in life is when we can give to others and make a difference in their lives.

As we begin to heal, process the pain, and get beyond it and break free from the past, we will begin to see ourselves differently; we will begin to see a bright and brilliant future. Continue to seek out opportunities to find, define and refine who you are in the new season. Explore and expand the gifts and talents that you are equipped with. Reframe your world. Live your life on purpose and fulfill your destiny. Live in the power of now and experience an abundant life of prosperity in the mind, body and spirit.

Transformation is the process of changing in form, nature, direction or function. We all have the ability and the potential to recover every ounce of health, strength and emotional wellness. We have the power to reconnect to our future and a fulfilling destiny.

I have been transformed and empowered with increased self-knowledge, more understanding of the love and power of God, and greater appreciation for others. Therefore, I am grateful for coming through the storms of life with a clear and sound mind, renewed physical strength, a strong sense of balance, emotional wellness, and an absolute commitment to fulfill the purpose of my life! May you be encouraged and blessed to do the same.

"You cannot change your past, but you can create your future with your thoughts, words and actions!"

Bonus Exercise:

List *5 Self-Pampering* ways you will take care of yourself and YOU are the only beneficiary:

1. ____
2. ____
3. ____

4. ____
5. ____

Recommended Reading:

Creating and Maintaining Balance, A Woman's Guide to Safe, Natural Hormone Health by Holly Lucille, ND, RN

You're All That! Understand God's Design for Your Life by Paula White

Sacred Pampering Principles, An African-American Woman's Guide to Self-Care and Inner Renewal by Debrena Jackson Gandy

ABOUT THE AUTHOR

CELESTE HAMILTON, MMATH

Celeste Hamilton is the founder and CEO of The Hampton Educational Services Group, Inc. and Hampton Group Management Company. She received a Masters of Mathematics at Nova Southeastern University in Ft. Lauderdale, FL and a Bachelor of Science in Engineering Technology at Florida Agricultural & Mechanical University in Tallahassee, FL. Ms. Hamilton has worked with the Public School systems in Miami-Dade and Broward Counties as a State Approved Contractor for the school districts in the state of Florida. Prior to this, she taught students at the secondary and tertiary levels for over 10 years. Ms. Hamilton has been nationally recognized for three consecutive years in the "Who's Who Among America's Teachers" and Cambridge "Who's Who Among Executives, Professionals and Entrepreneurs". During her career, Ms. Hamilton has made significant contributions in education and has significantly impacted the lives of her students and members in her community.

Ms. Hamilton is a devoted and committed educator and community activist, who strongly believes in helping others to identify and accomplish their goals and aspirations. Her vast range of services to her community includes providing group and one-on-one mentorship for children, families and adults. Ms. Hamilton is passionate about working with disadvantaged groups and has invested great effort in providing social support to women, especially single mothers. One of her many goals is to establish and maintain services to help women handle day to day issues, overcome obstacles and achieve their goals.

Ms. Hamilton is a member of several professional organizations such as The Professional Woman Network (PWN), National Association of Female Executives (NAFE), Cambridge Who's Who Among Executives, Professionals and Entrepreneurs.

Contact:
The Hampton ESG, Inc.
celestehamilton@comcast.net
(954) 435-1098

NINETEEN

SURVIVING YOUR PAST

By Celeste Hamilton

Surviving past experiences is paramount in all of our lives. Each of us has had experiences that have impacted our lives both positively and negatively. Learning to accept my past has been based on an old saying, "What doesn't kill you makes you stronger." My experiences have shaped every aspect of my life. Over the years I have learned to put everything that I have been through in perspective. In retrospect, what didn't kill me did in fact make me stronger.

Like many women, I was abused as a child. This is a horrifying nightmare that no one should suffer, especially not children. I endured this abuse from a close family member in my home. I was three years old when this began and today, at thirty-nine years old, I am still learning how to process this. As a result, I learned to live in fear from an early age. Fear turned into anger, despair and bitterness. I hated the fact that I had to be the one to experience this. But most of all, I learned to distrust and fear getting too close to people. Throughout my childhood and way into adulthood, my self-confidence was severely affected. I did not share my abuse with anyone and I suffered in silence, feeling terrified and absolutely alone.

At eight years old my family moved to a new neighborhood. It was a predominantly white neighborhood miles away from my friends, my school, what I considered to be my home. I was the only little black girl on my side of the neighborhood, which was divided by a school and a park. My new friends used to openly make racial comments through humor. They made jokes based upon my color and, although it was not funny, I did not let them know how I felt. Being the only black child in a white neighborhood was a daunting experience for an eight year old trying to adjust to a new neighborhood. Their passive racism became blatantly overt one day when I took a black doll to play at a friend's home. I was told that they did not want to play with my doll and they made me feel that there was something wrong with my black doll. This made me so angry and hurt because my black doll was a representation of me, and if they didn't approve of my doll, they did not approve of me, a little black girl.

I wanted to be accepted so badly and constantly sought validation from my so-called friends. After the incident with the doll, I began to distant myself from them and started to play with other children that lived on the west side of the park, the 'black side'. I thought that if I played more with black children, I would be accepted and valued as a friend, but most importantly, as a person. I was sadly mistaken when I realized that one of my new friend's parents did not approve of me. They did not hide their disapproval, and when I went to their home, I had to stay outside on the porch. Other children from the neighborhood, however, were allowed to go inside their home.

When we went to church on Sunday evenings, my friend's parents would pick up other girls and when I asked for a ride, they would tell me no, I had to walk. The service ended at night and they would drive past me while I was walking home in the dark. The unbelievably awful thing about this was that they had to drive past my house to get home. The humiliation escalated when they verbally berated me, with expletives, for being at their home, and told me that my parents did not care about me. The parents also told other parents in the neighborhood that I was a disrespectful child that was a bad influence on their children. I was eventually told that I was not welcome at their home.

From that time, I tried to become the perfect child who would make every attempt to please the adults around me. I waited patiently for time to pass for the parents to tell me it was okay for me to come back over. I was too embarrassed to tell my parents for fear of losing my friends. My thought process at this time was that I if I tried hard enough, I could make them like me and I would gain their acceptance and approval.

My past was, therefore, characterized by enduring verbal, physical and emotional abuse with the hope of being accepted. As an adult, I have tried to identify what made me accept so much unnecessary abuse. To this day, I am still learning how to process abuse, disapproval, shame and hurt. I have come to realize however, that 'hurt people hurt people'. People who abuse others in any way often times have been abused and hurt themselves. While this and other realizations do not take away the anger and the pain, it helps to put my experiences into perspective.

Over the years, so much has been revealed to me through constant prayer, self-evaluation and validation. Survivors (yes…that is what we are) learn to transcend hurtful experiences and grow from them. They somehow manage to transform anger and pain into fuel that drives them to either succeed or surpass restrictions that others attempt to place on them. This is a survival mechanism that drives me to this day. At times, there is this little girl deep inside me that is so damaged and in pain, but a long time ago, I decided that on the outside I was this invincible fighting machine that would succeed beyond anyone's wildest imagination. I was determined to show the world that people may hurt me, but they cannot stop me.

Although I still have a need to please others, I have accepted that the only entity that I need to please is the Lord. Feelings such as self-doubt, blame, shame, bitterness and anger are familiar feelings to persons who have been victimized in any way. But I am proof that you are only a victim if you choose to see yourself as one. Another survival tool is to reframe your situation and look at your experiences as just that…experiences. I suggest that if you have been wronged in any way, the first step to moving on is to acknowledge what you experienced. If you were hurt, abandoned, abused or experienced pain of any sort, do not blame yourself. Abused persons often do that in an effort to rationalize what happened to them. Humiliation and fear of reprisal are issues compounded by their pain and are heavy burdens that they suffer in silence.

If you learn to reframe your situation, however, you will realize in time that not only do you <u>not</u> have to bear the burdens alone, but also that what happened to you was not something that you chose. In other words, it was not your fault. Talking about the embarrassing details involved in any abuse can be very difficult and humiliating and brings back painful memories. My memories made me so angry, but I learned that anger allowed me to express my emotions and it was ok to be angry.

After my anger turned into rage, something great happened. This reaction allowed me to gain the strength and courage to take control over my life. This is a remarkable feeling to have, especially since I felt so helpless for so many years. Although that little girl emerges every so often, the stronger, more self assured me is able to put her into perspective. She reminds me of how far I have come and helps strengthen me to continue to grow. If you can relate to my story, there are so many feelings that you may be experiencing. These revelations took years for me to realize; they did not happen overnight. To help you to process your emotions as they relate to any past abuse, complete the following exercise.

Exercise:

1. Write down the abuse you survived and, during the time of the abuse, the reason you continued to accept it in your life.

____

____

2. Is fear related to your past? If so, who or what do you fear most and why?

____

____

3. Do you feel any guilt about the incident(s) that occurred? Why? What would you have done differently?

____

____

4. If you are angered by the events that took place, who or what is the source of your anger?

____

____

5. Are you feeling humiliation? Tell why you're so embarrassed and ashamed of what happened to you. Remember, you are not responsible for someone else's actions upon you.

___

___

6. Did you feel betrayed by the abuser? Explain why you felt so betrayed. Was it a relative or trusted family friend?

___

___

7. As a result of your abuse, do you now have a lack of trust in others, especially those who appear to be similar in statue or have the attributes of your abuser?

___

___

8. Did you feel powerless and fall into a deep state of depression? Do you still feel powerless or are depressed today?

___

___

After making a truthful assessment of your anger and pain, try to connect with your past experience and relive it. Keep in mind that the hardest part has been done because you owned your experiences. You can begin the healing process and take control of your life by following a few suggestions. Reliving your past is paramount as it helps you understand why things happened and allows you to release the pain and anger tied to your experiences. For example, if the source of your pain and anger is still around, tell him/her how he/she made you feel and let him/her know you don't hold any grudges against them (face your demons). The next step is to release your pain and anger without the outburst; come up with ways of expressing your emotions without anger. It is important that you are truthful and honest about the origin of your pain and anger in order to fully understand it. I know that admitting the real truth about your past experiences can be devastating, and can and will cause you to feel pain, especially if you have tried to forget some of the details. But it's important that you face your demons to understand that you are not responsible for what someone else chose to inflict upon you.

Lastly, learning to forgive yourself and the perpetrator of abuse is the final step of beginning your healing process. Forgiveness is a powerful tool for any survivor. It is the only way you will be able to begin healing from the trauma that you have experienced. Forgiveness is going to be a key step to surviving your past. I have learned that you cannot continue to live your life hating others for what they did to you, as it will destroy you physically, emotionally and mentally. They win if you are still angry with them. "A fool gives vent to his anger; but the wise holding it back quiets it." —Proverbs 29:11) Once you've forgiven yourself and the persons who hurt you, the source of your anger, pain, and/or fear, the process of you surviving your past, begins and you embark upon healing.

Remember, there is no one way to survive your past, and each person deals with their experiences in their own way. My efforts to survive my past and achieve some level of successful healing depended on how much I really wanted to heal. If you can move on, by letting go of the past, healing will ultimately take place. While the emotions associated with hurtful experiences do not completely vanish, they decrease with time. My suggestion to you for getting through the healing process is for you to pray without ceasing; to ask God to give you faith and courage to continue to go on in your life after reliving your past experience. This could be very challenging, but keep the faith and God will see you through it all. Surround yourself with positive people that are supportive and understanding.

Use the chart below to help you identify the source of your pain and anger, and how to answer some questions that can help you cope and get on with your life by beginning to love yourself through healing, change and acceptance of what happened.

Facing Your Demons

Traumatic Event and Age of Incident	Source: Who is Responsible?	Do You Blame Yourself? Why?	Have You Confronted the Person/ Persons?	How to Cope (Briefly state things that will help you cope with the event and get on with your life).
Sexual Abuse				
Verbal Abuse				

Domestic Abuse You or Parent?				
Rape by Family or Friend?				
Death of Parent				
Divorced or Separated Parents				
Extreme Poverty				

God has always kept his promise. *"I'll never leave you, nor forsake you."* —Hebrew13:5. I prayed daily and pleaded with Him to help me get through the things I was going through, and to help me have understanding of what was happening in my life and why it was happening. Keeping God first in my life and doing His will, especially during what seemingly appeared to be daunting trials, has helped me become the woman I am today, with great strength and more courage than I've ever had before.

Sometimes it may take weeks, months, or even years for you to realize you were internalizing anger from your past. At some point, you realize that you don't like the person you are and then decide you could no longer go on living in the rage that you are living in. There are times when you will be confronted with some kind of provocation from something or somebody (the devil) that is going to cause you to explode. I asked God for strength, guidance, and direction to make it through each day. I knew that I had a long road of healing ahead of me with learning to cope with my past. To date, I am still healing, but long forgave those involved in making my life miserable. I have moved on and, as a result have been able to accomplish many of my goals. You can learn to survive your past just as I did and realize that it is past.

The following are some steps that you can take to learn how you can survive your past and move forward with your life:

- Reflect on your past and determine what circumstances standout in your mind.

- Accept the past events that took place in your life.

- Upon accepting the past, begin learning how to cope.

- Don't allow your past experiences to make you feel shameful, embarrassed, or as if it was your fault.

- Communicate with family or trusted friends and establish a support structure.

- Believe in yourself. Do not believe the negative things people say or think about you.

- Maintain relationships with positive and supportive people to help build your self-confidence and self-esteem, not bring you down.

- Map out a plan as to how you will cope.
- Learn to forgive your abuser.
- Put your past experiences behind you and get on with your life. I did not say forget about your past because you can't do that, it's a part of your history, but put it behind you.

Learning to cope with your past is a very daunting task. Like me, I lost all trust in the people I should have been able to trust. You may feel the same way because of experiences you've had that made you realize it's going to be extremely challenging to regain your trust in people. Research has indicated that any harrowing events occurring in the first ten years in a child's life will have a deep impact on how they will view and deal with life. Your life experiences do shape your life, however they do not define it.

To help you get on your way of surviving your past, take the Lord with you, as I did. I didn't say it was going to be easy. But if you stick with it, you can and will succeed beyond your imagination. Below are a few suggestions to better help you understand yourself:

- Is keeping your faith and trust in God the most important thing for you?
- Do you have a time and place for daily Bible devotion, which is a critical tool for you to find understanding of what the will of God is for your life?
- Have you dedicated a time and location for daily prayer?

- Do you stay true to your convictions? If a circumstance aroused and challenged your convictions, how would you or did you respond? Do not let negative people discourage you or bring you down with them. They are miserable, unhappy beings and do not want to see you doing better for yourself.

- When someone says you can't do something because of your past mistakes or inabilities, what do you tell yourself? Are you up for the challenge to prove that person wrong?

- Do you stay focused and set goals continually to improve yourself?

All of the above mentioned are some questions for you to answer to see how you feel about yourself to date. The questions should also be used to help you learn some things about yourself that you may not even know until answering them. I feel in answering the above questionnaire, it could help you learn to cope with the unpleasant memories of pain and anger that you had experienced in your childhood or young adult life.

Notes:

ABOUT THE AUTHOR

KERRIAN LAFAYETTE, MS MFT

Kerrian Lafayette is President & CEO of KTL Management & Logistics LLC and The Lafayette International Institute. Ms Lafayette is a dedicated professional who has a strong sense of social responsibility. She has worked in social services providing clinical intervention and prevention programs for at risk youth and families for over 10 years. Ms. Lafayette has made a significant impact on the lives of the families that she has worked with. Her professional experience includes providing therapeutic services in a community based private practice, developing and implementing therapeutic, behavior modification, afterschool and educational programs and grant writing.

Through the Lafayette International Institute, Ms. Lafayette provides professional Consulting services that include personal and professional development, corporate training, capacity building and strategic planning, organizational leadership and development and personal and professional workshops.

Ms. Lafayette currently resides in Florida but was born and raised in Jamaica. She conducts business internationally through her logistics management company where she establishes and maintains professional relationships with business owners.

Kerrian Lafayette holds a Master of Science in Psychotherapy, with a specialization in Marriage and Family Therapy and an MBA Specialization in Human Resource Management. She also holds a Bachelor of Science in Psychology and International Relations and Political Science. She is a certified trainer and holds certifications in Dispute Resolution, Mediation and Conflict Analysis, Solution Focused Intervention and Strategic Planning.

Contact:
Kerrian Lafayette MS MFT
KTL Management & Logistics LLC
Miramar, Fl
954-394-8126
kerrian1@gmail.com

TWENTY

JOURNEY OF SELF-DISCOVERY: THE PATH TO FINDING YOURSELF

By Kerrian Lafayette

"The self is not something that one finds; it is something that one creates."
—Thomas Szaz

At some point in our lives, we all ask ourselves the age old, somewhat rhetorical question: Who am I? Some of us ask that question more often than others, and most times there is no simple answer. Defining oneself can be an overwhelming task that does not have an easy explanation. There is no definitive answer, as we define ourselves according to so many factors: our past and current experiences, our jobs, our families and interactions with the people around us.

We all play a multitude of roles that provide a combined description of who we are: mother, daughter, sister, friend, co-worker; the list can go on to include a description of every role ever played in one's life. I have asked myself this question numerous times, and each time my answers vary to include a new situational definition of myself. In retrospect, I realize now that I have asked this question to make sense of the transitions that I make at different times in my life. In an effort to process change, I wonder who I am. Do I respond to each new situation in the best way possible?

After constant self-evaluation, I realize that a metamorphosis takes place the older I get. I have come to the realization that I am indeed a work in progress. No one remains the same day after day, year after year. Each and every experience creates a kaleidoscope of characteristics that makes us who we are.

As a Psychotherapist, it was my responsibility to help my clients 'find themselves' and identify tangible solutions to address or process situations, experiences and/or problems. Most clinicians are advised to go through the therapeutic process themselves to fully understand their role, and experience what it would be like to 'sit on the other side of the couch'. I avoided counseling and decided that I did not need to explore my issues with anyone; I can handle it. That was my motto, "I can handle it." This is the reality of the classic superwoman syndrome. I will face any situation head on, and I will find a way to deal with everything.

My situation is similar to that of many persons who decide to work in social services. We become psychotherapists or counselors, specifically, because of a desire to help others and give of ourselves. We also choose to this because we have unresolved issues in our own lives, and we hope deep down inside that by helping others heal, we can, in turn, help ourselves to heal. I chose to work with some of the most difficult populations because I wanted to essentially help myself.

As a professional, I was on point; as a person, I felt like I was drowning inside. Superwomen don't get defeated, they find solutions; they put on their armor and they keep fighting. As a person, I was a scared little girl who was not really sure if she was making the right decisions. You see, if I was to ask myself the question, "Who am I?" at certain times in my life, I would have said 'Superwoman'. If I were to really answer that question and be brutally honest with myself, I would have said that I did not know.

Looking back, I am now able to acknowledge that I neglected myself to play the roles that I thought I had to play. I was an educated professional who had everything going for her. I had the potential to 'conquer the world'. I was a dedicated friend, obedient daughter, supportive sister, and the list goes on. I tried to ignore that little voice in my head that said, "I am scared, I am hurt, I am not happy, this is not what I want, this is not me." But I was a professional and I had responsibilities.

I had many life experiences that ultimately defined me, and my view of life, in general: some were good and some were absolutely awful and traumatic. There were times when I felt completely incapacitated when I thought about those experiences, and there were other times that they fueled me to be the best at every endeavor that I pursued. I didn't feel like I had anything to prove to anyone. Instead, I felt the burning desire to succeed for me; I had something to prove to myself. Ultimately, we are our hardest critics.

Exercise:
What experiences did you have that significantly impacted your life?

____

____

____

Once again, as a clinician, my first inclination is to examine family of origin issues, once I think of the journey of self-discovery…start from the very beginning. A person's first concept of self is developed in infancy and continues through adulthood. The first contact with the world begins with the family of origin. The way in which one was treated as a child impacts one's views on the world and on him or herself. The way in which needs were met, the emotional attachments made and physical treatment experienced, will create the development of a belief system that will impact the concept of self. This belief system and developing self-concept will determine the way in which we make decisions and life. Ethics, values and morals learned will determine our personalities. According to Freud, we are born with our id, the part of our personality that is developed at birth, according to how our basic needs were met. Within the next three years, as interactions with the world increase, the second part of the personality, the ego begins to develop. The ego meets the needs of the id. By the age of five, the superego develops; which is the moral part of us, and develops due to the moral and ethical restraints placed on us by our caregivers. The superego helps us determines right from wrong.

When you think about the stages of development, the growth process does not end with adulthood. Personal growth, whether positive or negative, is an on-going process that only ceases at death. As a result, your journey of self-discovery begins at birth and ends at death: the cycle of life. What differs from person to person is how we embark upon the process. We all make the decisions on how to live our lives based on our personalities, life experiences, and concept of self in relation to our views of the world.

When I think about my family of origin, everything in my life falls into place. My family is the most wonderful, supportive and dysfunctional set of people that I have been blessed with. No family is perfect, and I love my family with all their imperfections. My parents are simply AMAZING, and they have worked so hard to ensure that I was given all the tools to be the best person that I can be. My values, beliefs and my concept of self were, and still are, a direct result of the way in which my parents raised me. Therefore, in my efforts to chart my journey of self-discovery, I must acknowledge the role of my family. Because of them, I can balance the pain and hurt that I experienced with positive affirmations and the comfort of knowing that at my lowest points, I AM LOVED.

Exercise:

Examine your family of origin and identify the people who have significantly impacted your life, both positively and negatively.

____

____

____

What are the values and beliefs that guide your actions and decision-making process? What do you believe in that makes you who you are?

____

____

____

Self-reflection is a powerful thing. Our greatest hero and our worst enemy are often times ourselves. Now, I realize that my story is similar to that of so many women. The person that I chose to be and the person that I want to be are sometimes conflicting and contradictory; like night and day. At thirty years old, I have finally accepted that there is no one characteristic that makes me who I am. I am a combination of personalities that address the different experiences that I have had and situations that I have to deal with. Self-reflection allows us to really examine our selves and leads to self-awareness.

Exercise:

1. What do you really think of yourself?

____

____

2. Do you like who you are? Why or why not?

____

____

3. What are three of the major things that you would change about yourself to become the person that you want to be?

____

____

4. List three things that you would have done differently in your life. Why?

____

____

____

5. How would you describe the person that you want to be, and how is that person different from the way you are now?

____

____

I will be honest; sometimes I do not like myself very much. I look in the mirror and I do not recognize the person that is looking at me. I am not speaking in terms of my physical appearance, but in terms of who I am...deep inside my mind…my heart…

One of the most profound things that I have discovered on my journey is that I do not need to be all things to all people. While I think it is important to value the opinions of those around you, it is more important to value yourself and what you think about you. According to Carl Jung, the goal of life is to realize the **self**. As we get older, most of us come to be more comfortable with our different facets. Many of us live our lives according to the way that we are perceived by others and our day-to-day roles—parent, employee, boss, friend….

A part of my self-reflection process included self-evaluation. I examined my strengths, weaknesses, fears, skills and talents. I also thought about what words my friends and family would use to describe me. This allowed me to focus on the positive attributes that I have and identify areas that needed improvement. My self-image became more apparent, and I then had to ask myself the question: Do I love myself? Am I happy with the person that I am? Am I maximizing my full potential in all areas of my life? Am I making enough effort to actualize my personal goals? I had to think about self-sabotaging behavior and other factors that affected my personal growth. I also examined the things that I was passionate about, and how they translate into my actions and thoughts. It is evident that there are many questions that one has to ask of themselves on this journey.

Exercise:

What do I love about myself?

____

____

What do others love or admire about me?

____

____

At different times in my life, I was so focused on establishing my career that I became disconnected from me. I used to journal every day, and yet for years I made no effort to do so. I remember writing one day that I just didn't have time to think about anything. The truth was that if I were to actually take the time to journal, I would have to reflect on my day and focus on myself. I was so caught up with the day-to-day responsibilities that I lost focus of me. I defined myself in terms of the roles I played, and I took very little time to stop and take a look at the inner me. The outer me was accomplishing the goals that I had set for me, but what about the inner me? I was unbelievably unhappy, and I no longer found joy in the career that I worked so hard to establish.

During this time, my mother was diagnosed with kidney failure. My world pretty much crashed. I was in such a bad place mentally and emotionally that my health was being affected. I was experiencing a great deal of confusion, and I had to reflect on my life and the direction I was going in. Then I found out I was pregnant. This was a bittersweet situation because I always wanted a family, but I was also at a turning point in my career and I was in an unhealthy relationship. Being the superwoman that I am, I devised a plan that would guide me through this new phase of my life. I realized very quickly that this was one situation that I could not control. I was not prepared to have a difficult pregnancy in the beginning, and I was forced to stop and once again re-evaluate myself. During my pregnancy, I had to learn to be still. I had to learn patience, and my faith in God grew to tremendous heights. I had to let go and let God take control of my unborn child and me. This was the beginning of a new stage of my life… I now had to learn that I am not in control and I have to accept that which I cannot change.

This was a difficult lesson for me to learn. I was becoming a mother, and this was a new role that did not come with a blue print. I was anxious and terrified, but at the same time, I was excited and ecstatic that I was going to be a mother. My journey took on a new momentum. I was determined to find myself quickly, so that I could be the best mother that I could be. I was going to resolve all my issues within a specific timeframe, and I was going to embark upon this path of self-awareness, self-discovery and any other self-related activity that I could think of. Self-discovery is a subjective experience that is determined by each person's perception. For me, it meant understanding and accepting the person that I was at that time. It meant 'fixing' my problems and being absolutely honest with myself.

Exercise:

What life lessons have you learned that have changed your life?

____

____

Here I had another revelation, I cannot fix me overnight. Self-discovery, self-identification, self-actualization of goals and all the other selves, do not just happen overnight.

Then came parenthood. No amount of planning could have prepared me for the birth of my child. Everything that I thought I knew about life changed. This tiny person changed my very core. This initiated the beginning of my spiritual journey. I have learned, through great adversity, that when all else fails, there is God. I now have a new and wonderful definition of myself: Child of God.

I learned so much about myself during my pregnancy. I also learnt that circumstances do not make a person; they reveal who they are. I learned that I am resilient and incredibly strong. I also acknowledged that I am vulnerable, and it is ok to not have all the answers.

My journey of self-discovery is ongoing. I have finally accepted that my experiences, both good and bad, do not define who I am, just what I had to overcome. They do, however, impact the way that I see myself and interact with others. I am indeed a work in progress.

Take time to reflect on who you are and where your journey will take you.

Self-Awareness Inventory

1. What factors in my cultural background have influenced me the most?

____

____

____

____

2. What factors in my environment have influenced me the most?

____

____

____

____

3. What person or persons have had a real impact on my life?

____

____

4. What experiences have I had that have shaped me as a person?

5. What activities of mine define me as a person?

6. What type of influence has my work had in shaping me?

7. Do I have a goal or purpose in life that shapes my behavior?

8. Do I have special values that influence my life?

ABOUT THE AUTHOR

Claudia White

Born on the west side of Chicago, Claudia White graduated from Purdue University with a BS in Business and minors in Marketing and Psychology. Her extensive career as a sales representative began with American Hospital Supply. She then broke into the field of advertising with the Leo Burnett advertising agency in Chicago, IL. After Leo Burnett, Claudia White became a Marketing Communications Specialist for General Electric Medical Systems in Milwaukee, WI. Claudia then joined Bristol-Myers Squibb in the Princeton, NJ headquarters as a Marketing Communications Manager. In this role, Claudia was responsible for placing, originating, and evaluating print advertising and visual media advertising for ostomy, wound care, and specialty product lines. She is currently a Senior Hospital Sales Specialists for King Pharmaceuticals in the Columbus Ohio market. There, she is charged with penetrating teaching hospitals in the Columbus area, and orchestrating/executing sales agendas for multi-million surgical and infectious disease products lines. She gives thanks to her niece Whitney Clair White, an undergraduate at Northwestern University for contributing to this project.

Contact:
Positive Pathways Unlimited
1209 Hill Road North #249
Pickerington, OH 43147
(614) 570-2057
Wcdub11@aol.com
www.protrain.net

TWENTY-ONE

THE SPIRITUAL COMPASS: FINDING DIRECTION ON YOUR LIFE PATH

By Claudia White

It is not often that today, in the modern world, we find the need to use a compass. Unless one is camping, hiking, or doing some sort of outdoor sport, the function and use of a compass has all but been replaced by computers, GPS tracking systems, and other technological devices. It is simply a device that helps you find your way. You can hold a compass in your hand, stand in the middle of an ocean, in every direction you look there is nothing but water, it's overcast so you can't see the sun, and yet still a compass will always point North. When there is nothing in sight to indicate where you are, it can lead you in the right direction. But there are times in life when one looks around, reflects on experience, memory, work, the daily interactions one had with people, and get the feeling that there is nothing but water and chaos in every direction. With our fast paced lifestyles and growing desire for material possessions, many of us have lost our sense of direction. Our internal compasses have been completely demagnetized. One needs only to look to the news to see how misdirected our lives have become. Violence and distraction are everywhere. We are constantly driven, particularly in western society, to work and work as our quality of life degrades every day. You may ask yourself, how can I find my way? Where is my center? which way is north?

These are questions that I have contemplated in my life. Being a normal person living in the world, I have experienced crises. There have been times in my life when all I could see was water in every direction, with neither land nor person in sight willing or able to help me find my way. In these times, I have realized that without direction, it is almost impossible to live a fruitful life. It is my belief that we as spiritual beings need direction in our daily lives—a tool to help guide us on our life path towards our soul's purpose.

What I have thus devised is what I refer to as a Life Compass. Each directional point is replaced with four essential aspects of life. Instead of north, there is Perfect Self-Expression. Instead of south, there is Love. For the west point there is Wealth or Prosperity, and toward the east there is Health. By making sure these four areas of your life are in order, you may discover, as I have, the power of being centered on your Life Path. We shall refer to this compass as our "Spiritual Compass". Over the course of this chapter, I hope to demonstrate that, by having balanced these four parts, it is possible to live a more productive life. First, let's explore each of these components individually.

East – Health

The first point of reference I would like to discuss is the point to the east, Health. Being in good health is something that anyone can benefit from. It is difficult to work on having a fruitful life without the physical ability to sustain and support oneself. However, what is important about this spiritual point is that being healthy concerns much more than wellness of the physical body. Rather, health also concerns emotional wellbeing and the mind. I can only tell you basic advice on maintaining physical health; things that you have probably heard before. Regular visits to the doctor, exercising, and making a systematic and daily effort to eat well are the basics. There are countless manuals on how to maintain physical wellbeing with regard to these activities. But how to maintain a healthy emotional life is less clear.

As women, being nurturing and giving creatures, it can be easy to forget to take care of our emotional selves. Putting ourselves first is a positive and initial first step. Learning to take optimal care of oneself before taking care of others, including loved ones, is essential to maintaining emotional health.

In many situations, you must think as if you are on an airplane that has begun to malfunction. If the oxygen masks fell, and if we listened to our instructions from the flight attendant before takeoff, we must put on our own oxygen mask first before assisting anyone else, even if you were traveling with a small child. This is not to say that you shouldn't help others, but that we need to do as much for ourselves as we do for others.

Another step to developing emotional health is to make efforts to better understand our decision making process. What this means is being able to say yes or no, and learning to be okay with these choices. It is not often that we actually *do not* know what it is that we really want. It becomes, however, more difficult to optimize our true preference through choice when influenced by others, distracted by fear and doubt, and in the face of stress. However, we must get better at saying NO. Though pleasing the crowd and the desire to be liked and accepted can be strong, it can often sabotage what it is you really need. How can we really find our life path if we are easily swayed by external choices and are not committed to our true desires? Emotional health is about living with great passion and desire. It is about being awake in our daily lives, instead of asleep. As Benjamin Franklin once said, "Most men die at age 25 but are not buried until they are 70." This is an important idea; despite circumstances, obstacles, or age, we cannot and must not stop dreaming and pursuing what it is we really want.

The thing to keep in mind is that we are all vulnerable to emotional ups and downs. It can be hard to really go after what it is that you want, and easier to settle for less. Challenges will present themselves that may render you less able to feel secure in your choices. Situations will arise when you will second-guess yourself. But, putting yourself first and having courage can help you develop your emotional and mental health. Every tough time we go through in life only makes us stronger.

West – Wealth and Prosperity

The next compass point I would like to discuss is that of Wealth and Prosperity. This direction is misleading; I am not saying that attaining money should be something that guides you on your life path. Rather, this point is about looking for a way to prosper as a well-rounded human being. The rich are those who sustain things of true value, such as friendship and family. Money does not and cannot bring you happiness. It can make life less stressful in some respects, but to be really wealthy is to discover the inert goodness in your life and do what is necessary to keep it in your life.

We've all heard the story of the very rich man who, after spending the long years of his life working and securing material wealth, while lying on his death bed, wished that he had spent more time with his family and friends. Well, this man was never really a wealthy man. He prospered materialistically, but the fruits of his labor could not make up for the fact that he was estranged from his loved ones and friends.

Fortunately, women tend to understand that the person that someone is should not be based solely on job titles and money. Instead, women are often more centered about relationships and communication. However, we too neglect what is really important in life for material things. Nonetheless, being willing to sacrifice the love of family and friends is to fall far away from our spiritual path.

South – Love

The southern point on our compass is Love. Love, as diverse as it can be, is one of the most important components of our spiritual compass. May it be pure, exalted, unselfish, and the strongest magnetic force in the universe, capable of uniting people for the better good. For the purposes of his chapter, I would like to focus on self-love. It is my strong belief that when you truly love yourself, everything else in your life will work and flow. In other words, self-love is the starting point for all the other parts of our spiritual compass to work properly. I'm not referring to completely self-centered and self-involved love. This will only foster arrogance and vanity. Self-love is what motivates you to do any and everything you can to help yourself, and in order to do so, you must recognize your flaws and strengths.

So many people in the world have difficulties loving themselves. It is my belief that self-loathing comes from the habitual experience of being mistreated. Many of us were raised by parents who were unaware of the impact that negative comments had on us. For women in particular, our lack of self-love can manifest in so many ways that it's obvious to even the most casual observers. These effects range from low self-esteem to being involved in abusive relationships.

I was at a party several years ago (and like many parties that I've attended, had a female to male ratio of 3-1), where there was a group of women discussing how lonely they were. At the time, I was not involved with anyone and could certainly relate to their frustration and pain. At one point, one of the women stood up with drink in hand and said, "You know what, a piece of a man is better than no man at all." Now, at first I thought this was an isolated incidence and that this woman had simply had too much to drink. But to my surprise, the other women all joined in with cheers of support. I thought, "Oh my God, they're serious." After giving them a piece of my mind, I politely removed myself from this madness to try to regroup. This incident made me think about how important it is to love yourself, and not to sacrifice your feelings for someone who is not there for you 100%. Some women would rather be in abusive relationships than be alone. They rationalize that things are going to get better, but unfortunately nine times out of ten, they do not. But, no one can teach you how to love yourself, and no one can make you love yourself.

There are many things that can be done to help foster a positive self-esteem and love for oneself. First, daily affirmations really seem to work for me. They serve as a source of encouragement. Here is an example of what I am describing. Stand in front of the mirror when you first wake up every morning and again before you go to bed at night. During these times, repeat positive words of encouragement to yourself. These words need be nothing more than a couple of phrases. Or, you could simply take these times to recognize good things you have accomplished in your life, or even that day. Phrases such as, *I am a beautiful person inside and out* or *I choose to be good to myself because I deserve the very best in life* are a good start. You can even write these affirmations down and put them someplace where you can see them everyday. I hang mine on my bathroom mirror, my desk in my office, and my nightstand near my bed, so that it's the last thing I see at night. Try this exercise for several weeks and I guarantee you will begin to feel a mental and physical change come about in your life.

Another simple action that can be done to encourage self-love is to be conscious of negative self-given judgments. We are often our own worse enemies. Remember that words and thoughts are extremely powerful. The phrase "you are what you think" is directly applicable here (See Emotional Wellness for Women - Volume II). Treating yourself with the same forgiveness and kindness that you would treat your best friends can have extreme results. Be forgiving; everyone makes mistakes. If our best friend made a silly mistake, we wouldn't ridicule them and make them feel worse, so why do it to ourselves? Remember, when you truly love yourself, your natural instinct will be to take great care of yourself and to avoid abusive people and situations. This connects deeply with the first compass point discussed, that of emotional health.

Overall, here are some other simple things that can be done to make it easier to remember that you deserve to love and take care of yourself.

1. Make a list of things you genuinely like about yourself.

2. Ask a loved one that you trust to tell you several things that they like about you.
3. Find things you can compliment yourself about every day; use this as part of your affirmations.
4. How well do you feel you really know yourself?
5. Determine what is the biggest obstacle standing in the way of you loving yourself right now.

North – Perfect Self-Fulfillment

The final compass point I would like to discuss is that of Perfect Self-Fulfillment. This compass direction is the most difficult to understand at first glance. Perfect Self-Fulfillment is the northern direction on our compass because it is the guiding principle. It means, we must understand that there is a place we are to fill that no one else can fill. There is something we are to do that no one else can do. This concept requires an understanding of how all the points, Health, Love, Wealth-Prosperity and Self-Fulfillment, are intertwined. They work together, enriching our lives and grounding us on our life path. When fostered, these points render a person emotionally stable, capable of loving themselves, possessing the means to prosper, and able to truly value that which is most important. Perfect Self-Fulfillment requires us to get in touch with our own spirituality, becoming able to appreciate our true talents, to be trusting, and strong. When you recognize where you are in your current life, what you are truly capable of, and that with a conscious effort you can fulfill your soul's purpose on this planet, you will undoubtedly be able to move forward in the right direction.

What all this amounts to, the examples I have given, my personal accounts, and the Spiritual Compass itself, is a method of dealing with the feeling of being lost and unsure of what path to follow. This is a universal experience. Ultimately, for the journey that is life, no one can make clear how life should really be lived because there is no perfect ideal. Life is an experience unique to every human being. However, by incorporating these four directional points into your daily life, you will be better able to maintain your direction. The Spiritual Compass is something that I believe in because it can always guide you back to your *core; it will always point you North. As a closing, I offer this poem:*

DEFINITION OF A SUCCESSFUL LIFE

To laugh often and much;
To win the respect of intelligent people
And the affection of children;
To earn the appreciation of honest critics
And endure the betrayal of false friends;
To appreciate beauty,
To find the best in others;
To leave the world a bit better,
Whether by a healthy child,
A garden patch or a redeemed social condition;
To know even one life has breathed easier
Because you have lived.

—Ralph Waldo Emerson

ABOUT THE AUTHOR

Ms. Cheranissa D. Roach

Cheranissa Roach is President and Chief Executive Officer of CDR Consulting, LLC. She conducts seminars and workshops for corporations and individuals. The seminars and workshops include Diversity and Multiculturalism, Women's Issues and Women's Journey to Wellness, Mind, Body and Spirit. Ms. Roach is a certified Diversity Trainer and a Certified Wellness Trainer with the Professional Woman Network.

Ms. Roach's knowledge of business and professionalism is supported by working with corporations, non-profits and faith-based organizations for over 15 years. She has over 10 years in Human Relations and Customer Service and over 5 years in Operations Management with the State Government. She has also participating in Leadership Teams and Training and Development of staff.

Among her accomplishments are co-authoring the soon to be released book, "Emotional Wellness for Women volume 3". She also holds a Master of Science Administration degree with specialization in Public Administration from Central Michigan University.

Ms. Roach is a wife, mother, daughter, sister, aunt, but most of all a friend. She enjoys traveling, entertaining family and friends, and good conversation. She is a believer of Christ and lives her life based on Philippians 2:4, "Each of you should look not only to your own interests, but also to the interests of others." It is this sprit that she seeks to encourage and empower women.

I would like to dedicate this book to My husband, Brett and our children. To my nieces, mother and family I love you and thanks for believing in me.

Contact:
CDR Consulting
PMB 214 2080 Whitaker Rd
Ypsilanti, MI 48197
734-644-2245
cdevon71@yahoo.com
www.pwnbooks.com

TWENTY-TWO

SELF-FORGIVENESS

By Cheranissa Roach

I made a mistake. I made a mistake? I made a mistake! This is the same sentence expressed three different ways, two of which can damage the heart and spirit of a person forever. Everyone makes mistakes, but not everyone is aware that mistakes do not make us, they *teach us*, if we let them. Mistakes guide us onto the right path because when we err, we already know where the wrong path will lead us. They can shape our habits, thoughts, character, lives and ultimately destinies, if we dwell on them far longer than necessary.

Experience is said to be a good teacher, but I believe that a mistake is a better teacher. Thomas Edison was asked the question, "What did you learn from all your mistakes." His reply was, "I learned what would not work." In spite of mistakes, he kept pressing on and eventually invented the light bulb. He learned the most important principle of success: *self-forgiveness.*

Mistakes are defined as misunderstanding the meaning or intention, according to the Webster-Merriman dictionary. Mistakes are going to happen just as sure as the sun gives off light and heat; mistakes are a way of life. How we *react and deal* with them can be the lessons of a lifetime. The way we *interpret* a mistake is just as critical as the mistake made. Whether large or small, our self-image is tied to them. If we have a healthy self-image, we can process the mistake and forgive ourselves quickly, but if we are in a "bad place", it takes longer for both the mistake to be processed and self-forgiveness to occur.

Exercise:

What opportunities have you missed out on due to not forgiving yourself for mistakes?

____

____

____

How has your life been affected by lack of self-forgiveness?

____

____

What life mistakes do you dwell upon?

____

____

Mistakes are a way of life, just like red lights when you are in a hurry, or a bad hairstyle on a very important date; they will happen. The art is to learn from them, release yourself and then move on to the eternal purpose for which you were born. Matthew 21:22 states,

"*And whatever things you ask in prayer, believing, you will receive.*"

About two years ago, I was in a very painful, unpleasant situation. I was in a job (notice I did not say career) that was not right for me, pregnant with our second child, unhappy with just about everything in my life and making a ton of mistakes. This was the most stressful time I have experienced in my life. I was looking at everyone and how they were mistreating me, not supporting and misunderstanding me, and least of all, not helping me get on with my purpose. I blamed others, but never looked within. You see, that is the hardest thing to do when you are going through a crisis, to look within.

I was making the huge mistake of giving the power of my life to others and letting their opinions of situations determine my future. Our peaceful home became a bitter, resentful atmosphere, where ignoring stares and silence ruled the days and nights. The intimacy once shared by soul mates was cooled and even nonexistent for months on end. I kept blaming myself and felt so hopeless, lonely, depressed, angry, bitter, and anxious. I was a mess.

What I learned from this experience was that I had to offer myself the one thing that I would offer a friend in the same situation, forgiveness. I had to give and receive the one thing I needed most. I had to act as my own best friend and speak kind words, think loving thoughts, and act with great care. In essence, I had to practice self-forgiveness for my actions and hateful thoughts. I had been so full of blame that I didn't take the time to open my mind to loving words and encouraging thoughts; I had poisoned my own mind. In essence, I acted as if I despised myself.

According to author Dr. Ilenya Marrin, self-forgiveness is defined as a **gentle method** for releasing self-judgments that stand in the way of your authentic expression of joy, loving and peace. If you can remember to release self-judgments that stand in the way of your authentic self being expressed and hold inside the positive elements of your life, you will begin overcoming many of the mistakes you have made. When we do not give self-forgiveness, we are in fact making life a prison for ourselves, all the while *holding the keys* for release. I learned this lesson the hard way and I will hopefully never repeat it.

Exercise:
What is your definition of self-forgiveness?

____

List the ways you have forgiven yourself in the past:
1. ______________________________________
2. ______________________________________
3. ______________________________________

List people you have forgiven in the past:
1. ______________________________________
2. ______________________________________
3. ______________________________________

If you continue to live with unforgiveness toward yourself (or others), the toxic thoughts and emotions can eventually lead to health-related illness such as depression, headaches, shame, guilt, regret, and heart disease. According to Dr. Don Colbert in his book *Deadly Emotions and Understanding the Mind-Body-Spirit That Can Heal or Destroy You,* unforgiveness produces toxic emotions that work like poison. My personal feeling is that since we have the choice to forgive or not forgive, and that unforgiveness can rob us of our health, we need to take personal responsibility and release the toxins within us.

The Benefits of Forgiveness

Let it go! Learn from your mistake no matter what it was, and free yourself! There are wonderful benefits that come from being free from guilt and anxiety:

- Begin to forgive others
- Peace
- Happiness
- Joy
- Unconditional self-love

Exercise:

Think of someone you have never forgiven. Name the person and your feelings toward them. What happened? Why won't you forgive them? How does it make you feel, holding the bitterness within?

____

____

____

____

Name someone you have forgiven. Who were they and what happened? How do you feel now that you have forgiven them?

____

____

____

Taking a Step

According to Gwen Nyhus Stewart, B.S.W., M.G., H.T., educator and freelance writer, these are practical steps to self-forgiveness:

1. Examine how you perceived a certain situation and how you can choose to change your perception. Remember that the thoughts we think create the feelings, and it is our perception that creates our interpretations of the situation.
2. Accept yourself and your humanness.
3. Admit when you make a mistake.
4. Confront your emotional pain.
5. Appreciate the lessons that have contributed to your growth and made you who you are now.
6. And another step I have personally added: Say, "I forgive myself for ____________________________" (Insert whatever you need to.)

Exercise:

So now, what will you do to start the process of learning from your past mistakes? What do you think is the most important first step?

____

____

List a mistake you have made in your life. What did you learn from it?

____

____

____

If this situation presents itself again in the future, what will you do to avoid this mistake again?

____

____

____

In your lifetime, you will have many successes and a number of failures. Take a moment to consider the successes you have had in your life. List them here.

Successes:

____

____

____

How did you contribute to your successes?

____

____

____

List the failures you have had in your life:

____

____

____

Embrace both the successes and failures of life. Take *responsibility* for your successes and your failures. The beauty of forgiving your failures is that someday with enough perseverance, the failures of yesterday may be the successes of tomorrow. However, these failures can only become wonderful, positive successes someday when you have learned a lesson, forgiven yourself, and moved on.

Every person has failed at something. The greatest presidents, mothers, fathers, corporate CEO's, and ministers have fallen. It is not so much the fall, as how we pick ourselves up. For whatever has happened in your lifetime, dust yourself off, talk to yourself as a best friend, and continue on with life with a forgiving heart.

To err is to be human; to forgive divine. —Alexander Pope

Notes:

ABOUT THE AUTHOR

Sunni Boehme, MSP

"Oh, boy! More Joy!" are Life Success Coach Sunni Boehme's favorite words. Sunni has helped thousands of women find more joy and fulfillment in their careers, relationships, and other important areas of their lives. With a Master's degree in Spiritual Psychology, she has dedicated her life to overcoming the major life issues that impact women everywhere in today's fast-paced world. Sunni is the author of *Mirror, Mirror... True Stories of Manifestation to Inspire the Magic Within You,* spinning delightful and captivating tales of overcoming fears and making her dreams reality while traveling throughout Europe and the Middle East.

Her book "Mirror,Mirror"…..true stories of adventures and manifestation to inspire the magic within you. She wrote it to help women to conquer their fears and learn to trust that they can manifest a life to fulfill their dreams.

She was an award-winning Mary Kay Director until 1983 when a major car accident changed everything about her life. A Reiki Master since 1981 she has been teaching manifestation, healing and metaphysics in business and relationships for over 36 years. Ms. Boehme is a member of the National Speakers Assoc. of Wisconsin, Women's Information Network, Women Business Owner's Network, The Breakfast Club Network, and The Professional Woman Network. Her energizing and dynamic programs offer women the wisdom she has garnered as a teacher, business owner, speaker, and world traveler. She has been teaching the "Laws of Attraction" for over 30 years and is best known for her workshops on "How to Get What You Want NOW" and the Women's self esteem building workshops "Awaken the Goddess Within You".

Contact
Global Goddess Enterprises
PO Box 070125
Milwaukee, WI 53207
(414) 482-8971
sunniboehme@hotmail.com
www.sunniboehme.com

TWENTY-THREE

RELAX, NOURISH AND REVIVE: CREATING A LIFE YOU LOVE

By Sunni Boehme

Imagine walking along the beach, filling your lungs to capacity with the fresh, clean air, delighting in delicious fragrances wafting from the flowers along the path, and then letting out a deep sigh of complete release.

Imagine reveling in the sunlight on a spring day as the snow is melting under your feet and your dog is thrilled to be running along beside you while sniffing the journal of interesting messages from furry friends along the footpath. Experiencing the joy and happiness of being alive today, being able to drink in the exhilaration of renewing life. Take some time to look at every tree you pass and be thankful for the fresh air and beauty it provides.

Thankfulness restores the soul. It lifts the spirit as we focus on the good in our life. It gives us hope for even better things. As you take a 10-minute walk, fill your mind every step of the way with things you are thankful for, such as, "I am thankful for being able to walk because I am unencumbered and free to discover every inch of the world. I am thankful for my eyes because I can see the beauty in all of God's creation. I am thankful for my sense of smell as I inhale the freshness in the damp, earthy smell of the ground as it is breathes new life from beneath the melting snow.

Do you already feel refreshed and renewed as you read? Can you feel and smell and visualize through the power of thoughts and words? Relaxation and restoration starts with making the choice.

I choose to take time to relax and restore myself NOW. I choose to let go and relax because it allows fresh, new thoughts to flood into my creative mind. I choose to feel joy and to focus on what I am thankful for today and my day becomes more fulfilling.

We don't have to wait to take a week's vacation on a Caribbean island. We can simply use our senses to heal and restore ourselves. We can go to the island this very moment in our minds, and exactly what we create in our mind is felt on an emotional and healing level in our bodies.

Listen to your biorhythms to discover the best time to make "Time for ME" each day. I have discovered that between 4 and 5 p.m. is a wonderful time to take for myself. I actually write into my appointment book ME. Yes, I need to take a power nap to recharge because I often teach classes in the evening and, if I just have 20 minutes to a half hour in the afternoon, I am restored and well able to teach from 7 to 9 in the evening, after working with clients and preparing for classes during the day.

By paying attention over the years, I found that listening to some kinds of music distracted me. However, I found a wonderful piece that instantly relaxes me. I have used the same piece of music for 30 years: Paul Horn, playing the alto flute in the Queen's Chamber of the Great Pyramid of Giza in Egypt. When I put that on, I immediately relax and go into a 5-minute, deep, meditative, restorative state of mind. I have programmed myself to know that I will be revitalized and renewed when I awaken.... and so it is. You, too, can find a piece that works for you, and program yourself to release all your worries and to-dos for a brief moment of your day.

We can get so distracted from what true peace and contentment is. Do you indulge yourself by luxuriating at least one hour a day thinking about what you really want? Or do you choose to use that hour instant replaying something miserable that happened at the office. Are you allowing yourself time to be daydreaming about the ideal life you want to create? Are you thinking about how much you are loved and appreciated by your friends and co-workers? Or, are you choosing to spend that time worrying?

Perhaps you have heard of the Law of Attraction. It says that what you focus your attention on, you will create more of. Do you want more good things in your life, or are you focused on the bills, the economy, or the grumpy neighbor?

Is the TV controlling your mind and your wants? Is the TV on in the background as you are working in your house? Do you spend one hour a day watching TV? Watching TV or reading the newspaper actually causes more stress. The trauma in the murder scene or the ER operating room actually induces adrenal overload. The stress that the advertisements cause creates wanton consumerism, "I want that ... I can't afford that ...oh well, I'll put it on my credit card." That causes worry and stress. If you already work in a high-stress environment, watching TV may be burning you out. Turn off that TV. Read or relax or take a walk. Do some writing. Choose to use that hour to daydream about your ideal life …and you will be creating it.

Let's think of some ways that we can truly nourish and restore ourselves within our bodies, minds and souls. I asked my clients to share with me things that they have learned in the coaching sessions and classes they continue to use to restore themselves and continue to heal and renew their vitality. You might find some that work for you. (Only the first letters of their names have been used to protect their privacy.)

G is a bright, spirited, dynamic and warm woman. She always looks like a million bucks and lifts the energy in a room with a ready laugh and playfulness that is a perfect fit for the career she has chosen. Over the past 25 years, she has built a satisfying business and trained other women to develop their own sales based on genuine warmth and great service. She was beginning to feel some burnout when she started taking some "How To Get What You Want NOW" classes. She shared the following "personal recipe":

1. Take time each day to stay present in my body and nourish it. I love to feel my vitality as I walk, work out, and stay present in my affirmation of robust health.

2. Schedule ME time in my day, week and month with massage, pampering, walking in nature, smelling flowers, playing games, and spending time with my grand children.

3. I have said "**no**" and found out…I am still loved after having said it.

4. Sometimes my attitude stinks or I have a pity party. When I pause to DREAM… I remember that my TODAY, this moment reality, can be used to make my dreams come true TOMORROW. Snap out of it!

5. Breathe! I have learned to love using it. Often, when driving, toweling off after a shower or getting through my body stiffness, I will deep breathe frequently before I walk into a meeting or feel like something is upsetting me. In meditation, I have learned to breathe deeply, right down to my diaphragm, exhaling slowly and fully. After a while I just watch it, as breath becomes my body's natural tranquilizer and makes a delicious connection to my soul.

6. "Every day my life gets better and better. Every day in every way" is an affirmation I use when I am walking, but especially swimming, as laps get boring. I may change the affirmation to help me with something I'm manifesting on a particular day… to give me hope for the best possible result! It is amazing how it works.

7. Laughter! It's what I love to do the most! I experience such great joy when I can share my laughter, hugs and smiles with everyone I meet. I think it is how our souls talk to each other. Laughter and touch are so cleansing for me.

V is full of energy and vitality with a house full of kids and some major challenges to overcome. She came to classes determined to squeeze all the good she could out of the lessons. Something in her life had to change. She proved that she was willing to put everything she heard into action and she has created miracles. V says: "The thankfulness exercise changed my life. I used to worry all the time. I am so much more appreciative of all the good things in my life. I used to focus on what was wrong or upsetting me. Now I start off the day....while I am in the shower, thanking God for everything and focusing on why."

Here are some examples of what V appreciates: "I am so fortunate, because life always blesses me with more of whatever I sincerely appreciate. I really appreciate unseasonably warm days in the middle of winter, *because* it feels so wonderful to go outside and to enjoy the sun as it gently warms every cell of my body."

"I am so grateful for the things that I used to take for granted, such as clean air, pure water, nutritious food, and adequate shelter, *because* these things are absolutely essential to my existence, and some people in the world aren't as fortunate as I am right now."

"I am so grateful that I have the power to choose where I take my attention, *because* I can choose to focus exclusively upon solutions, thereby attracting whatever is needed to quickly regain my balance."

"I think of even the littlest things and I have become so much more full of hope and believing in miracles."

"I am grateful that I have developed a much more positive vocabulary. It reflects back to me in things I hear my children say. We have all benefited from the work I have done on myself. I go back to look at it a few weeks later I am amazed at how much I have already manifested."

"I created my own little booklet from affirmations and that I continued to write down, affirmations and ideas that were important to me from the classes. I keep it in my purse and I read it when I am waiting in the car for one of my kids or when I am upset. It makes me forget what I was upset about and focus on what I am happy about. I know it keeps the lines open to the universe for good things to come to me and my family. The speed of the leader is the speed of the gang."

P has been in the mortgage banking field for more than 20 years (we won't say how many more). She conquered cancer years ago and reclaimed her health to be able, literally, to climb mountains. Some of the mountains she has also overcome are the ups and downs in the mortgage industry. She is a strong, determined woman with a heart of gold and a giggle that sends waves of joy through a room. P didn't want to be "fixed" when she started attending my classes. She has a powerful, positive attitude and simply wanted to be around more positive people because she knows how easy it is to get dragged down into the fears of the world. One evening, she marched in and said, "I want more."

Here is how P got more, by asking for more:

"I learned that I control my universe by the thoughts I think and I learned "again" that I can be my own best friend or worst enemy. Bringing meditation back into my life gave me the most peace. Going into my own stillness and connecting with my soul brought peace, joy and happiness back into my life."

"I was feeling overwhelmed with some big concerns, and I was able break them down into smaller segments to make the task or the problem something I could easily tackle. I learned to make goals for myself again. I used to do that, but I forgot and got caught up in taking care of everyone else first."

"I learned to give something to myself every day, whether it's 10 minutes in the morning to write down my affirmations, write in my 15-minute workbook, walk, or just be quiet. I began to sleep more peacefully by looking back on all the small or big things that I have to be grateful for. I am truly blessed and being thankful keeps me healthy."

Does it make you feel better just to read these true stories that confirm miracles in people's lives? Has it lifted your energy and made you think…."I want more of that, too"?

Have you watched or read "*The Secret*" or "*You Can Heal Your Life*" by Louise Hay? Even if you only devote 10 minutes a day to either one of those, you will be energized and find your own positive attitude restored.

Are you willing to take some new action? Here is a fun one. Write down 60 things that you want to BE, DO or HAVE before you die.

For example:

I want to BE content, peaceful, loved, loving, forgiven…..etc.

I want to HAVE plenty of money, peace of mind, a (certain) car, great health etc.

I want to DO….hot air balloon, Mediterranean cruise, help humanity, travel…..etc.

Now, decide what you want from this list in the next four months and watch how magically it appears in your life. Look at it and read it regularly and tell yourself, "I deserve it." What are you willing to change about your life to have these things come true?

Exercise: (adapted with permission from "*The 15-Minute Miracle Workbook*" by Jacquilyn Aldana)

15 Simple Ways to Miracle-ize Your Life

1. **Focus** primarily upon that which you **DO** want to experience.
2. **Notice** how wonderful you feel when you express **gratitude.**
3. **Envision** life as you **prefer** it to be for at least 15 minutes a day.
4. **Appreciate** everything you **already** have before asking for anything else.

5. **Learn** to work in **harmony** with the natural laws that govern the quality of your life.
6. **Decide** what you want to experience, then step aside and allow life to take care of the **details.**
7. **Understand** the Law of Attraction that says, "What you **think** about is what you **bring** about."
8. **Release** resentments – holding on to them is like drinking **poison** and expecting someone else to die.
9. **Allow** life to consistently and abundantly fill **your** cup so that you can help others to fill **theirs.**
10. **Remember** to be proactive; being **for** something greatly strengthens you and attracts solutions.
11. **Accept** others just as they are by completely releasing your desire to **judge** and **control** them.
12. **Commit** your goals to **paper** and you will likely achieve them more quickly and easily.
13. **Recognize** how you love to **feel** and ask to experience more of this feeling.
14. **Emulate** the positive qualities you **admire** in highly successful people.
15. **Create** a specific **intention** prior to taking action on things.

ABOUT THE AUTHOR

Linda Hart Streeter

Linda is founder and president of Radiant Living Life Management Systems, and specializes in individual interventions, designing programs to help people learn more about themselves that they recognize their strengths and weaknesses and find greater satisfaction in life as a whole. As a consultant, she functioned as a part-time Adjunct Professor for Valencia Community and Seminole Community Colleges, and as an instructor/facilitator for LifeWorks, a Division of Ceridian Corp. In her capacity as professor and consultant, Linda excels in developing training curriculum and facilitating training programs. She possesses over fifteen years of experience in the Human Resources and human services fields, and has experience managing, and training in corporate settings. Organizations she provides professional training to have ranged from small companies to large corporations, to professional organizations and ministries.

She holds an Associate Degree in Business Administration and in Marketing/Management; Bachelors Degree in Theology and Psychology; upon completion of her practicum, a MA Counseling/MFT and currently pursuing a PhD opportunity. She is a co-author of one of a series of Emotional Wellness books for Women, a Certified Diversity Trainer with the Professional Woman Network (PWN); a Certified Trainer for Achieve Global (Zenger Miller) Leadership and Workforce Development Programs; and a Certified Instructor for Development Dimension International's (DDI) Interaction Management Strategies for High-Involvement Leadership Programs and other programs. Linda is a motivational speaker, an associate minister, a Metropolitan Orlando Urban League Guild member, Member of Association for Marriage and Family Therapy, and functioned as a mentor/coach for The Jobs Partnership of Florida, and currently serves as the Program Director of a women and children's shelter.

Whether from a personal or professional perspective, individuals and team members will enjoy their learning experience with Linda. She has a unique teaching and training style that is pleasant and fun. Linda says it this way, "My passion is to inspire individuals to develop physically, mentally and spiritually, maximizing their potential." She believes an organization is as good as the individuals who make up families and organizations. Therefore, maximizing ones potential is maximizing personal wellbeing and performance.

Contact:
Linda Hart Streeter
P.O. Box 547548
Orlando, FL 32808
321.438.3051
lstreeter@radiantlifemgmt.com
www.LindaHartStreeter.com

TWENTY-FOUR

IN SEARCH OF MEANING: PERSONAL SPIRITUALITY

By Linda Hart Streeter

"Sometimes people get the mistaken notion that spirituality is a separate department of life, the penthouse of existence. But rightly understood, it is a vital awareness that pervades all realms of our being."
—David Steindl-Rast

How do you find meaning in life to a life that makes no sense? The vicissitudes of life are an ever-moving force that constantly creates shifts and changes in life, demanding that we make adjustments. So how do you stay afloat, or remain positive? Or as some would say, how do you keep the faith? How do you achieve a sense of wellbeing and ultimate living in every aspect and dimension of life? We are triune in make-up. There is the physical self—a composite of blood, tissue, muscles, fibers, nerves and organs; the mind or psyche—a conscious and unconscious system of thoughts, emotions and beliefs; and then there is spirit—the creative, original, all knowing source that makes you a living being. The source that never dies or sleeps. This source of power provides the ability to bounce back from life's tragedies and bitter circumstances, as well as triumph to celebrate life's victories. Spirit is the source and power of all energy that creates and gives life, regardless of age, race, ethnicity, conditions, circumstances or geographical location. Through spirit, we find meaning in life when we turn off the external conditions and tap into the divine, connecting with the all-knowing, omnipotent, omniscience, omnipresent source from which all of life and creation emanates.

We can't always predict the chain of events that occur in life. Tragedy, as well as success can strike at any given moment, creating a domino affect of emotions, reactions and change. My most recent moment happened on Friday evening, March 8, 2008, just two days before the deadline of this writing project. I was preparing to leave work when I received a called from a stranger, asking if I was Charlotte's sister. He said that the reason for his call was to inform me that my sister had been badly hurt. Well, the rest became a blur, yet a lasting event. I was told that Charlotte was hit by a car. Upon arriving at the scene, blue lights flashed rapidly and streets were blocked off for several blocks. As I approached the block where debris scattered the streets, my heart begin to melt. I could only think, "Is she alive?"

Officers were demarcating restricted areas. When I stepped inside the yellow streamed boundaries, I was quickly warned that I should not be in that area. I pleaded, "I just need to get to my sister." By then an officer approached me and asked if I was the sister he had spoken with and that he needed me to confirm her identity. With some relief, I quickly answered, "Yes" and asked if she was nearby. "No, miss she is not here," he replied. "Take a look at my monitor. Is this your sister?" "Oh my God! She's dead," were my exact thoughts. I was about to fall apart. Restricted areas? Confirming her identity? He then told me to drive to the hospital and that both my sisters had been transported to Orlando Regional. It was at that moment that I realized that the car (which had lost the entire front end and right side) was my sister Eva's Chrysler 300. There was not one sister injured, but two. I then began what seemed a long journey back to my car.

Observers stood by asking if I needed help and if I was OK. I was in an absolute daze. I didn't quite know what to expect. Well, I managed to drive to the hospital emergency. Bewildered, I asked a lady in guest services for the two ladies transported from an auto accident. The attendant made a few calls and advised that both were in trauma divisions and that a chaplin team member would be out shortly to speak with me. It seemed this was the longest wait of my life. About an hour or so later, a doctor from one of the trauma teams came out and explained that he could only report on my sister Charlotte. Charlotte had suffered some very serious injuries. More than likely one of her legs would be amputated; she was on a respirator, had multiple acute lacerations over most of her right arm and hand, fractured ribs and was undergoing a blood transfusion, due to a massive loss of blood. I was petrified and cried, "Surly there is something you can do to save her leg!" The doctor then clearly stated that it was highly unlikely because the bone in that leg was shattered and that the muscles, nerves and ligaments were ripped and torn so badly that reattachment was 95% unlikely. The team was preparing her for surgery. What a blow. I could not fathom my sister without a leg, or possibly dying. He had no report on my oldest sister Eva, as a different team was working with her.

I'm from a family of faith. Prayer and faith has been our greatest source of survival and ability to bounce back from all of life's bitter challenges. I'm from a family of thirteen siblings, so that alone conveys that life has not been an easy ride for us. But I've learned when nothing makes sense any more, finding meaning in your sufferings, struggles and disappointments is the key to resilience, enlightenment, fulfillment and hope. Life lessons are great teachers when we choose to learn from every experience—good or bad.

Personal Spirituality

I've learned that I am a co-creator and co-author of my life. I've learned to get the most out of life, even during times of hardship, difficulties, disappointments, lack, crisis, family tragedies, brokenness and despair. If I should experience this particular incident with a sense of hopelessness and despair from losing someone dear, I would miss the opportunity to inspire you to a well of hope and to ignite the spirit of life lying dormant within you.

The conceptualization of personal spirituality and meaningful living demands the will of power that transcends our limited view of who we think we are, and causes us to rely upon the infinite source of power made available in the earth. Humans are a spirit living within a body, embodying the fullness of a living, creative God. You're not significant because of material possessions, but rather significant because you are a part of God. You don't need Hollywood glitz and glamour, a perfectly shaped body, hairstyle, nails, or clothing, nor do you need to have a glorified reputation to travel the road to spiritual perfection. You are a spirit with purpose and that cannot be diminished because of your looks, gender, age, color, creed and religion. Your spirit connected to the divine is the gateway to the world of healing that manifests abundant living.

Connectedness – Personal spirituality is not all abstract, ambiguous or elusive. Remember you are spirit. You are a spirit being having a human experience. Personal spirituality is about connectedness. Connected to God through an inner knowing and wisdom, a quiet strength and assurance that all is well. The Spirit of God is the third

person of the trinity available to connect with your spirit to give you wisdom, insight, knowledge and guidance at all times, throughout each transition of life. Therefore, you must be aware of and sensitive to the spiritual guidance provided by your source; otherwise you slip into worry, doubt, anxiety and emptiness. So how do you know when you are spiritually connected? What does it feel like or look like in your life? Presently you may feel you're in a pit, awaiting rescue from someone who has failed to meet you at your point of need. May I suggest the lifeline of the Spirit as a source of rescue? Connecting to God, you see impossibilities as possibilities and authentic living instead of merely existing. Here are seven clear indicators I've used to assess my spiritual connectedness at different times in my life, especially during this period.

Living above the line is to emanate and move toward God, living above circumstances, bad emotions and finding meaning.

Indicator #1 – Enlightenment

Enlightenment is the purest way to experience God, other human beings and creation. This demands liberation of the senses from thoughts. By doing so, you experience life at the highest level of spiritual awakening. You're able to tap into the rich resources of love and happiness. Enlightenment is the ability to capture reality untainted and enjoy each moment. Enlightenment is oneness with God. It's the ability to experience heaven on Earth. Step into God's REALITY. Abandon negative thoughts and increase your ability to see, feel, touch, smell and taste the beauty of God and the essence of His love in everyday living. So it is, I see and feel God in every situation. My thoughts and vision transcends the current family conditions. Plainly put, I see God. I see restoration and joy!

Indicator #2 – Freedom

"*...they [prisoners] offer sufficient proof that everything can be taken from a man but one thing: the last of the human freedom—to choose one's attitude in any given set of circumstances; to choose one's own way.*" (Viktor Frankl, *Man's Search For Meaning*). God has granted to every human being the power to choose his or her own way. Freedom is taking responsibility for your life. I'm reminded of a niece who shared the story that while visiting with her uncle, she noticed the family dog was always left in his cage, especially weekdays due to school and work. She felt sorry for the pup and decided she would open the cage and let him have his freedom. She beckoned for him to come out. He didn't move. She literally pulled him out of the cage and he would return to the cage. At this point, her patience grew short and she replied, "Silly dog, I'm trying to let you go free and you keep running back into the cage." I hope you got that! Don't forfeit your freedom. Stay out of the cage. Repeat this daily affirmation, "I have the power to be, to have and to become. I exercise this FREEDOM today!

Indicator #3 – Wisdom

Wisdom is the judicious application of knowledge. The spirit of wisdom fosters prudence, discretion, and reverence for God. Wisdom is a virtue to be embraced and is gained through experience and spirituality. Esteem wisdom and she will exalt you, embrace her and she will honor you. Trust the wisdom within, as wisdom represents willpower and connectedness to the divine.

Spirit is the lifeline that pulls you out of every pit.

Indicator #4 – Vision

Vision in this sense is the ability to see spiritually what the natural eyes can't see. Vision is a clear or deep perception of a situation; a feeling of understanding, revelation, visualization. It's the ability to see yourself and present situations not as they appear, but as God intend them. Frankl sited that a man who could not see the end of his provisional existence was not able to aim at an ultimate goal in life. Thus, he ceases living. Structure of his inner life changes and signs of decay begin to set in. What are signs of decay? Depression, inactivity, mental anguish, passive living, hopelessness, going through the motions, negativity, pessimistic outlook, inability to dream, apathy, worry, sickness, loss of gratitude, loss of identity and loss of purpose. Does this sound familiar to you? Get back into the race. Pick yourself up. See yourself in a perfect state of being. I end this note of vision with a poem written by Kalidasa centuries ago.

Listen to the Exhortation of the Dawn!
Look to this Day!
For it is Life, the very Life of Life.
In its brief course lie all the Verities and Realities of your Existence.
The Bliss of Growth,
The Glory of Action,
The Splendor of Beauty;
For Yesterday is but a Dream,
And To-morrow is only a Vision;
But To-day well lived makes
Every Yesterday a Dream of Happiness,
And every Tomorrow a Vision of Hope.
Look well therefore to this Day!
Such is the Salutation of the Dawn!

Indicator #5 – Courage

I shall begin with a quote from Dorothy Thompson, "*Courage, it would seem, is nothing less than the power to overcome danger, misfortune, fear, injustice, while continuing to affirm inwardly that life with all its sorrows is good; that everything is meaningful, even if in a sense beyond our understanding; and that there is always tomorrow.*" Need I say more? Walk boldly. Take charge of your life and live meaningfully. Change will happen as a result of new thoughts, ideas and willingness on your part to take action. God grant YOU the courage to change. Exercise good faith, the greatest source of courage. Bad faith destroys trust in God and self. Work through the activity at the end of this chapter to identify and replace bad faith statements.

Indicator #6 – Purpose

Follow the path of purpose. Purpose in its most general sense is the anticipated aim that guides action. Rick Warren's book, *The Purpose Driven Life*, continues to be a top seller. He gives profound wisdom of God's intended purpose for mankind. God created everything with purpose and when he created you, he had a specific task in mind that no one could do but you. Purpose guides decisions we make, keeps us focused, and often time keeps us alive, as it is the "will to power" in your life. Purpose keeps you alive and keeps you out of the pit. Want to be great? Live with a purpose in mind! Complete the "Living With Purpose" exercise at the end of this chapter to assist you in identifying and clarifying purpose and meaning in your life.

Indicator #7 – Fulfillment

Is life empty? You will never look good enough, have enough money, surround yourself with enough important people, or be important enough to achieve inner fulfillment without your spiritual source. At midnight, when the lights go out and you're all alone, what are you feeling? Now that you finally arrived on the red carpet, did you experience the blissful epiphany you strived for? Was the sacrifice of your family, relationships and struggles worth the journey? These are questions only you can answer. Does the path you've chosen or the people you surround yourself with invite inspiration or perspiration?

Your spiritual depthness is an indicator of your strength during stormy seasons of life. Allow your roots to grow deep. Harness the power of spirit from the source that never runs dry. You've been granted great abilities and power. If you're suffering in any area of your life, stop asking why and pursue meaning so that you may experience the fullness of GOD.

Search For Meaning

Life only has the meaning you bring or give to it. Meaning to life is discovered through the processes of suffering, work and love (Frankl, 1965). There is a constant struggle within us to grow toward maturity and independence, yet we realize that expansion is often a painful process. Thus we struggle between the security of dependency and the delights and pains of growth; when nothing, absolutely nothing produces a greater sense of being and meaning in life than hard times. Suffering, though quite discomforting, yields a deeper relationship with God. We discover meaning and develop character. Personally, I've discovered my calling through suffering, which is to inspire others to become. I only wished there was space and time to say more, but this chapter must come to a close. Remember, God meets us daily with love, gratitude, giving, mercy, kindness, longsuffering and gentleness. Choose today to live life above the line. Take time now to consider thoughts you hold in your mind and heart to completing the bad faith/good faith chart.

Hope*Love*Peace*Fulfillment*Revitalization*Expectation*Optimism*Transcendence*Meaning

Despair*Hate*Chaos*Depression*Disappointments*Unexpected Change*Hopelessness*Suffering

Bad Faith Thoughts	Good Faith Rebuttal	Idea for Creating Your Destiny

Living With Purpose

Most people struggle with three basic issues in life: Identity, Value, and Contribution to self and others (humanity)

1. **Identity**: Who Am I?

____

____

____

____

____

2. **Importance/Value**: Do I matter? In what way?

____

____

____

____

____

3. **Contribution**: In my search for personal spirituality, I intend to reach out and contribute to others in the following ways…

My Life Purpose Statement: Write one paragraph about your life mission. How will you live your spirituality?

4. Spirituality for me is this… *Describe in detail or draw a picture of what Personal Spirituality looks like.*

5. List your unique personality traits, gifts, talents, abilities, and virtues. *Do not focus on whether or not you are well developed or proficient in these areas at this time.*

____

____

____

____

____

6. How can you live your life of purpose and vision using the strengths, talents you listed in #5?

I,________________________________, will live my life filled with purpose and vision by sharing my strengths, talents and gifts with the following people in these ways:

Gift I Will Share:	**With Whom:**
1. ____________________	____________________
2. ____________________	____________________
3. ____________________	____________________
4. ____________________	____________________
5. ____________________	____________________

May you live your life's journey filled with your own personal spirituality. Take time daily to reflect upon your life purpose and whether your choices and decisions mirror your values and spiritual depth. Remember the importance of sharing your strengths and gifts with others. This will give greater meaning to your purpose and vision.

Recommended Reading:

Man's Search for Meaning **by Viktor E. Frankl**

A Year to Live **by Stephen Levine**

Escape From Freedom **by Erich Fromm**

The Power of Intention **by Dr. Wayne Dyer**

Awakening To The Power of Personal Spirituality **by Linda Hart Streeter**

Notes:

ABOUT THE AUTHOR

Terry L. Hairston

Terry L. Hairston is the President & CEO of Quality Business and Technical Solutions (QBTS) a business solution provider of Quality Assurance and Information Technology Training services, since 2004. Her experience in Quality Assurance has allowed Terry to successfully spearhead process improvement and training activities for several Federal Government and Commercial clients. She has performed internal Quality Assurance Audits, developed Gap Analysis documentation, and performed training activities, which have allowed her clients to prepare for software capability evaluations and receive their CMM/CMMI Certifications. These clients have also established company wide best practices with the expertise of Terry.

Terry has traveled locally and worldwide to support software applications for Government Contract organizations. Terry has also trained government and private sector employees in Technical and Soft Skills training courses. She is a platform presenter, facilitator, and team builder. A very passionate Instructor, Terry believes that "teaching is touching lives" and she desires to continue to impart a wealth of knowledge through training all mankind.

Terry is a member of the Professional Women's Network and she is a Certified Workforce Diversity Trainer with emphasis in Women's Issues (Self Esteem, Assertiveness, Diversity, Leadership and Business Etiquette). Terry is also a member of Delta Sigma Theta Sorority Inc., the Federal City Alumnae Chapter. She is a very active member, supporting several committees and she is co-chair on the Audit Committee.

Terry holds a Bachelor of Arts degree in English and Mass Communications from Virginia State University in Petersburg, Virginia.

Terry L. Hairston is available to train, consult and also speak to audiences nationwide.

Contact:
Terry L. Hairston
Quality Business and Technical Solutions (QBTS)
P.O. Box 5841
Capitol Heights, MD 20791
(301) 613-8147
QBTS@comcast.net

TWENTY-FIVE

THE FINAL ACT: DEALING WITH DEATH, GRIEF, AND LOSS

By Terry L. Hairston

Death, Grief, and Loss are three events in life that are part of the Final Act. This "Final Act" is that time in our lives where life terminates or ends. The Final Act is a pretty serious deal and the three events in this act will ultimately occur when we least expect them to. We don't ask for them, but day by day death, grief, and loss seem to "just happen". There's not a magic potion to drink, or a magic wand to raise to prevent them. Oh, wouldn't it be nice, though, if we could be assured from this day forward that we'd have no more tears to cry, no more sadness, frowns, or despair. We'd only have joyful and happy times, equipped with smiles, laughter, and peaceful pleasantries for everyone. Instead, reality deals us with loss as well as joy. What's going to be extremely important is the way in which we actually deal with the three events of Death, Grief and Loss when they happen.

I experienced death in my life and it involved three close family members. My sister, at age 52, died of lung cancer six years ago on April 1, 2001. It took me by surprise, but I know that I will never forget the last six months of her life and the time spent with her in her last days. Then, my brother, at age 55, died of a heart attack nearly two years ago on May 9, 2006. His death occurred very suddenly, while working at a Giant Food store, and we didn't even get to say goodbye. My brother went to work that morning and never came home that evening. Now, what was even worse than that was losing one of my best friends, my dad. I am actually named after his father who was Terry Melvin. Dad told me many stories about my granddad, and often I think about our exciting talks about him. My dad, at age 88, died of complications from Alzheimer's disease and an infection on December 9, 2006, just seven months after my brother's death.

'Sugar and spice and everything nice' was characteristic of my grandmother, who at age 97 died of natural causes on December 15, 2007. She had resided in a nursing home in the mountains of Welch, West Virginia for four years. The nursing staff told me at least one year before her death that they thought that she just wouldn't make it. Well, she sure proved them wrong. She closed her eyes when she was ready, about 15 days before the start of 2008.

I had to participate in writing a summary about my loved one's lives, and then work with my family to place them in the local newspaper. The longer details were written in their obituaries. The words didn't come so naturally as I thought they would at that time. Fortunately, I had a close relationship with my sister, brother, father and grandmother, and I had a wealth of history I could provide about my family members. If

I didn't quite remember information for myself, I could call on other relatives like my mom, other siblings and my niece or nephew because they were just as familiar. At the outcome, I was the one, the baby girl, that the family wanted to help provide the loving and inspirational words about my sister, brother, father, and grandmother, along with their pictures, to be posted for the world to see.

Dealing with Death

Imagine that "death-related thoughts" came to you one day when it was a beautiful day in your neighborhood and about 65 degrees outside in the middle of March. The sun was shining very brightly and you were strolling in your neighborhood getting your walk and exercise. Yes, this is a beautiful Saturday morning about 8am. You walk into the 7-Eleven store right near your home. You begin having an emotional moment because you are remembering a loved one. Your head is a bit cloudy, you feel weak, and you are very teary eyed. You pick up and begin to read the Washington Post daily newspaper and it's at that very moment that you turn to the obituary column and all of a sudden Death hits you right in the face. While looking at the obituary column, you see the bright smiles on the pictures of the people that are being remembered and you begin to verbalize these great words shown with the various pictures. The words are written by a sister, brother, mother, father, niece or nephew, good friend or companion. It seems like just yesterday you were trying very hard to pull the words together about your loved ones.

Today there are still questions in your mind about Death. The questions are very common, yet they are answered very differently, depending upon religious beliefs and culture. There are also known facts about Death that we must at some point understand and accept:

Death is a Permanent Condition.

Feelings may start to become spared about death because we'd rather say the person has just "gone away" or "gone to sleep". Often this may happen when explaining death to young children or adults who might have difficulty dealing with the death.

Death is Irreversible.

You may hear about a doctor performing surgery and "healing or bringing someone back to life." Death, in and of itself, is very permanent. Once someone is dead it's a permanent condition, for they have actually passed away and are gone for good.

Death Requires Support.

Staying connected to the people that have lost a loved one is going to be a huge help. It's essential and allows them to focus and move forward with successfully making arrangements, and handling the business matters. They feel better knowing that someone understands and is in their corner.

Dealing with Grief

Grief is often described as intense sorrow caused by the loss of a loved one, or when something else causes us real unhappiness. When you really think about it, grief can be more complicated than that. The very thought about someone close to us dying may cause us to spend weeks, months, and even years dealing with our own feelings.

We are all truly unique, and we all grieve differently and for varying amounts of time. Just the same, there are parts of the grieving process common to most everyone:

1. **Sad Feelings**:

- "There's not a day that goes by that I don't shed a tear since my mom's death."
- "I'm having nightmares all the time since my dad died."
- "Will I ever stop feeling so sad about losing my husband?"
- "There's a pain deep within just thinking about the death of my infant child."

Losing someone is truly a sad experience and sadness is a large part of the grieving process. To lose someone close to us may cause us to have an "out of control" type behavior and can even cause us to become depressed at times. What do you remember about the death of your loved one and the sadness that you felt?

2. **Disbelief and Shock**

- "All this just doesn't seem real to me."
- "When do I wake up from this nightmare?"
- "I feel like I'm in a fog ever since my sister died."
- "Will I ever feel happy after losing my best friend?"

Often, right after the death of a loved one, it's quite normal to find that some people have no emotional feelings at all. It's as if they are "sleep walking" or having a dream where they just can't wake up. The emotion felt may allow us to feel overpowered and we may just "shut down" without realizing why we're acting that way.

Grief can also cause:

- A lack of energy
- No appetite
- Weak feelings
- Loss of interest in normal activities
- Problems in school or at work

Dealing with Loss

Losing someone is difficult, but we must recognize that this is considered a life-changing event. By all means, give yourself the time to deal with the situation emotionally, and also try to cope during your healing process. Like clockwork, you can definitely expect to feel some of these emotions during your grieving and loss process:

- **Denial** – You may have a reality check and begin to ask if the individual that died is really gone or wonder why something like this could happen to you.

- **Anger** – You may begin to feel anger toward those involved in the loss, such as doctors, caregivers, medical staff, or family members.

- **Bargaining** – The angrier you get, the more you may find yourself trying to bargain with God, or with whatever universal power you believe in.
- **Depression** – You may be easily distracted and uninterested in normal activities. Consider professional help if you continue to feel so sad that you are finding it too difficult to function.
- **Acceptance** – At some point, you will eventually accept your loss, but it takes time. When you accept the loss, know that it will still hurt, but you will begin to move forward and be hopeful.

To be able to predict the length of time it will take you to cope and deal with the loss of your loved one would be ideal, but there really is no timetable. It's recommended that you try and locate people with whom you can discuss your feelings. This will allow you to face your grief openly and with honesty. Be sure to allow yourself to seek professional help if you are finding it difficult to discuss your loss openly. Try finding some support from the following after a loss:

Friends	Consider letting people who care about you handle some things for you. Let them help and wipe the tears away.
Family	When a death occurs in the family, it creates a path for a reunion, and allows the living relatives to reconcile differences and build a stronger bond.

Support groups	Many support groups are available to assist you with your grieving process. There are specialized groups, depending on the type of loss, as well. (e.g. loss of spouse, children, coworker, etc.)
Therapists and other professionals	If you can't deal with the grief, talk with a therapist or specialist, especially if time goes by and you're not feeling any better.

I want to feel better and I want you to feel better about how to deal with Death, Grief and Loss. A friend of mine provided some encouragement about a year ago and she sent me a very special and inspiring card that reads:

"You Can!"

Whatever you're faced with, you can handle.

Whatever you're feeling, you can cope.

Whatever you fear, you can conquer, as long as you believe in yourself as much as I believe in you."

At the time that these words were delivered to me, I was making some life changes and I was also dealing with the loss of my loved ones. These words gave me a true since of hope and inspiration to start looking within myself and getting a grip. They also provided some real credence for how I would cope, how I would handle my business, and how I would move forward with life. When I wanted to just throw up my hands and give up, because my big sister lost her fight, I handled it. When I could no longer joke with my big brother, because he went to see the Master, I persevered. When I could no longer hear my dear sweet granny tell me to press on, because she had gone on to glory, I dealt with it. Finally, when I wanted to just give up because I had lost my best buddy, my dad, I stayed strong and coped with it. You can too.

ABOUT THE AUTHOR

Karen R. Freeman-Moore

Karen R. Freeman-Moore, President and Founder of The E.T.N. Group, believes wholeheartedly in the power of self-discovery and action planning. Her strong background in human services, human resources and training provides her with an excellent foundation to assist her clients with their stated goals.

The E.T.N. Group is a personal and professional development company designed to "unlock" the client's potential for further growth and fulfillment.

The E.T.N. Group workshops are designed to provide a higher level of awareness-whether for a business professional seeking better customer relation skills, a mother-daughter who want to enhance their communication, or a child who has questions about those different from his/her.

She lives with her husband, John, and daughter, Victoria, in Charlotte, North Carolina.

Contact:
The E.T.N. Group
Karen Freeman-Moore
P.O. Box 480635
Charlotte, NC 28269
704-264-9059
ETNgroup@bellsouth.net
www.protrain.net

GUEST

SELF-LOVE: 15 WAYS TO PAMPER YOURSELF

By Karen Freeman-Moore

In, Out, In, Out, In, Out… Breathe, Breathe, Breathe… R-e-l-a-x. Yes, that's better! Standing in front of my bathroom mirror, slowly breathing is how I often begin and end each day. I just breathe, concentrating on me – no one else. That is **my time**, in that tiny bathroom… my alone moment. My breathing space! Sometimes, it doesn't take a lot to pamper oneself!

How do you pamper yourself? What calms you, excites you, renews you? How is that working for you? Do you put as much energy into self-love as you put into loving and caring for everyone else? Taking care of **you** is vital. How can you create a life of self-love? Throughout this chapter, we are going to explore some conventional and not-so-conventional ideas for you to experience and live a life filled with "me time".

1. **Breathe** – Let's try a little self-love, right now. Stop everything and just BREATHE with me. You know how… *In, Out, In, Out, In, Out. Breathe.* Close your eyes… forget that report due to your manager, forget the carpool, and forget the pain in your lower back. *In, Out, In, Out, In, Out. Breathe.* Aah! You can experience a great deal of peace by just listening to yourself breathe.

2. **Dance and Sing** – Do you ever just dance around your house when no one else is home? It feels GREAT, doesn't it? Even though I can dance a little, sometimes I'll just jump around without any sense of rhythm whatsoever! Now, I add in vocals to the song and before you know it, there's a concert going on in my home! It's amazing how those few moments can bring such joy to your day. Once you've mastered your "in-home" routine, take your show on the road (so to speak) and join a dance class to hone your skills. Not only is this great exercise, but a wonderful opportunity to meet new people. *Go, Tango!*

3. **Laugh** – Just last week, my good friend, Penny, and I were coming from lunch and something I said struck her as funny. As we walked back into the office building, she was laughing so hard that tears were rolling down her face and she could hardly stand up. So, what did I do? I egged her on by repeating what I had said. It was so funny, just to watch her. The best part of all is that her laughter was infectious. People on the elevator joined in, even though they had no idea what was funny! We've all had those moments, haven't we? Making sure that we have more of them is the key. Maybe we don't need to have those, "hold my side" bouts of laughter all the time. But, finding something to laugh about every day relieves stress, is

calming and simply fun! After all, laughter is the best medicine. *Ha! Ha!*

4. **Alone Time** – How many times have you wanted a few moments by yourself, to do something for yourself? I'll bet it was just yesterday! You owe it to yourself to find the "me time" that you deserve so much. Your first task for the day (ok, after the kids are off to school, or the baby is sleeping, or after the next conference call – smile) is to look at your day with a critical eye. Where can you realistically carve out 1 or 2 hours for you? Turn the phones off, stop reading e-mail for a little while and just BREATHE. You know how - - *In, Out, In, Out, In, Out. Breathe.*

5. **Take a Sabbatical From Your Job** – Pamper yourself by going on sabbatical. Discover your passion, your ideal career, or a new way of doing something. In this current state of the U.S. economy, it may be a little scary to take extended time off from your job. But, if you can afford it, then make it happen. Reflect on where you are in your career. Is it just a job or is it the career that you always wanted? Do you really believe that you can't be fulfilled in your current job? Take a sabbatical and explore a new career path.

6. **Be a Little Indulgent** – What is that one thing that you really want, but you just will not allow yourself to have? Maybe it's a massage, a pair of designer shoes, or time away from your children. Whatever it is that you think is indulgent, you have to figure out a way to have it. You may have to save a little longer to pay for the all day spa day or barter for babysitting with your sister. Remember, you are worth it, your deserve it, you need it! Ok, maybe you don't really NEED a pair of designer shoes…but, you definitely are WORTH it!

7. **Ask for Help** – When was the last time you actually admitted to yourself that you are not Superwoman? Never, I'll bet. Are you one of those people who feel that the more that's on your plate, the more you're capable of juggling? So, you live each day running and juggling, juggling and running. The more balls in the air, the better. Well, let me just give you a little wake up call…Superwoman is not REAL! Pamper yourself - - - ask for help. Ok, you can go back to juggling now.

8. **Learn to Say No** – Self-love sometimes can begin with a "no". Are you someone who takes on whatever people ask, whenever they ask, with a smile? You are probably stressed out, run down and grouchy (beneath that smile). Saying no to someone in a non-confrontational tone will allow you to add more hours back to your day for "me time" and hopefully, will gain respect from the person who is always doing the asking. So, the next time your neighbor asks you to care for her two dogs and twelve cats while she's out of the country for a month, just say NO! You will love yourself for standing your ground.

9. **Make a Nostalgic Recipe** – When was the last time you made your grandmother's pineapple upside-down cake recipe? You know, the one with the two sticks of butter and all that yummy brown sugar. That's right…you remember…it smelled so good as you walked up to her front door. Heaven? Almost. Pamper yourself by reliving and honoring some of those special times with your loved ones by re-creating a family recipe. Hmmm!

10. **Take a Class** – There are hundreds of learning opportunities in every city and online. Maybe you have always wanted to earn a degree or learn to fence or learn how to build a website. Once you've carved out the time and you've saved up the money, don't let anything stop you.

11. **Go On a Day Trip** – If you drove just fifty miles, in any direction, outside of your hometown, where would you be? Maybe you know the name of the location, but have you spent any time there? I love to "get lost" and go on day adventures. It allows me an opportunity to get away and experience some place new and different. Even if you think you know a city, there's always something new to discover. *Go forth and explore!*

12. **Spa Day** – There's hardly anything more enjoyable than to have someone rub fragrant oils on your body while you do nothing at all, but lie there! Whether you go to the spa alone, with friends or with your partner, there's absolutely nothing better. If you can't get to a spa, invite your better-half to rub your feet and back (after a hard day at work). Don't forget to return the kindness. Ooo Aah! Ok, enough said!

13. **Book a Hotel Stay in Your City** – You've secured a babysitter or dog sitter for the night and the city is waiting for your arrival! Enjoy an overnight stay at a local hotel and go out on the town. Or, if it's just peace and quiet you need, stay inside and call for room service.

14. **Candles, Wine (or Hot Chocolate) & Music** – Imagine…a cold night, a bottle of champagne, a roaring fire, Will Downing's CD is

playing and the children are all in bed. You can *R-E-L-A-X*! Maybe that can't happen every night or every week, but it CAN happen with a little planning. *Cheers!*

15. **Get Some Sleep!** – Drum roll, please! The best way to love yourself…get some sleep! I don't think a day goes by when someone isn't telling me to get some rest. It's often my husband saying it as he heads to bed, but I'm still watching television or working on something. Doctors on the morning shows tell us time and again that sleep is vital to all aspects of our health. It's true. We simply cannot "catch up" on lost sleep. Be kind to yourself, renew yourself, love yourself…go to bed! *Nighty, night!*

Self-love begins in the mirror. Look at yourself closely, look at yourself honestly, and look at yourself lovingly. You must make time for YOU. If you don't, then who will?

Breathe.

Notes:

ABOUT THE AUTHOR

C.M. Johnson

C.M. Johnson graduated with honors from Coppin State University in Baltimore, Maryland. During her college years, she lived in Petach Tikvah, Israel for several months, where she carried out research for the University of Maryland and The Rabin Medical Center. Her professional certifications and experiences are in the areas of Life Sciences and Secondary Education. Her training has afforded her the opportunity to work in the areas of Biological Research, Statistics, and Animal Dissection/Minor Surgery (National Institutes of Health, Veterans Hospital of Maryland, and Johns Hopkins University), Microbiology (Howard Hughes Grant Program and Johns Hopkins University), Research Science and Epidemiology (University of Maryland and the Rabin Medical Center), and Education and Student Enrichment (Baltimore City Public School System, Baltimore County Public Schools, The Calvert School, The Newton Learning Program, and FSK/Middle Grades Partnership). Along with features in various newspapers and magazines, her publications include "Detection of Human T-Cell Lymphotrophic Virus Type-1 by particle agglutination, Western Blot, and rp21e ELISA Tests and HTLV-1 antigens by p19 ELISA Tests." JAAMP. Vol. 9, No.4, Oct. 1998. She is a member of Beta Kappa Chi Honor Society for Natural Sciences and Mathematics and the Professional Woman Network. She is also certified by The Professional Woman Network as a Youth Trainer and Professional Coach.

She is founder and president of Out Da Box Ministries, Inc, a non-profit, 501(c)3 organization that uses the Arts to educate youth and their families about their individual worth in order to increase healthy self-awareness and positive self-development. Incorporating Biblical lessons and her life's experiences, her outreach includes workshops, seminars, musical concerts and a full-length theatrical production, entitled "More Than Conquerors: A Hip-Hop Musical." Out Da Box Ministries, Inc. has performed at various locations and was given the opportunity to perform at ARTSCAPE (a cultural arts festival that has an audience of over 100,000 over a three-day period). With over a decade of training and experience in Biological Research and Secondary Education (along with training as a professional singer, actress, and model), she is currently using her skills as a homemaker and writer. She is also a God-fearing, happily married mother of two who is expecting in April 2008.

Contact:
C.M. Johnson
P.O. Box 1646
Owings Mills, Maryland 21117
(443) 867 – 2938
(888) 318 – 7282 Fax
johnson.outdabox@yahoo.com
www.outdabox.org

GUEST

EMBRACING THE BEAUTY OF CHANGE

By C.M. Johnson

"May the words of my mouth and the meditations of my heart be pleasing unto you, O Lord."—Psalm 19:14

Life

It was a quarter after six on a Friday morning before, a long-awaited, winter break. My 10-month old son and I were preparing to leave the house, *ahead* of schedule. My morning was booked with a before-school parent conference, followed by a first period observation.

As we reached the front door, an odor attacked my olfactory glands. Lifting my son's rear-end to my nose, his diaper needed to be changed. With record speed, I changed a soiled diaper and outfit, and wiped out the inside of a snowsuit—all while singing the theme song to Sesame Street.

Finally, my son and I were ready. We rushed to the car, buckled up, and began the twenty-minute drive to daycare. I drove defensively, *safely* negotiating traffic, and with ten minutes to spare, we arrived to an empty parking lot and a lifeless daycare.

Five…six…seven after seven and the director arrives with the morning assistant (who usually opens up at 6:30 AM). After a quick greeting, the director apologized for being tardy while I removed outerwear and put lunch in the refrigerator. As Murphy's Law would have it, the morning assistant had a flat tire a few blocks from the site and phoned the director to pick her up on the way.

I kissed my son and said a quick farewell to the director and her assistant. And with ten-minutes to spare, I dodged in and out of traffic to make it to my classroom one minute before my student's mom.

Well, the parent conference went very well and my first period observation was excellent. Even with the shoestring surprises, the day's end was "normal." But, within a period of six months, my son's father and I will have separated; my son and I will be living in the front room of my parent's one bedroom apartment; the department of education will inform me that my teaching certificate will expire at the end of the school year and will not be renewed without two additional post-graduate classes; my son will be rushed to the hospital; and I will lose my car because I, eventually, become jobless and—before it is all over—homeless.

Life!

100 Percent Guaranteed

Life for most of us is like a roller coaster. Ups and downs, twists and turns, blinding inclines and dips through dark tunnels. Sometimes, no matter how much you have in savings or how much insurance you have set aside, you may not be prepared for life's unexpected changes.

The loss of a job, the death of a loved one, moving away from your family and friends, divorce, becoming disabled due to an accident, the birth of a baby, and marriage can all be changes that occur in life. Some of these changes occur by our **choice,** while others occur by **force**.

There are two types of change. I've named them *Choice Change* and *Force Change*. ***Choice Change*** occurs when an event or situation is not imposed upon a person and the outcome (whether positive or negative) can be altered based on one's decision-making ability.

Examples of Choice Change
Loss of a job (due to tardiness, poor performance, duty negligence, etc.)
Moving away from family and friends
Planned parenthood
Marriage
Change in lifestyle (diet, sleep pattern, exercise, etc.)

Force Change occurs when an event or situation is imposed upon a person and the outcome (whether positive or negative) cannot be altered due to one's decision-making ability.

Examples of Force Change
Loss of job (due to lay-off, downsizing, phase-out, etc.)
Death of a loved one
Illness
Divorce
Becoming disabled due to an accident or illness

No matter your gender, age, race, religion, or socioeconomic status, change does not discriminate.

C.H.A.N.G.E.: 6 Strategies for Surviving Change

One of my favorite poems is actually an excerpt from Reinhold Niebuhr's sermon that has been adapted and used by Alcoholics Anonymous and other Twelve-Step Programs. Bartlett's Familiar Quotations (1992) states, "The Serenity Prayer," as it is commonly known, was written as a prayer in the 1930's.

God grant me the serenity
To accept the things I cannot change,
Courage to change the things I can,
And the wisdom to know the difference

My prayers about my experiences have led me to come up with an acronym, **C.H.A.N.G.E.**, which may assist you in *surviving* change. More than just dealing with or tolerating change, *surviving* change allows one to become at peace with life's many changes. Consider "The Serenity Prayer" when reviewing **C.H.A.N.G.E.**

C – Control
H – Humility
A – Anticipation
N – iNspection
G – Goals
E – Endurance

C = Control

When analyzing the idea of *control*, the results prove contradictory or incompatible in nature. However, the sooner you realize that you *don't* have control over every event in your life, the sooner you will be free to embrace change. Human nature causes one to resist this truth while fighting to maintain a false sense of control. Still, facing the fact that you cannot control every aspect of life will facilitate a healthy transition when dealing with changes.

When analyzing the idea of *self-control*, the results are more harmonious with human nature. Self-control being one of the key elements to a fruitful spirit, when facing change, it is healthier to concentrate on *your* reactions, rather than on the outward situation.

Does the kindergartener in you surface when change occurs? Does optimism take a back seat when you are dealing with change? Do you throw in the towel or persevere when challenges arise? Take a moment to reflect on your reactions to some of the changes that have occurred in your life. Whether large or small, evaluate how you reacted to these changes.

- List three changes that have occurred or are occurring in your life. List ways you expressed emotions during these changes.

____

____

____

- List three things you can do to maintain self-control when changes occur.

____

____

____

H = Humility

The greatest story ever told was of a man who was born in a manger, who healed the sick and raised the dead, who taught the truth with love, who served his friends and family, who was wrongfully arrested and tortured, who was judged and sentenced to death, who was striped of his clothes, crucified and killed, who was buried in a borrowed grave, and who defeated death—rising three days later. From a very humble beginning to an exalted end, there has been no other life that has impacted the world to such a great extent than that of Jesus Christ. His life was the ultimate example of humility.

From an early age, many are taught that being number one is the best state. We award excellence in athletics, academics, and so on. And do not misunderstand my point; praising someone for a "job well done" can be a wonderful gesture. However, achieving so many good things without the proper mindset may fuel one's pride. Pride can blind one from truly seeing the most important things in life. Remember, *those that humble themselves will be exalted*!

Take a moment to think of the last time you were deliberately humble or served others without being asked to do so. Think about how you feel when you are around others. Are you satisfied with, sometimes, being "one-of-the-crowd" *or* do you have to be the center of attention? Review your thoughts and actions when exhibiting humility or pridefulness. Determine if lessons in humility can be learned while going through your life's changes.

A = Anticipation

Predict, plan, prepare, promise, and pray and changes are still likely to occur. A proactive individual will do their best to anticipate change. There is a saying that states, "It is better to be prepared for a situation or an opportunity that never arises than to have a situation or an opportunity arise and not be prepared." So, by all means, purchase that insurance policy, invest in that retirement plan, save for your child's college education or for your next family vacation. But, remember the *Fine Print Times.*

The *Fine Print Times* are moments when no matter how well one has anticipated a situation, change happens; companies fold, natural disasters occur, insurance companies include policy exclusion clauses, loved ones may become hospitalized or unable to work. Whatever the change, do your best to anticipate it. Nevertheless, know that there are times when you are unable to do anything in your own strength. It is in those times that your faith is being tested and faith produces patience.

N = iNspection

"The truth shall set you free."

This is the time to be <u>honest</u>. It's time to analyze what the change may be able to tell you about your life's direction and purpose.

Ask yourself the following:

- Is the change a *situation* that I have not previously dealt with (an event that is resurfacing because of my delay in handling it)?
- Is the change a *challenge* to overcome (an event that will mature and strengthen me)?
- Is the change an *opportunity* to meet (an event that will add to my life's direction and purpose)?

Change is often a catalyst for new opportunities. For that reason, whatever the circumstance, be honest with yourself and be open to changing directions, starting over, moving onward, or just being still for a "season."

G = Goals

Although my faith teaches me not to worry about tomorrow, thinking about and planning for tomorrow is a part of life. This brings us to one's purpose in life. *What is your purpose in life?* Knowing your purpose will keep you anchored. And though many of our purposes are continuously unfolding, having a central purpose will assist you in determining short-term and long-term goals.

When setting goals, it is important to remain focused, but realistically flexible. Forsaking all others to achieve your goals has never been a good idea. Just ask the children who grew up without a relationship with a parent or loved one. Neglecting your family, disregarding quality time with loved ones, and transgressing to gain popularity or position, are sure ways to be deficient of true love, joy, and happiness.

Set goals based on sound judgment and morals. Enlist the assistance of wise counsel; people who are attempting or have already achieved the goals you have in mind. These people will prove to be great resources for accountability, assistance, and encouragement. Also, think about what you will do if any or all of your goals are off-schedule or delayed. And finally, don't forget to be realistic and enjoy the process!

Here are a few things to consider:

- Think about your **belief system**.
  - Do you have a spiritual center?
  - What are your beliefs?
  - What do you value?
- Think about your **Short-term goals**.
  - Write a list of your short-term goals.
    - One-Month: ______________________________
      ____
      ____
      - List objectives you must accomplish in order to meet your one-month goal(s).
        ____
        ____
        ____
      - List the resources you will need in order to meet your one-month goal(s).
        ____

____

____

- Six-Month: ________________________________

  ____

  ____

  - List objectives you must accomplish in order to meet your six-month goal(s).

    ____

    ____

    ____

  - List the resources you will need in order to meet your six-month goal(s).

    ____

    ____

    ____

* Complete a list of objectives and resources for your twelve-month plan.

- Think about your **Long-term goals.**
  - Write a list of your **Long-term** goals.
    - Two-Year: ________________________________

      ____

      ____

- ◻ List two objectives you must accomplish in order to meet your two-year goal(s).

  ____

  ____

  ____

- ◻ List the resources you will need in order to meet your two-year goal(s).

  ____

  ____

  ____

- ■ Five-Year: ______________________________

  ____

  ____

- ◻ List two objectives you must accomplish in order to meet your five-year goal(s).

  ____

  ____

  ____

- ◻ List the resources you will need in order to meet your five-year goal(s).

  ____

  ____

  ____

* Complete a list of objectives and resources for your ten-year plan.

- Are your goals measurable and attainable?
    - How will you evaluate whether or not you are on track to reach your goals?
        - If you are not on track to reach your short-term or long-term goals, what are your alternatives?
- Review your objectives.
    - Are your objectives clear and specific for the time-frame allotted?

E = Endurance

Referencing Ecclesiastes 9:11, an unknown author is recorded to have stated, "*The race is not to the swift, but to the one who keeps on running.*" This reference is helpful when changes come in the form of trials and tribulations in one's life. While weeping on my parent's sofa bed—just a few years ago—with my oldest son in arm, I never imagined that, although my plans for my life were crumbling before me, God's plan for my life was perfect.

Are the struggles over completely? *No.* Will more changes occur in my life? *Yes.* But, because of the changes that have occurred thus far in my life, my faith is stronger than it has ever been. Experiences shape and mold us into the individuals that God wants us to be.

Endurance is not a very common quality these days. It takes commitment, long-suffering, and a willingness to stick with something—no matter how tough the circumstances. When changes occur, it's easier to give up than take the harder, more rewarding, road less traveled. So, "keep your eyes on the prize" and stick to the fight!

Now, when changes occur and you just don't know how you will make it through, there are several simple things that you <u>must</u> continue to do. Take care of yourself by doing your best to continue to eat a healthy diet, get enough rest, and remain active. It may not always be in your budget or ability to eat lobster dinners, attend the spa on a regular basis or purchase a membership to your local gym. But, take some time to reflect on your lifestyle.

- Think about your diet and resting patterns. Are they adequate for a person of your activity level?
- Think about your daily routines and activities. Do they include adequate time for relaxation, exercise, and "U-time?"
- Think about how you relax. Do you set aside adequate time to pamper yourself and rejuvenate?

In some instances, it may *seem* unrealistic to think about your diet and rest patterns, daily routines and activities, and relaxation. But, you're a human being. And the last time I checked, part of being physically healthy included doing things to keep your energy levels up. Also, maintaining your spiritual and mental energy will help you endure. And when your endurance is developed, you will become stronger in character and more ready to embrace change!

In conclusion, life happens, change occurs, and you will have to come to grips with it sooner or later. Think of it like this, everything you use has to be tested; vehicles go through mechanical and safety tests, computers and others devices are tested for functionality and quality, animal food is even tested—by human tasters—for quality. And so, in life, *we* have to be tested and proven. "Fire tests and purifies gold—and your faith is more precious than mere gold." So, remember to acknowledge that life can be unpredictable, be flexible, "tighten up your boot straps," and use the C.H.A.N.G.E. paradigm. "*Get ready--get set--go!*"

Change—Embrace it!

Recommended Reading

Getting Through the Tough Stuff by Charles R. Swindoll

Facing Your Giants and *Captured by Grace* by Dr. David Jeremiah

Who Moved My Cheese? by Spencer Johnson, MD

Notes:

ABOUT THE AUTHOR

Treivor Branch

This chapter is dedicated to my grandmother Leola McNeil and my mother Mary Branch for their support, faith and inspiration.

Treivor Branch is the President and Founder of *Success Her Way,* an international coaching and training network for women. She conducts workshops focused on life skills and self-empowerment which have been presented throughout the United States and abroad. Ms. Branch founded *Success Her Way* based on her passion to help women reach their full potential and improve their quality of life by transforming challenges into opportunities for success. Through individual and group coaching sessions Ms. Branch provides strategies to develop a life plan, overcome obstacles and achieve goals. Ms. Branch has a warm inviting demeanor which helps her get to the heart of the issues her clients face.

Ms. Branch has over 12 years of experience in the field of human resources management with specializations in employee relations, staffing, global deployment, and training and development. She graduated cum laude with a Bachelor's in Business Administration and is a certified professional development trainer specializing in women's issues, diversity, and conflict resolution. Ms. Branch is also a certified life coach and human resources consultant.

Professional Affiliations

The American Society for Training & Development (ASTD)
The International Coach Federation (ICF)
The National Association for Female Executives (NAFE)
The Professional Women Network (PWN)
The Society for Human Resource Management (SHRM)

Contact:
Treivor Branch
Success Her Way
P.O. Box 3685
Milford, CT 06460
Email: tbranch@sucessherway.com
Website: www.successherway.com

GUEST

LETTING GOD LEAD THE WAY

By Treivor Branch

"I feel lost! I'm afraid! I can't do it by myself! Where Can I Find Help?" When we were children we would seek the guidance of our parents to deal with pressing issues, but since we are no longer children and, in many cases parents ourselves, where do we turn now? As children of God, we should seek the direction and guidance of our heavenly parent. Just as children ultimately trust the guidance and direction provided by their parents, we should trust and let God lead the way.

Accepting the Invitation

"Then Jesus said, "Come to me, all of you who are weary and carry heavy burdens, and I will give you rest."
—Matthew 11:28, New Living Translation (NLT)

When we receive an invitation, the first thing we consider is who it is from and of what benefit is the event. Is this someone I know and is this something I want to participate in? One of the greatest invitations of all is given to everyone who is willing to accept it. The invitation is from God to get to know him and let him lead the way. He lets us know right away what's in it for us, He will give us rest. This invitation yields no ordinary rest for those willing to accept; it yields a rest that results in deep inner peace – peace of mind, body and spirit.

Virginia was what some might call a woman of the world. She loved to gamble, drink and party. Even as a young girl, she was always wise beyond her years and lived her life in a manner that demonstrated this. She was a great hustler and even taught others how to make *fast* money. As a result, she lived a very comfortable lifestyle. She was always the topic of conversation amongst those in her neighborhood and the God-fearing women. Virginia was not completely against anything holy, but she wasn't the first to embrace it. She would tell others they should go to church and listen to the Lord, but refused to step foot in one.

One day a woman named Susan, a God-fearing woman who lived in Virginia's neighborhood, unexpectedly decided to stop talking *about* Virginia and began talking *to* her. Initially, Virginia was taken aback by Susan's sudden neighborly demeanor, but as time passed they formed a friendship. Susan began sharing with Virginia some of the ways God helps her cope with life. You see, Susan had been married for only two short years when her husband became an alcoholic and, while there was no physical abuse, there was emotional abuse. However, Susan always seemed to have herself pulled together, very calm, relaxed and self-assured. Virginia would sometimes tease, "*I know a way you can get rid of that husband of yours for good,*" and Susan would always reply, *"I've tried everything, so now I'm leaving this one in God's hands."* Virginia would listen to this reply and think to herself, *"This woman is fooling herself."* As time went on, Virginia noticed she no longer saw Susan's husband, or so she thought, so on Susan's next visit to her home, she asked her where her husband was. Susan replied, *"He's still around, haven't you seen him?"* Virginia's reply was of course, no. Susan pointed out, *"You probably haven't noticed him since at his new job he has to wear suits."* Virginia was shocked. She blurted, *"You mean the clean shaven man I saw the other day with the three piece suit and the fancy car?"* Susan shook her head with a big smile. Virginia had seen this man twice in the last month and thought he was a tax collector or a banker coming to foreclose on Susan's home. Virginia inquired of Susan what happened to the shabby unkempt man she would see lounging around, sitting on the porch scaring the neighbors. Susan took this opportunity to enlighten Virginia on the power of prayer.

Susan had been praying to God and talking to her husband, encouraging him to draw close to God. Susan knew the problems her husband was going through which led to his drinking. She would leave him a note each day focusing on one of the problems they were facing in their lives and in their marriage. She included in the note scriptures which her husband could read and meditate on to see how God could help them, if only he would accept God's invitation. She also left him notes about how God says husbands should treat their wives and care for their families. Susan did this for over a year and eventually her husband responded. He accepted God's invitation and changed his life. Susan's situation so touched Virginia's heart that she asked Susan to show her how to pray and share with her some of what she shared with her husband. Virginia, too, came to accept God's invitation and found true rest. She was so rested and at peace with herself that she was able to convince Susan to help her start a support group for women that helped them find rest and inner peace by *accepting the invitation*.

Exercise

When you think about your life, are you rested in mind, body, and spirit?

____

What are some areas of unrest? Be specific.

____

____

____

Is the invitation from God appealing to you?

____

Have you accepted God into your life? Why or why not?

____

Are you willing to let God lead the way?

____

Releasing Control

"I know, LORD, that our lives are not our own. We are not able to plan our own course."—Jeremiah 10:23, NLT

"If you want to make God laugh, tell him about your plans." Likely you are familiar with this quote, courtesy of Woody Allen. However, have you ever thought of how true it is? For many people, success means climbing the corporate ladder. We hear it all the time; reach the pinnacle of success. However, how many of us take a step back and ask if this what you really want? And if it is what you want, then at what cost?

During my career, I met a woman named Amy who had achieved a great deal of success in her career and was on the path to a senior level at her company. However, I listened to her lament about the direction she had taken which led her to relocate. She now sees her two young children mainly on weekends because of her extensive travel and her husband's refusal to relocate the family for a second time to support her in her plans. Through further discussions with Amy, I learned the reason for her unwavering pursuit was because she wanted *success*. She wanted to help her husband provide for her family, as well as have a sense of achievement and purpose. However, Amy wore the turmoil of her decision. You could see the stress, the struggle, and the inner conflict she was living with because of her decision. As time passed, Amy and I became friends and I would provide her with my two cent*s* on the situation. Amy was an ambitious woman who was always in the driver's seat. Even at the urgings of her husband, who also had a successful career, she was not willing to change her course. Time passed and I lost contact with Amy, perhaps because she was on the road yet again.

Shortly after my last contact with Amy, a situation arose which greatly impacted my family, and required me to make a crucial decision that ultimately led to our relocation. I prayed to God and released control so that He could direct my steps on the matter. I had a plan for my career, but I put that aside and focused on the needs of my family. In the new location, I accepted a position that I knew was a slight departure from the path I was initially following and took me in a new direction. However, that was of little concern to me because, while I am ambitious, I had resolved long ago to leave things in God's hands and to never put career before family. As I faced this crucial time in my life, Amy came to mind. I wondered what caused her to sacrifice the joy and well being of her family for her career. I wondered how she and her family were doing.

I'm not sure if it was my deep thought or some other force behind it, but several years after my relocation, I crossed paths with Amy at a networking event sponsored by an organization it turned out we were both members of. Something was very different about Amy. She appeared happy and had a radiant glow. Her spirit was even different. To speak with Amy before, you could tell her spirit was full of unrest, however, now she had a calm refreshing spirit. When we met later that afternoon over a quick meal, I mentioned to her the noticeable change since we had last seen each other and inquired as to what caused this. She admitted she was caught up in the *ideal* of climbing the corporate ladder. This ideal remained a constant in her life. Then she said, one day you asked me simply, *"Is this the success YOU want or is it someone else's idea of success for you?"* A question she had never asked herself. She thought about the distress her family was in and she knew deep inside she was failing herself and her family. However, because she became caught up in the hype to pursue what someone long ago decided was the peak of success, she lost sight of what success meant to her.

Amy confided that her family life was out of control and she had finally reached an emotional breaking point. She recalled how I had once talked to her about God and shared a scripture with her of Proverbs 17:1. *"Better a dry crust eaten in peace than a house filled with feasting - and conflict."* NLT. She also remembered my story about the responsibilities I was carrying and the distress I had caused myself when I refused to release control. How I had to pray for faith and learn to let God lead the way. I had told her that when I learned to do this, God always led me to where I needed to be. At times the path had unexpected twists, turns, and hardships, but at the end there was always enlightenment, fulfillment, and most of all, success. She said the question I asked her and my willingness to share with her some of the details of my life helped her to pray to God for faith and let Him show her the way to a life of success and purpose. When she released control and let God lead the way, oh what joy she found! God brought her family back from the brink of destruction. She made a shift in her career which no longer required extensive travel and relocation so she was able to be with her family regularly. Despite this shift, she continues to have a successful career. However, most of all, she has a successful family life. She is able to be there for her children, actively guiding them through life. She is also able to maintain a strong loving relationship with her husband. This involvement in the success of her family life gives her the sense of purpose and achievement she so desires. She let God take control and He helped her achieve her own success.

Reflections:

What are some areas in which you can release control and let God lead the way?

____

____

____

What are some self-imposed burdens that can be removed by letting God lead the way?

____

____

____

What guidance is God giving you to improve the quality of your life? Consider each area including at home, at work, and in relationships.

____

____

____

Daily Following God

"Your word is a lamp to guide my feet and a light for my path."
—Psalms 119:105, NLT

God has provided us with a book of life lessons. He so lovingly leads us on this path of life with examples of those who came before and how they dealt with the very same situations that we face today. In the book of Ecclesiastes, wise King Solomon revealed, *"There is nothing new under the sun."* When we consider that there is nothing new under the sun, we have to ask, what lesson is there to be learned from those who went through this before me? How did God lead them?

Leola is a woman from the south who was married at the age of 13, and over the years gave birth to 16 children. She was responsible for the needs of her children, her husband, and her home. Leola was a strong sprightly woman who went to work everyday, sometimes with one or two of her children in tow. Leola believed in two things, "*the good lord and the good book.*" She was seldom found without the good book in her hand held close to her chest. As Leola faced the difficult challenge of raising sixteen children, she often turned to *the good book* for guidance. She read the example of Moses and how he had to lead the people of Israel through the wilderness. You see, Leola felt as if she was raising a small village and leading them through a world akin to a wilderness of uncertainty. She learned through the trials of Moses how to call upon God and let him lead the way. When people would meet Leola they often asked, *how do you do it?* Leola would respond, *"The good lord lights my path and I make sure my feet keep on following that light."* She then proceeded to share with them a scripture or passage from *the good book* to encourage them as they went throughout their day. Leola is over 90 years old and she continues following that light by reading the word of God daily and letting God lead the way. She credits her longevity to her unwavering zeal to *follow the good lord and read the good book.*

Reflections:

1. Schedule time to read the word of God daily.
2. Meditate and reflect on the guidance given in the word of God. Examine how you can apply this guidance in your life.
3. Share instruction from the word of God with family and friends, and encourage them to read the word of God.

Overcoming Discouragement

"All Scripture is inspired by God and is useful to teach us what is true and to make us realize what is wrong in our lives. It corrects us when we are wrong and teaches us to do what is right."—2 Timothy 3:16, NLT

The stress and anxiety of caring for our families, protecting our children, and simply making a living in a world of increasing fear and uncertainty is, at times, difficult to bare. Although we have accepted God's invitation, let Him lead the way, and follow His path daily, we are not immune to discouraging thoughts. There have been times in my life when I have let my emotions and discouragement throw me off course. However, I've learned it's in these times of discouragement and despair that we need to be fervent in our prayer and dig into the word of God to find direction and encouragement to continue following Him. We also need to talk to others who are letting God lead the way. These individuals can provide support and encouragement as we keep following His path. While letting God lead the way and reflecting on His word, take time to make note of scriptures that highlight how He encourages and instructs us:

When We Say	**God Says**	**Support from God's Word**
I am lost.	I will guide you.	Proverbs 3:6, NLT *Seek his will in all you do, and he will show you which path to take.*
I am afraid.	Be courageous.	2 Timothy 1:7, NLT "For God has not given us a spirit of fear and timidity, but of power, love, and self-discipline."
I can't do it by myself.	I will help you.	Luke 18:27, NLT *"He replied, "What is impossible for people is possible with God."*

Reflections:

Write down some of the discouraging thoughts that may be holding you back.

____

____

____

Study the word of God and keep a log of scriptures that can provide you with support and encouragement to continue letting God lead the way. *

* *If you are not familiar with the word of God, pray to God and ask for His assistance in helping you locate someone who can genuinely assist and support you as you seek to become familiar with Him and His word.*

ABOUT THE AUTHOR

Jo Anne White, PhD

Jo Anne White, PhD, is President and CEO of Doc White Consulting Services, LLC, a corporate consulting and training company strongly committed to excellence and achievement. As a personal & business coach and corporate trainer, she empowers and inspires women, their families, businesses and corporations to achieve greater health, wellness and success.

Her expertise in training and coaching has motivated organizations, groups and individuals to be more effective and successful, and to create more satisfaction in their lives and businesses. Corporate clients include hospitals, banks, universities and organizations that desire the best in Strategic Planning, Image, Performance and Achievement.

Formerly a professor at Temple University's Dept. of Education, Dr. White has been featured on the Internet and in local, national and international publications including Web MD, Woman's World and Women's Day. She's appeared as a frequent guest on radio and television networks such as NBC and CN8, World Talk Radio and WYSP.

Dr. White is a radio host for "The Good Life Show."

Jo Anne White, PhD has also developed seminars and curriculum on Self Esteem and Self Empowerment for girls and women and has offered private counseling to women and their families for over fifteen years. As a therapist, and hypnotherapist, she specializes in an integrative and holistic approach to wellness. Doc White currently resides in New Jersey.

She is a member of The Professional Woman Network Speakers & Authors Bureau and a contributing author in: *Emotional Wellness Volume II & The Baby Boomer's Handbook for Women..*

Additional Books:
Sense Your Way to Life Satisfaction
Secrets to Lasting Relationships

Contact:
Dr. Jo Anne White
Doc White Consulting, LLC.
PO Box 176
Haddonfield, NJ, 08033
856-795-5854
1-877-DOC-WHITE
joanne@drjoannewhite.com
www.docwhite.org

GUEST AUTHOR

SELF-EMPOWERMENT: CREATING PERSONAL MASTERY

By Jo Anne White, PhD

Do you know who you really are and do you have a strong sense of purpose and a clear vision of where you're going? Now is the time to detail what you desire to create and make it happen. Believe in you, your ability and your choices; take credit and responsibility for them and for your life with confidence and integrity. Knowing that you're responsible for you can be very life affirming once you become accustomed to the idea that you're in charge of you. You can take active and decisive steps to empower you to reach your maximum potential and achieve personal satisfaction.

Abraham Maslow, a respected American psychologist, studied exceptional people to examine the interaction between personality and motivation. In his theory, the Hierarchy of Needs, self-actualization was defined as a basic human instinct that motivates us to maximize our unique abilities and aim to be the best that we can. You feel this need for self-actualization in you, too. When empowered, you are self-motivated and you motivate and inspire others to reach higher levels of achievement. You take charge of your life and your direction with more confidence and ease. To feel, know and be in control, where control is possible, is what personal mastery is about.

You create and exert energy and influence in those areas of utmost importance to you and feel good about you and your choices. Decide to advance you, while staying true to your values and your special talents, and with respectful regard to others and to a greater purpose. Develop and enhance your ability to dream and imagine and to act with clarity, optimism and positive intent for you and your vision. Personal Mastery doesn't just happen without your conscious effort, conviction and will. Create personal mastery right now by taking charge of your life, thoughts, actions and dreams. Include the following seven essential elements into your **Personal Mastery Plan** to steer you into your personal and professional power while enjoying the process: Integrity, Self-Acceptance, Vision, Commitment, Motivation, Action, and Optimism.

Personal Mastery Plan

- **Integrity:**

Accept personal responsibility for you and live true to your moral code and core values. Are you honest with you and do you tell yourself the truth? Do you deflate or inflate the truth to suit your whims or the moment? You practice integrity when you adhere to your principles with words and deeds and when you treat others fairly and tolerate differences. Become self-aware and know what's valuable to you and be introspective. Frequently examine how you're doing and what's driving you. Practice daily reflection for personal evaluation and discovery. When you understand you, you can act honestly and plan according to what's really important to you and not be swayed by other's expectations. Recognize your shortcomings and your abilities without illusion and without boasting or diminishing the worth of others. You display a confidence without the need to overpower or overshadow other people and you trust in the valuable interrelationship among you and them. Your work and life ethic are positive and non-defeating, while inspiring others to rise above their limitations and succeed.

- **Self-Acceptance:**

In each of us is the need for respect and recognition by others, and also from us. You are self-accepting when you honor your feelings and believe you are worthy, despite your mistakes and shortcomings. You feel confident in your judgment and in your ability to handle life challenges and to defend your interests and your needs. Your thoughts about you and how you define who you are contribute to your self-esteem. They have been shaped by other people such as your parents and teachers and by the past. You may have to let go of old, limiting beliefs programmed by others. Update them to make them more current with your needs and goals. Only you can decide if you must change them. Feeling good about you is up to you and is a choice you make every day. If your attention is on the gloomy, hopeless side of living, change it. Remember, you always have a choice. Self-appreciation is ideal in increasing your upbeat feelings, so practice activities that promote your appreciation.

Self-Acceptance Strategies:

- Be kind and compassionate to you.
- Become more self-aware.
- Don't take you so seriously; laugh at your mistakes and you.
- Change your judgmental thoughts and words about you to be more respectful.
- Stand up for your interests and your needs.
- Remember, you have the right to be happy.
- Appreciate the uniqueness that is you.
- Create a sense of inner peace and well being.
- Gently update the outdated versions of you.
- Tell yourself the truth.

- **Vision:**

Your vision is a roadmap that helps you navigate life events and challenges with purpose and direction, and is fueled by your core values and your mission. It outlines where you're going with clarity and belief and inspires you to move forward and take the necessary steps toward that dream whether personal, professional, familial or more. Hopefully, your vision stretches you and pushes you to grow beyond external or internal limitations. When you do, there's excitement and more enthusiasm as imagination becomes reality and you're living your vision. Every vision needs a plan to set the intentions and direction and a mapped out strategy to guide you forward. Keep your vision close to you always and don't let anything block you from your plan unless it's a better plan. Learn to say no when there's goal interference and set boundaries with others without feeling guilty. Guilt serves no one; practice self-acceptance, instead.

Vision Plan:

1. Your personal vision is a clear and credible picture that captures what you want from your life, job and relationships, and includes how you plan on realizing them.
2. Create a vision statement that is flexible and adaptable.
3. Make sure you include a practical timeline and a framework for outlining your dreams for you, your family and your world.
4. Take purposeful and concrete steps toward your vision and write them down.
5. Stay on track by setting boundaries when necessary and sticking to them.
6. Keep you eye and mind on the desired future while continuously re-evaluating the present.

7. Be flexible and ready to adapt to any necessary changes that adhere to your goals.

8. Keep your inspiration strong and your imagination open to all possibilities.

9. Ensure that your vision excites and inspires you and those you need to share it with.

10. Infuse your vision with passion and commitment.

11. Assess what works to bring that vision closer to you.

12. Visualize, Visualize and Visualize.

- **Commitment:**

Your dedication and devotion to you and to your vision is what keeps the embers glowing, even when you feel that the fire's gone out. This unshakeable determination is a conscious decision that you make and keep throughout any hesitation and momentary doubt. We've all had our share of those nagging thoughts, but with your persistence, you strive forward and keep that vision in the forefront of your mind.

Passion fuels commitment; so, get excited about what you're currently doing and what you're creating. If you can't; maybe it's time to rethink why and make some changes that excite you. The alternative is not really living to the full strength and capacity of who you are. Make sure that in life, relationships, love and work you are moved and your heart's engaged. Discuss your dreams with people who desire to see you excel and ask them to help you stay on track while you do the same for them.

- **Motivation:**

Be a self-motivator and act like you're creating your life day by day, because you really are. Your motivation is an outgrowth of your desire to identify and achieve your goals, and rooted in the belief that you're capable to accomplish what you set out to do. You set short and long-term goals and you are action oriented. Dreaming is wonderful, as you create with your imagination, but dreaming isn't enough. To power you into success, you must be able to advance into action when necessary with quick and accurate assessment of each situation and the corresponding response. Become inspired, whether by you or other people, or by whatever gets your energy flowing in the direction of your vision. Motivation can wane, so know what increases your motivation. If your motivation temporarily wavers, tap into a motivation strategy that will energize you into purposeful activity.

- **Action:**

A major difference between successful and unsuccessful people is their ability to act. Back up your ideas and goals with action and initiative. You may not have all the information and you may lack courage, yet become accustomed to moving forward, past your fear, and become action-oriented. When you do, the fear disappears, confidence grows, and new ideas are continuously being born. Act boldly rather than wishing that you did. If you never act, you'll never know what great feats you can accomplish. Sometimes you must seize the moment and bolt into action without too much forethought to discover the opportunity that awaits you. Do so with positive expectation and accept full responsibility for the consequences. Redirect your activities that aren't working well into new projects that can build and sustain your vision. If you're constantly waiting for you to be perfect or to come up with the perfect solution, your action may be stalled. Instead, don't overanalyze or dwell on the need to always be right. Practice action and you'll discover that you're acting more appropriately and swiftly than ever.

- **Optimism:**

Your outlook is essential and can't just be left up to chance. It is a life approach in the way you view you and your world. Even during uncertainty and disappointment, optimism is necessary to keep you on a path of positive expectancy. You anticipate self-affirming results, yet are realistically aware that challenges exist. Nevertheless, you trust that you can and will handle them to the best of your ability to ultimately produce what you desire. Optimism drives your motivation and encourages purposeful activity toward your goals. Your focus is on constructive problem solving rather than pessimism and worry. Optimistic people cultivate self-reliance, yet also trust that their positive action and that of other likeminded people will create a better life for them, their business and their community. Within them is a strong faith in their own efforts, in other people, the future, and in something beyond them: a universe and a Higher Power that is supportive, loving and affirming.

Remember that self-empowerment is a choice and a determination to continuously grow you and become more self-actualized. It doesn't happen overnight, nor is it neglectful of your responsibilities or genuine care of others. It relies on an inner strength and belief in you and in your ability to make the right decisions and take correct action. You recognize your worth and feel yourself as powerful over your life and circumstances so that you can make a major difference in them and in your world — and you do.

Self-Appreciation Activities:

- Keep a self-appreciation journal and jot down when you do something large or small that you appreciate.
- Include activities in your busy schedule that honor you: yoga, spa, meditation, prayer, relaxation, music, nature, reading, writing, painting, sports…
- Reward pleasant outcomes and all the little steps along the way that lead you ahead.
- Find out why others appreciate you and appreciate you for the very same reasons.
- Be your best friend, critic, advocate and cheerleader — all at the same time.
- Direct yourself, yet do so with love, understanding, encouragement and optimism.

Increase Your Motivation:

- Join a mastermind group.
- Be specific about what you want.
- Create a step-by-step action plan.

- Visualize your goals as already achieved.
- Cultivate self-discipline.
- Listen to or read motivational material.
- Celebrate your successes.
- Associate with people who share your optimism and enthusiasm.
- Get excited about your goals and your vision.

Motivational Strategies:

- Keep your goals and visions current and believable.
- Know when to act and act decisively and courageously.
- Be well informed, yet also rely on your intuition.
- Share your goals with people who support you.
- Encourage your ideas and rally behind your efforts.
- Plan ahead, yet focus on today.
- Decide to challenge yourself often.
- Get into the habit of putting your ideas into action.
- Complete your tasks to create more confidence and positive feelings.
- Believe in you and stay committed to what you believe.

Personal Mastery Inventory:

Rate yourself gently but honestly:	Never	Sometimes	Always
1. I treat myself compassionately.	☐	☐	☐
2. I am satisfied with the present.	☐	☐	☐
4. I am optimistic about the future.	☐	☐	☐
5. I live my life with integrity.	☐	☐	☐
6. I am true to myself and my beliefs and values.	☐	☐	☐
7. I feel in charge of me.	☐	☐	☐
8. I like who I am.	☐	☐	☐
9. I have a vision and goals for my life.	☐	☐	☐
10. I can laugh at myself and at my mistakes.	☐	☐	☐
11. I act when I need to.	☐	☐	☐
12. My actions correspond with my words and values.	☐	☐	☐

Note: Decide to incorporate these empowerment tips into your life more often. If never or sometimes is your rating, take one bold step each week toward more self-mastery.

Action Questions for Self-Empowerment:

- What do I need to do more of?

- What do I need to do less of?
- What can I do right now to bring me closer to my vision?
- How can I help empower others?
- What must I let go of right now to reach my vision?
- How can others help empower me?
- In what way can I share my vision with others?
- What beliefs stand in the way of my vision?
- What beliefs support my vision?
- What motivates me towards my goals?
- What deters me from my goals?

*** Make a habit of frequently asking these questions and acting on your responses.

Recommended Reading:
As A Man Thinketh by James Allen

The Art of a Leader by William A. Cohen

The Magic of Believing by Claude M. Bristol

The Charisma Factor: How to Develop Your Natural Leadership by Robert J. Richardson & S.

Katherine Thayer *Toward a Psychology of Being* by Abraham Maslow

Notes:

THE PROFESSIONAL WOMAN NETWORK

Training and Certification on Women's Issues

Linda Ellis Eastman, President & CEO of The Professional Woman Network, has trained and certified over two thousand individuals to start their own consulting/seminar business. Women from such countries as Brazil, Argentina, the Bahamas, Costa Rica, Bermuda, Nigeria, South Africa, Malaysia, and Mexico have attended trainings.

Topics for certification include:

- Diversity & Multiculturalism
- Women's Issues
- Women: A Journey to Wellness
- Save Our Youth
- Teen Image & Social Etiquette
- Leadership & Empowerment Skills for Youth
- Customer Service & Professionalism
- Marketing a Consulting Practice
- Professional Coaching
- Professional Presentation Skills

If you are interested in learning more about becoming certified or about starting your own consulting/seminar business contact:

The Professional Woman Network
P.O. Box 333
Prospect, KY 40059
(502) 566-9900
lindaeastman@prodigy.net
www.prowoman.net

The Professional Woman Network Book Series

Becoming the Professional Woman
Customer Service & Professionalism for Women
Self-Esteem & Empowerment for Women
The Young Woman's Guide for Personal Success
The Christian Woman's Guide for Personal Success
Survival Skills for the African-American Woman
Overcoming the SuperWoman Syndrome
You're on Stage! Image, Etiquette, Branding & Style
Women's Journey to Wellness: Mind, Body & Spirit
A Woman's Survival Guide for Obstacles, Transition & Change
Women as Leaders: Strategies for Empowerment & Communication
Beyond the Body! Developing Inner Beauty
The Young Man's Guide for Personal Success
Emotional Wellness for Women Volume I
Emotional Wellness for Women Volume II
Emotional Wellness for Women Volume III

Forthcoming Books:
The Baby Boomer's Handbook for Women

These books will be available from the individual contributors, the publisher (www.pwnbooks.com), Amazon.com, and your local bookstore.